MAR   1987

IRISH LIFE AND TRADITIONS

a book about life in contemporary Ireland - the forces that shape its character, the variety of its preoccupations and passions.

CONTRIBUTORS

SHARON GMELCH: anthropologist; associate professor at Union College, Schenectady, New York; author of *Tinkers and Travellers* and *Nan: The Life of an Irish Travelling Woman*.

ANTONY ORME: professor of geography and dean of social studies at the University of California, Los Angeles; formerly lecturer at University College Dublin; author of sixty publications, several dealing with the Irish landscape.

OSCAR MERNE: naturalist; works with the research branch of the Forest and Wildlife Service, Dublin; author of *Wading Birds*.

JOSEPH RAFTERY: former Director of the National Museum of Ireland and former President of the Royal Irish Academy; author of *Prehistoric Ireland*, editor of *Christian Art in Ancient Ireland*, Vol. 2.

PATRICK SHAFFREY: architect and town planner; author of *The Irish Town: An Approach to Survival*, and (with Maura Shaffrey) of *Buildings of Irish Towns* and *Irish Countryside Buildings*.

EDWARD MACLYSAGHT: journalist, archivist, historian; best known for his work on Irish surnames; author of fifteen books.

GEORGE OTTO SIMMS: former Archbishop of Armagh and Primate of All Ireland; publications include *The Book of Kells: A Short Description* and *Christ Within Me*.

BREANDÁN Ó HEITHIR: journalist, writer, broadcaster; has published *Lig Sinn i gCathú* (translated as *Lead Us Into Temptation*), a collection of short stories, his reflections on the GAA, and has written many film scripts.

NELL MCCAFFERTY: freelance journalist, living in Dublin; her main interests have been malpractice in court and feminism; publications include *The Best of Nell* and *A Woman to Blame*.

GARRY REDMOND: sports commentator and editor; formerly with *The Irish Press, The Observer* and the *RTE Guide*, currently on the staff of *Radio Telefís Éireann*.

SEÁN MACRÉAMOINN: head of external affairs at *Radio Telefís Éireann*; interested in the Irish language, religion, politics, the arts and in 'talking about them all'.

MAEVE BINCHY: one of Ireland's most popular journalists; publications include *Light a Penny Candle* and *Echoes*.

SEAN MACBRIDE: recipient of the Nobel Peace Prize, the Lenin Peace Prize and the American Medal of Justice; has had a long career in Irish and international politics.

IRISH LIFE
AND
TRADITIONS

Edited by

SHARON GMELCH

Syracuse University Press · The O'Brien Press

IRISH STUDIES

Irish Studies presents a wide range of books interpreting important aspects of Irish life and culture to scholarly and general audiences. The richness and complexity of the Irish experience, past and present, deserves broad understanding and careful analysis. For this reason an important purpose of the series is to offer a forum to scholars interested in Ireland, its history, and culture. Irish literature is a special concern in the series, but works from the perspectives of the fine arts, history, and social sciences are also welcome, as are studies which take multi-disciplinary approaches.

Irish Studies is a continuing project of Syracuse University Press and is under the general editorship of Richard Fallis, associate professor of English at Syracuse University.

Irish Studies, edited by Richard Fallis

Published in Ireland 1986 by The O'Brien Press, 20 Victoria Road, Dublin 6.
Published in the United States 1986 by Syracuse University Press, Syracuse, New York 13244-5160.

First published in Ireland 1979, as *Irish Life*.
First paperback edition published in Ireland 1982.

ISBN 0-8156-2367-4 clothbound edition, Syracuse U.P., USA.
ISBN 0-8156-0201-4 paperback edition, Syracuse U.P., USA.
ISBN 0-86278-109-4 paperback edition, The O'Brien Press.

Design: Michael O'Brien. Typesetting: Redsetter Ltd., Dublin.
Printing: Richard Clay Ltd., England.

CONTENTS

ABOUT THIS BOOK

Irish Life and Traditions springs from a great personal affection for Ireland and a desire to capture on paper some understanding of the country and its people. The book deals with many topics that impress the visitor, but only those that also have meaning to the Irish. As a cultural anthropologist I am interested in the culture of different peoples, in the complex whole of their history, habits, and habitat. The organization of *Irish Life and Traditions* reflects this broad interest by dealing both with Ireland's physical landscape and with its people and their traditions.

It begins with a discussion of Ireland's natural environment, from its rugged coastline and abundant bog to the plants and animals that give life to the landscape. Next, an archaeologist and an architect talk about the man-made environment - the meaning of the ring forts and passage graves early peoples left behind and the history and character of Ireland's modern cities.

Most of the essays have been written by Irish people and thus provide an insider's understanding of Irish culture. The four essays in 'Growing Up' - written by an historian, a Protestant archbishop, a writer and Gaelic-speaker, and a feminist - paint an uniquely vivid and intimate portrait of what it is like to be socialized into Irish culture. They also reveal the country's diversity - the regional, religious, class and generational experiences that cross-cut an otherwise homogeneous population.

The Irish are a warm, gregarious people. The essays on ancient fairs and religious pilgrimages, modern festivals, sport, and 'words' reflect their intense interest in people, conversation, and social life. These essays also reveal the enduring significance of tradition in their everyday lives. In the concluding essay, one of Ireland's leading statesmen gives his personal assessment of his country's recent past and its contemporary policies.

Although no single book can provide a comprehensive picture of an entire country and its people, *Irish Life and Traditions* aims to give a realistic and personal glimpse of modern-day Ireland.

Sharon Gmelch

Part One

THE PHYSICAL SETTING

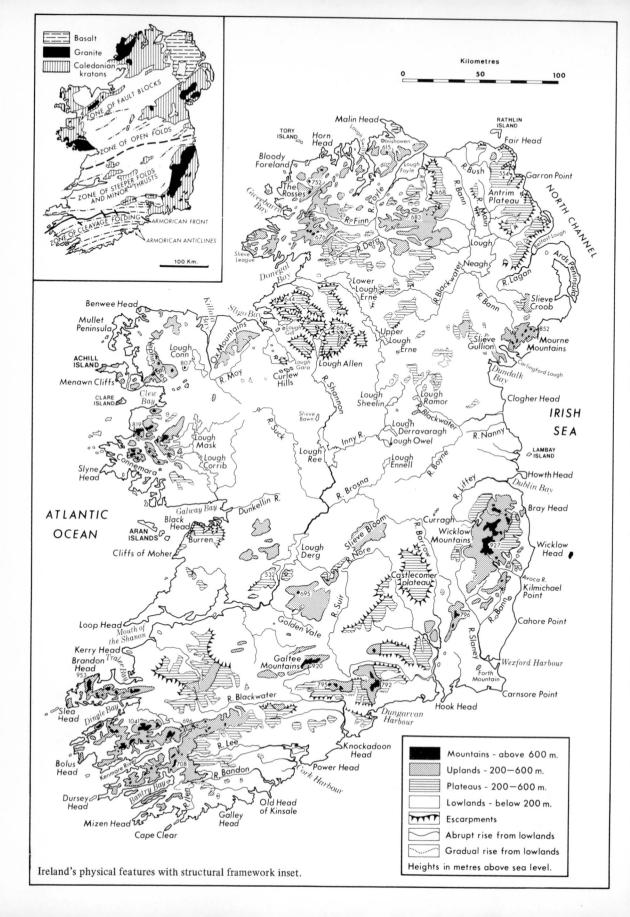

Ireland's physical features with structural framework inset.

Inset legend:
- Basalt
- Granite
- Caledonian kratons

ZONE OF FAULT BLOCKS
ZONE OF OPEN FOLDS
ZONE OF STEEPER FOLDS AND MINOR THRUSTS
ZONE OF CLEAVAGE FOLDING
ARMORICAN FRONT
ARMORICAN ANTICLINES

100 Km.

Main map labels:

Kilometres 0 50 100

Malin Head
TORY ISLAND
Horn Head
Bloody Foreland
The Rosses
752
676
683
468
Giveebarra Bay
R. Finn
R. Derg
R. Foyle
Inishowen 615
Lough Swilly
Lough Foyle
RATHLIN ISLAND
Fair Head
R. Bush
554
Garron Point
Antrim Plateau
R. Bann
R. Main
Lough
NORTH CHANNEL
A
Belfast Lough
Ards Peninsula
R. Lagan
Slieve Croob
Slieve League
Donegal Bay
Sligo Bay
644
Lough Gill
666
Lough Allen
Lower Lough Erne
Upper Lough Erne
R. Blackwater
Neagh
Lough
R. Bann
852
Mourne Mountains
Slieve Gullion
Carlingford Lough
Dundalk Bay
Clogher Head
Benwee Head
Mullet Peninsula
Ox Mountains
Killala Bay
Nephin Beg
Lough Conn 807
ACHILL ISLAND
Menawn Cliffs
CLARE ISLAND
819
Clew Bay
Connemara
Slyne Head
Lough Mask
Lough Corrib
R. Moy
Curlew Hills
Lough Gara
Slieve Bawn
R. Shannon
Lough Sheelin
Lough Ramor
R. Blackwater
Lough Derravaragh
Lough Owel
R. Nanny
IRISH SEA
LAMBAY ISLAND
Howth Head
Dublin Bay
Bray Head
R. Liffey
Curragh
Wicklow Mountains
927
Wicklow Head
Avoca R.
Kilmichael Point
R. Bann
Cahore Point
R. Slaney
Wexford Harbour
Forth Mountain
Carnsore Point
ATLANTIC OCEAN
ARAN ISLANDS
Black Head
Burren
Cliffs of Moher
Galway Bay
Dunkellin R.
Lough Ree
Inny R.
R. Suck
Lough Ennell
R. Boyne
R. Brosna
Lough Derg
Slieve Bloom
R. Nore
532
695
R. Barrow
Castlecomer plateau
796
R. Suir
Golden Vale
Loop Head
Mouth of the Shanon
Kerry Head
Brandon Head 953
Tralee Bay
Galtee Mountains 920
795
792
Dungarvan Harbour
Hook Head
Slea Head
Dingle Bay
1041
696
R. Lee
R. Blackwater
Knockadoon Head
Power Head
Bolus Head
708
Kenmare R.
R. Bandon
Cork Harbour
Old Head of Kinsale
Dursey Head
Bantry Bay
Galley Head
Mizen Head
Cape Clear

Legend:
- Mountains – above 600 m.
- Uplands – 200–600 m.
- Plateaus – 200–600 m.
- Lowlands – below 200 m.
- Escarpments
- Abrupt rise from lowlands
- Gradual rise from lowlands

Heights in metres above sea level.

LAND AND SEA

Antony Orme

LTHOUGH PEOPLE fashion a nation's personality, it is nature, initially at least, that provides the stage and backcloth for their activities. Nowhere is this more evident than in Ireland where more than 8,000 years of human activity have been played out on a damp but lush lowland stage backed by stark mountains, where nature has in places been bountiful with its resources but elsewhere harsh and miserly, and where the encircling seas have provided both a link and a barrier to human endeavour. Since prehistoric time, nature has provided man with a challenging range of opportunities and limitations which he has exploited according to his needs, skills and traditions. Indeed, much of the fascination of modern Ireland lies in the legacies of the landscape that reflect several thousand years of interaction between successive generations of men, women and children and the natural scene in which they lived. In a book of this kind, therefore, it is only reasonable to begin by reflecting on the character of the land that has provided the stage for so much subsequent human activity.

As with human affairs, where the recent past is more readily remembered, nature's record on the origins of the Irish landscape is most explicit for the last few thousand years and becomes much more difficult to interpret as we extend backwards through time. Thus, we know much more about the later stages of the Quaternary Period, especially the last ice age and its aftermath, than we do about earlier glacial stages and the shaping of the preglacial landscape. Going further back, our understanding of Ireland's origins as a distinct entity remains largely speculative, clouded in the mists of time and by major gaps in the geological record. Fortunately, it is the events of the last ice age and its aftermath, of the last 25,000 years or so, that are most important to our understanding of the present landscape. Thus, after setting the stage and describing briefly what may have happened in the distant past, we will look at these more recent episodes in earth history.

Ireland's physical landscape has often been likened to an old chipped saucer. Its broad central lowland is surrounded by a broken rim of uplands, the breaks in which allow the excess waters of the lowland to spill over into the sea. The flatter parts of this lowland, between Dublin and Galway, are rarely higher than 100 metres above sea level and abound with bogs, lakes and slow-flowing streams. Even the broken upland rim is comparatively low in elevation, reaching 1,000 metres above sea level only in Macgillicuddy's Reeks in Co. Kerry.

While the saucer analogy affords a useful mental picture by way of introduction, it also oversimplifies a varied and interesting landscape. In reality, the central lowland is rarely flat. Instead it is diversified by prominent hills and ridges, by bold escarpments sweeping up onto marshy plateaux and by subtle mounds of glacial debris. What Ireland's uplands lack in absolute height is more than compensated by their often abrupt rise from the lowlands and the coast, and by an appearance rendered infinitely more harsh and forbidding by drenching rains, high winds and blanket bogs. Mountains are not to be numerically defined. They are the products of man's perception and to Irishmen the rugged windswept hills that rise to form the bleak backcloth to so much lowland activity will always be known as mountainy land.

Around its edges, Ireland is trimmed by often violent seas that pummel stark cliffs and fashion majestic beaches along 3,000 kilometres of often deeply indented coastline. From the Atlantic Ocean in the west to the narrow seas that separate, for better or for worse, Ireland from Britain, no point is more than 100 kilometres from the sea. It is this nearness to the sea and the sea's pervading influence over Ireland's weather that gives the landscape its permeating wetness that is so germane to an understanding of the country's rivers, bogs, soils and plant life. Throughout the year, clouds drift eastwards across Ireland from the Atlantic, releasing their moisture over the hills and valleys and bathing the countryside in a soft misty light. Not all this moisture returns directly to the sea for much is locked up in the soil and in lonely tracts of bog, to be released but slowly to the lakes and streams in which the country abounds.

IN THE BEGINNING

Beneath the glacial debris and other rock waste laid down during successive ice ages of the Quaternary Period lies rock that ranges from 200 to 2,000 million years in age. Most, however, belongs to the Palaeozoic Era that began some 600 million years ago. These rocks bear the firm imprint of two major mountain-building events: one, known as the Caledonian, which began some 400 million years ago, and a second, known as the Armorican, around 280 million years ago. An understanding of these two mountain-building events goes far towards explaining the grain of the landscape — the orientation of present-day ridges and valleys.

Except in the extreme south, Caledonian folding along northeast to southwest lines crumpled the more ancient rocks and set the main

Above– Ireland's stage and backcloth. Although the landscape is not always so well organized, this view across the Glen of Aherlow towards the Galtee Mountains aptly captures the frequent contrast in Ireland between human activity on the lowland stage and the starkness of the mountain backcloth.

Right– Successive flows of dark coloured basalt lavas of early Tertiary age lie on white Cretaceous chalk near Garron Point in Antrim.

structural framework of the country. As the name suggests, the Caledonian uplands of northwest Ireland are an extension of the Scottish Highlands. Farther south, the direction of the Caledonian structures found from Down to Longford continues the line of the Southern Uplands of Scotland, while a similar zone in southeast Ireland is a continuation of structures found in the Isle of Man and North Wales.

South of a line drawn from Dungarvan in Co. Waterford to Dingle Bay in Kerry, the more recent Armorican mountain-building episode created a series of east-west folds in the earth's crust, continuing the trend of similar structures found in South Wales, southwest England and, indeed, Brittany. Because the Armorican movements died out northwards across Ireland, structures created at this time within the central lowlands were increasingly affected by older Caledonian elements, so that Armorican hills such as Slieve Bloom actually trend from northeast to southwest. In the north, from Sligo and Leitrim and extending northeastward to the North Channel and Scotland, considerable faulting took place. The Irish Sea basin may have originated as one or more structural troughs at this time.

During the Mesozoic Era, from 230 to 70 million years ago, the Armorican mountains and what remained of the Caledonian folds were worn down by erosion, at first under desert conditions and then by rivers and marine erosion. So little evidence of this Era survives today, however, that our understanding of exactly what occurred is highly conjectural. We think that as recently as 80 million years ago, Ireland was largely submerged beneath the sea. Small outcrops of Cretaceous chalk, a soft white limestone, in northeast Ireland and in Kerry provide a clue to this submergence. Offshore extensive deposits exist and it is reasonable to assume that the evolution of the Irish landscape as we know it today began with the country's uplift and emergence from beneath the Cretaceous sea.

The forces which finally raised Ireland from the sea were but one expression of a series of dramatic events which also led to the widening of the north Atlantic Ocean during the Cenozoic Era, the last 70 million years. As North America and Europe drifted apart, Ireland came to form part of the trailing edge of the European continental plate. It rose and probably tilted westward, while Britain rose and tilted east toward the subsiding North Sea basin. Between them, the Irish Sea, possibly the keystone in a former arch spanning the two countries, subsided through sagging and faulting around its margins.

Inevitably, the stresses involved in these earth movements were accompanied by volcanic activity. Lava spewed from fissures over much of northern Ireland and western Scotland; this helps to explain much of the present scenery of Antrim and Derry. The subsequent warping and faulting of these lavas created the Lough Neagh basin and the North Channel. Beneath the surface, granites and similar rocks collected in deep subterranean cauldrons at about this time, to be later exposed by erosion to form the Mountains of Mourne and the Carlingford hills. Although igneous activity diminished in importance later, crevices in other rocks were still being filled in by igneous rock to form geologic features known as dykes in southwest Ireland as recently as 17 million years ago.

Plant remains and pollen that have been preserved in soils between the lava flows and in crevices and caverns within limestone rocks tell us that Ireland was once clothed in luxuriant forest and that the climate was warm and wet, almost tropical, for much of the last 70 million years. Under these conditions, most rocks underwent rapid chemical decay. The resulting waste was either carried away by rivers or remained to form thick soils. Gradually, the Irish landscape was worn down at rates varying with the strength or weakness of its different rocks. This selective decay and erosion produced uplands composed of resistant sandstones and quartzites and lowlands of chemically weak limestones and granites. The survival of limestone plateaux in Sligo and granite uplands in Wicklow, however, suggests that block faulting and other major earth movements may have countered, locally at least, the trend towards landscape lowering during this time.

If, as many scientists think, the country's major rivers came into existence as Ireland emerged from the sea some 70 million years ago, this emergent chalk surface could not have long survived the onslaught of weathering and erosion. Rivers sliced through the chalk and were super-imposed onto the underlying Caledonian and Armorican framework with little regard for the grain of the structures thus exhumed. Superimposi-tion of this nature is thought to explain why many rivers, such as the Shannon, after following undistinguished middle courses, choose to cut seaward through bold ridges. Farther south, the Blackwater, Lee and Bandon are today mainly east-flowing rivers which abandon easy outlets and, just above their mouths, turn abruptly southwards to the sea. Such unusual patterns may have originated as part of a south-flowing drainage network whose tributaries, following superimposition, later adjusted in part to the underlying east-west Armorican structures. This explanation may not fit all Irish rivers, however, and it is possible that some rivers were able to maintain their courses through uplands rising in response to Cenozoic earth movements. In this way, the Slaney, Barrow and Nore may have cut the gorges which carry their waters seaward through the granite ridges of southeast Ireland.

Some 25 million years ago, Ireland's climate began to cool, signalling the beginning of climatic fluctuations that were to culminate in the dramatic glacial and interglacial stages of the Quaternary Period. Under conditions that had become temperate rather than tropical, rock weather-ing slowed down but the rivers continued to flush eroded rock waste seaward into basins around the coast which today reveal thick deposits of these sediments. Gradually, the landscape acquired its main features: mountains of resistant or recently uplifted rocks, broad plateaux at inter-mediate heights, and extensive lowlands. The plateaux, particularly those found between 200 and 350 metres above sea level in the southern part of the country were most likely sheared off by the prolonged weathering and river erosion which took place when the sea stood somewhat higher

Above– A corrie notched into the north slope of Slieve Corragh in the Mourne Mountains. Such bowl-shaped hollows were carved out by small masses of glacial ice and by frost action during Quaternary times in many parts of Ireland.

Right– The Giant's Causeway, Antrim. Basalt lavas owe their striking columnar appearance to vertical hexagonal joints that came into existence as the basalt flows cooled and contracted.

than it does today. Erosion by waves and currents may also have played a part in their shaping. By 2 million years ago, nature had painted with broad strokes the principal features of the Irish landscape. It remained for the fine brushwork of the Quaternary Period, the so-called Great Ice Age, to complete the picture.

THE ICE AGE AND ITS LEGACY

The dramatic changes of the Quaternary Period did not arrive suddenly, nor are they necessarily over. The cooler conditions of late Cenozoic times, from 10 to 2 million years ago, had already produced ice sheets in Greenland and the Antarctic, and glaciers in Alaska and the Arctic, but warm interludes continued to occur within the overall cooling trend and world sea levels rose and fell as the ice melted and then refroze. In Ireland, some cold stages were dominated by tundra rather than true glacial conditions and several warm stages were warmer than today and lasted much longer than the mere 10,000 years that have passed since the last glaciers melted. Throughout much of the Quaternary Period, therefore, the Irish landscape continued to be sculptured by rain and rivers, rather than by glacial ice which only accumulated in significant quantities during the last 200,000 years. Nevertheless, when the ice did eventually arrive, it left a rich legacy of minor landforms and soil-making materials of immense ecological significance.

Two major glacial stages are commonly recognized in Ireland: the older, Munsterian Glaciation whose surviving deposits are well weathered and rather featureless, and the younger, less extensive Midlandian Glaciation whose fresh hummocky debris widely mantles the lowlands. The Munsterian Glaciation probably lasted from about 175,000 to 130,000 years ago, the Midlandian from 70,000 to 10,000 years ago.

The existing topography of Ireland strongly influenced the growth and movement of glaciers. At first, local glaciers formed in the uplands, subsequently pushing their way down existing valleys onto lower ground. As these valley glaciers came together, a large ice cap formed over the central lowlands. From this, ice streams radiated outwards across the present coast. Meanwhile, Ireland's northern and eastern margins were periodically over-run by powerful ice streams originating in Scotland. As the main ice sheets waned, local mountain glaciers again predominated until, with a return to warmer conditions, they and the snowfields that fed them also melted away. Today, the uplands which nurtured this succession of local glaciers display scenery of remarkable beauty, whereas the lowlands exhibit accumulations of debris deposited both by the ice and by the outwash streams which drained the former glaciers.

The Munsterian Glaciation began with the birth of glaciers in the mountains of Donegal, west Connaught, Wicklow and southwest Ireland. These pushed downslope to form ice lobes at the base of the mountains and beyond. Large granite boulders from the Wicklow Mountains have been found in the stony glacial deposits plastered across the nearby coast, showing that one such ice lobe spilled into the Irish Sea basin at this time.

THE QUATERNARY GLACIATIONS OF IRELAND

Malin Head
Inishowen
NORTH CHANNEL
DONEGAL ICE CENTRE
LONDONDERRY
Sperrin Mountains
Lough Neagh
BELFAST
R. Lagan
R. Erne
Slieve Beagh
Armagh
Mourne Mountains
Erris Head
SLIGO
R. Moy
Nephin Beg
Achill
Clew Bay
IRISH SEA
Ben Head
R. Suck
Lough Ree
R. Boyne
DUBLIN
WEST CONNACHT ICE CENTRE
Lough Corrib
R. Liffey
Slyne Head
GALWAY
R. Shannon
Blessington
R. Barrow
WICKLOW ICE CENTRE
Wicklow Head
Aran Islands
Lough Derg
R. Nore
R. Slaney
LIMERICK
Kilkenny
Cahore Point
Loop Head
Listowel
R. Suir
Screen Hills
Wexford Harbour
Dingle Peninsula
Comeragh Mountains
Kilmore Quay
Carnsore Point
Killorglin
Killarney
R. Blackwater
Dungarvan
KERRY–CORK ICE CENTRE
R. Lee
CORK
R. Bandon
Power Head
Bantry Bay
Cape Clear

| 0 10 20 30 40 50 60 70 80 90 100 |
| KILOMETRES |

Drumlins
Eskers
Dead ice debris } MIDLANDIAN OR YOUNGER GLACIATIONS
Moraines
Till and ice flow

Till and ice flow } MUNSTERIAN OR OLDER GLACIATIONS
Unglaciated areas

Similarly, far-travelled boulders of Galway granite show that ice from the western mountains joined together to form a large ice sheet which fanned out south and eastwards along a broad front extending all the way from the Dingle Peninsula to Waterford. Another part of this ice sheet passed northwestward across north Mayo. Large though it was, this ice sheet probably did not bury the higher mountains of the south and west which became harsh refuges for a few hardy plants.

Meanwhile, powerful Scottish ice streamed across Ireland's north-east coast and into the Irish Sea basin. As the ice moved through the basin it dredged mud and shells from the sea floor and plastered these across the present coast as far south as Cork. This purple and brown shelly clay, so different from the stony debris laid down by local mountain glaciers and from the limestone-bearing rock waste of the lowland ice sheet, has been found near Blessington, west of the Wicklow Mountains, and as far west as Power Head in Co. Cork. Eventually, as warmer conditions returned, water from the receding ice fronts cut impressive channels in Munster and the glacial deposits left on the lowlands were exposed to weathering and erosion. During the subsequent warm stage, Ireland was probably clothed in a temperate forest, containing many trees and shrubs similar to those found in modern Ireland.

The Midlandian cold stage was ushered in by a return to tundra conditions with small mountain glaciers. Full glacial conditions only began to emerge some 25,000 years ago, and even then the glaciers were less extensive than during the earlier glaciation. Tundra conditions extended across much of the southern part of the country. As before, mountain glaciers joined together to form broad ice sheets. One such ice sheet stretched from Lough Neagh to Galway Bay. Its southern limits can still be clearly seen in the hummocky end moraines, or ridges, that fan out in a series of broad arcs across the south central lowlands. The ice failed to override the larger uplands around its margins and in wrapping around the Wicklow Mountains its meltwaters were impounded as proglacial lakes between the ice front and the hills, notably at Blessington and Glenasmole.

As the glaciation came to an end and the ice sheets melted, a series of ridge-like recessional moraines were left. Low, winding ridges, or eskers, were also formed as the sub-glacial river channels that had led to the ice front were filled in by sand and gravel. Esker chains are very noticeable in the Midlands, where they show that the ice mass sluggishly shrank from east to west. In north Leinster and mid-Ulster, hummocky spreads of sands and gravels show where ice masses more or less died in place, the hollows between the hummocks indicating where large blocks of ice were once stranded. At some stage during the Midlandian Glaciation, glacial currents moulded the clays and other debris beneath the ice into several thousand small hills, or drumlins, which today cover 10,000 square kilometres of Ireland. These streamlined hillocks, which from the air resemble schools of half-submerged whales moving over the glacial plains, reflect the path taken by the main glacial currents. Their blunt, steep ends point in the direction from which the ice came. Drumlins are spread across the north-central lowlands from Down to Sligo, and reappear in Donegal, north of Lough Neagh, in east Mayo passing seaward through Clew Bay, around the Shannon estuary, and near Bantry and Kenmare in Co. Kerry.

While the relatively large lowland and Irish Sea ice sheets expanded, pulsated and waned, smaller ice caps remained in the mountains of west Cork, Kerry and Wicklow. Smaller cirque and valley glaciers nestled among the mountains of the north and west. Cirques are basin-shaped amphitheatres scoured by glacial ice. The magnificent scenery of the Killarney area owes much to glaciation: the Gap of Dunloe was much deepened by ice, the Upper Lake, Long Range and Muckross Lake each occupy ice-gouged rock basins, while Lough Leane and Caragh Lake are held behind crescent-shaped ridges of glacial debris left at the mouths of mountain glens. In the Wicklow Mountains, glaciers were largely responsible for enhancing the scenery of the Annamoe valley, Glenmacnass, Glendalough and Glenmalure with their often precipitous sidewalls, cascading waterfalls, ice-scoured floors and masses of sand and boulders. The small cirque glaciers that nestled beneath Croaghaun on Achill Island and below Mount Eagle on the Dingle peninsula are the most westerly expressions of Quaternary mountain glaciation in Europe. Although cold snaps continued to affect glaciers during late Midlandian times, causing a re-invasion of north Ulster by Scottish ice as late as 13,000 years ago and a temporary rebirth of mountain glaciers about 10,500 years ago, the mountain ice finally disappeared 10,000 years ago and the land began to acquire the last remaining pieces of the puzzle.

In retrospect, we can see in the present landscape how the glaciers scoured the uplands of their rock waste and deepened many existing valleys, while their meltwaters carved such spectacular channels as the Glen of the Downs and the Scalp near Dublin and Keamaneigh in west Cork. The ice and its meltwaters also plastered clay, sand and gravel across the lowlands and mountain glens, thereby providing a wide range of materials for soil development and subsequent agriculture. As a consequence, the postglacial landscape inherited a physique vastly different in detail from what it had been before. Nearly everywhere, modern streams have had to adapt to physical circumstances much changed from those to which their ancestors were accustomed. Although the main preglacial drainage pattern re-emerged largely unchanged by the glacial interlude, some quite large rivers were in places deflected by heaps of glacial debris into new channels. The Liffey beneath Dublin and the Shannon near Limerick are two notable examples. Furthermore, the fluctuations of sea level caused by the growth and decay of the world's ice sheets, together with the gentle depression that northeast Ireland and the Irish Sea basin experienced under the weight of their glaciers, have all left their mark on the country's coastline.

THE BOGS AND THEIR RECORD

The present warm stage opened 10,000 years ago when temperatures rose and woodland trees began filling in the open tundra which was then

Above– Glengesh, a glaciated valley in Donegal whose slopes have been further modified by mass movement since the last glacier disappeared.

Left– An esker near Timahoe in the central lowlands. This is but one of many similar sinuous ridges which reflect the wastage of the Midlandian ice sheet in central Ireland.

(years)	GEOLOGICAL STAGE	CLIMATIC PHASE	CLIMATE	POLLEN ZONE	DOMINANT VEGETATION	TYPICAL PLANTS	CULTURES	OTHER ENVIRONMENTAL FEATURES
0				X	OAK ALDER BIRCH WOODLAND	Alien plants widely introduced Pedunculate oak on calcareous soils	Historic	Partial afforestation Plantations Anglo-Norman invasion Viking invasion Christianity arrives General deforestation begins
1000	POSTGLACIAL	Sub-Atlantic	Markedly oceanic- cool, wet and windy	IX				
2000						Durmast oak and birch on non-calcareous (acid) soils	Iron Age	Arrival of Celts and iron-working
3000		Sub-Boreal	Warm and relatively dry	VIII	OAK ALDER WOODLAND	Scrub and secondary woodlands expand Oak, holly and ivy widespread	Bronze Age	Metal (copper-tin) working spreads
4000								
5000						Alder, hazel, ash, elder, black-thorn spread Weeds spread Elm begins to lose ground	Neolithic	Early woodland clearance Agriculture introduced
6000		Atlantic	Oceanic- Warm and Wet	VII	OAK ALDER PINE WOODLAND	Holly and Ivy widespread Mixed oak-elm-pine-hazel woods enriched with elder Bog growth increases	Mesolithic	Sea rises to present level — drowning coastal woods to form submerged forests
7000								
8000		Boreal	Warm and damp	VI	HAZEL PINE WOODLAND	Heath plants Holly Ivy Yew Oak Elm Scots pine Hazel		Ireland finally cut off from Britain Man arrives in Ireland
9000								
			Cool and damp	V	BIRCH-HAZEL WOODLAND	Hazel Birch species		Most modern types of native plants and animals begin reaching Ireland
10000		Pre-Boreal	Temperature rising	IV	BIRCH WOODLAND	Tree birch Aspen Heather Willow species		Normal weathering and fluvial action become main geomorphic agents
	LATE GLACIAL	Arctic	Subarctic oceanic	III	OPEN TUNDRA	Dwarf birch Dwarf willow		Close of Midlandian cold stage Corrie glaciers reappear Strong solifluction
11000		Subarctic	Mild subarctic oceanic	II	BIRCH TUNDRA	Tree birch Juniper Crowberry heath Marsh plants		Running water replaces mass movement as major transporting process
12000								
		Arctic	Arctic oceanic	I	OPEN TUNDRA	Dwarf willow Crowberry Mountain avens		Frost disturbance and solifluction widespread Scottish ice-lobe invades north coast. Mountain glaciers elsewhere
13000								

The changing late-glacial and postglacial environment.

dotted with heaps of glacial debris and innumerable lakes — a landscape not unlike that of northern Canada today. As woodlands spread, many lakes were filled in and in time developed into bogs. Fortunately for us, pollen from the woodlands and some actual plants and animals were trapped in the accumulating sediments and decaying vegetation. By studying this entombed pollen and fossil record we can reconstruct the changing landscape after the glaciers disappeared.

Ten pollen zones are commonly recognized. The first three zones, ending around 10,000 years ago, reflect a late-glacial climatic fluctuation from open tundra to birch tundra and back to open tundra. The next three zones embrace the first 3,000 years of postglacial time and see the arrival of most trees and shrubs which were to reach Ireland naturally. First birch trees appeared on the open tundra. But they were soon overshadowed and disappeared beneath a higher canopy of pine and hazel, which in turn gave way to oak and elm trees. These were by no means the only plants, merely the most dominant. Alder, ash, yew, holly and many shrubs and heath plants also grew under favourable conditions.

Between 7,000 and 5,500 years ago, during pollen zone VII, the woodlands reached their maximum extent and vigour. The climate was warm, wet and oceanic, perhaps 1° or 2°C warmer than today in summer. Primitive hunters and fishermen had now arrived in Ireland but they had yet to make much impact on the landscape. About 5,500 years ago, however, this primeval scene began to change dramatically as farming methods were introduced to Ireland by Neolithic colonists. By girdling the trees and burning the brush, these early farmers and their Bronze Age successors cut inroads into the forest. In the clearings they pastured cattle, grew wheat and barley, and built homesteads, trackways and graves. The decline of elm, the expansion of hazel and thorny shrubs and the appearance of ribwort plantain, dock, nettle and other weeds in the pollen record of the bogs at this time all indicate increasing human interference.

Early Irish farmers practised shifting cultivation, abandoning one clearing for another as the soils became exhausted. Soon the landscape became a mosaic of virgin forests, tillage plots, rough pastures and secondary scrub in various stages of regeneration. This episode of sporadic forest clearance, pollen zone VIII, lasted until about 1,700 years ago. Then, with the adoption of more advanced farming techniques and organization, including the use of the plough, an episode of general deforestation began which saw most of the remaining lowland oakwoods destroyed. This, pollen zone IX, lasted until about 300 years ago. Since then, especially over the past 100 years, an attempt at reafforestation has been made. Meanwhile, around 2,500 years ago, the relatively warm climate gave way to the cooler, wetter, stormier conditions which have persisted ever since. Thereafter, even without human interference, many plants came under greater stress, the treeline on the uplands was lowered, and some species such as the Scots pine, an early postglacial arrival, virtually disappeared to be reintroduced later by man.

Such in outline is the story of the changing postglacial landscape as told by the pollen record of the bogs. But the bogs are important in their own right, distinctive features of the Irish landscape for both native and visitor alike. At their maximum extent, before their exploitation for fuel began on a large scale in the 1930s, bogs covered 1.2 million hectares or about one-seventh of Ireland. Cool temperatures, frequent rains, low evaporation, gentle slopes and often impermeable soils have combined, since the last glaciers disappeared, to impede drainage and create lakes and water-logged hillsides where, owing to the lack of oxygen, the principal bacteria that attack and break down dead plant matter cannot survive. As a result, bogs have arisen and peat has accumulated.

In essence then, bogs develop where the rate of accumulation of plant debris is greater than the rate of decay. In Ireland, this has happened in two areas and, accordingly, we distinguish between two kinds of bog. The raised bogs of the lowlands began life as poorly decayed plant debris that accumulated in lakes, river valleys and swampy hollows with considerable surface water and high water tables. The blanket bogs of the uplands and western seaboard began in areas where peat growth was facilitated by excessive surface water on sloping ground, notably in the west where rainfall is high and evaporation low. Despite their different origins, however, both the raised and blanket bogs eventually came to grow under conditions where the only water available for plant growth is rain that falls directly onto the bog surface.

Raised bogs are magnificently developed in central Ireland, notably in hollows among the glacial deposits left by the last ice sheet. As the open tundra gave way to forest, the large expanses of water which filled these hollows were invaded by fens and marshes. A succession of plants grew up along the lake margins, beginning with aquatics such as Bladderwort, Pondweed, and Water Lily, and then by such rooted marsh plants as Bulrush and Common Reed. These plants trapped the inflowing muds. Gradually fen-peats built up to the water level and were colonized by sedges, grasses and various marsh flowers. Trees such as alder, birch and pine might eventually invade the fen surface, creating a layer of wood-peat over the fen-peat. Commonly, however, the water table rose as the fens themselves obstructed the drainage pattern. As a result fen-peats and wood-peats grew upwards and outwards beyond the lake margins. As the fen-peat thickened, plants on its surface found it more and more difficult to reach down and extract nutrients from the soil beneath the bog. Gradually they were replaced by plants more suited to the changing conditions. Of these, the Sphagnum moss was especially suitable because it thrives when nourished only by rain. Sphagnum hummocks grew on the bog surface while other mosses colonized the scattered pools. Gradually, as knolls of moss replaced pools and new pools came into existence between the higher knolls, the growth of Sphagnum peat caused the entire bog surface and water table to rise upwards into a dome of spongy vegetation nourished only by rain. A raised bog had come into existence.

The above explanation, though simplified, may be illustrated from many of the raised bogs of the Midlands where a basal fen-peat and mud

The blanket bog south of The Twelve Pins in Connemara.

are overlain by wood-peat, which is in turn overlain by humified Sphagnum peat and the domed surface of the fresh Sphagnum bog.

The fen-peat began to form as the tundra disappeared some 10,000 years ago. Sphagnum peat began accumulating at least 7,000 years ago, slower under drier climatic conditions but accelerating under wetter conditions, especially after the climate deteriorated around 2,500 years ago. Today, some raised bogs occupy small basins a few hectares in extent; others cover many square kilometres, notably in the country stretching from the "Bog of Allen" in north Kildare to the Shannon and Suck rivers farther west. The larger bogs average 6 metres in depth and may reach 10 metres. Owing to their economic significance, however, few raised bogs survive in their natural state. For centuries they have been cut by hand for local use and since the 1930s a programme of large-scale mechanized removal for fuel and power purposes with partial reclamation of the cut-away bog for agriculture and afforestation has been followed. Early in the next century, Ireland's deeper raised bogs will have largely disappeared.

Although similar to the raised bog, the blanket bogs of the uplands and western seaboard began life in a different way. Blanket bog began forming between 4,500 and 2,500 years ago and may still be forming locally today. In many areas, the bog has developed on a landscape which was previously wooded and had been disrupted by Neolithic and Bronze Age farmers: here, bog can be seen overlying the stumps of trees and covering prehistoric field walls, graves and even homestead foundations. Some scientists in fact believe that human activity played a leading role in creating blanket bogs. Such a scenario involves the clearance of primeval woodland by early farmers, the cultivation of well-drained soils until they became exhausted, a change in the soil as valuable nutrients were washed out and the creation of a hard impermeable layer below the surface as less soluble iron and clay minerals accumulated. Above this layer, drainage would be impeded and fen and marsh plants would begin to colonize the abandoned and now waterlogged farmlands. Afterwards, the pattern of bog growth would resemble that of the raised bog.

Another scenario, however, ascribes greater importance to climate, especially to the climatic change of around 2,500 years ago. Today, blanket bogs are best developed in areas that have more than 250 rainy days and more than 1,250 millimetres of rain each year, namely the area west of a line drawn from Lough Foyle in the North to Galway Bay and then south to Cork Harbour. Isolated uplands farther east also carry blanket bog. In these areas, persistent drenching rain and low evaporation maintain a steady downward flow of water in the groundwater system throughout the year so that acids forming in the peat are never neutralized by mineral bases derived from underlying soils. Because persistent wetness, rapid leaching and increasing soil and groundwater acidity have come to typify the physical environment of Ireland over the past 2,500 years or more, some authorities believe that blanket bogs may represent the vegetation cover that is best suited to the climate of the west and the uplands farther east. As in many scientific controversies however, a compromise solution may best fit the facts, namely that many blanket bogs resulted from a combination of both climatic factors and human activity.

Blanket bogs vary from a few centimetres to over 6 metres in depth. They may occur on quite steep slopes but those more than 2 metres deep commonly become unstable after heavy rain. As internal stresses overcome the bog's inertia, masses of water and peat may be propelled downhill at speeds of up to 50 kilometres per hour over short distances. Bog flows engulfing sheep, farmlands and roads have occurred in the Glens of Antrim, the Wicklow Mountains and in Donegal. Elsewhere, notably in the Mountains of Mourne and on Achill Island, blanket bogs are being eroded by a combination of wind and running water. This may be due to local climatic changes which have dried out the bog surface, but peat cutting by man and sheep grazing can have a similar effect.

PHYSICAL PROCESSES AT WORK TODAY

As we have seen, long before man began carving his own unmistakable imprint on the landscape, Ireland was being kneaded and sculptured by a wide variety of physical forces, from mountain building and volcanic activity to river erosion and glaciation. Today, Ireland's mild and pervasively moist climate exerts a profound influence on the landscape, as seen in the prevalence of rivers and lakes, wet soils and frequent floods. By far the most important processes acting on the landscape today are chemical weathering and running water. Irish rivers carry several million tonnes of rock waste to the sea annually. Other processes are more limited in their effect. Spectacular landslides and bogflows may occur from time to time but most mass movement on hillsides occurs as an imperceptible downslope creep of soil and rock particles. Except along the coast, wind action is generally inhibited by the vegetation that now clothes and protects the soil. Frost action is now most evident only during the winter months and in the higher mountains. Waves and currents are mainly confined in their work to shaping the coastline, although they are locally important in the larger inland lakes.

Under the prevailing moist climate, chemical weathering exerts a pervasive influence on the Irish landscape, causing a slow but cumulative decay of the underlying rocks. The effect of chemical weathering is well seen in The Burren, the stark limestone country of north Clare. Here rainwater that has percolated through the soil becomes enriched with carbon dioxide to form a mild carbonic acid. This acid then reacts with the calcite (calcium carbonate) of which limestone is mainly composed to form calcium bicarbonate which is thirty times more soluble than the original calcite. Wherever pure limestones occur in gently dipping and well jointed formations, as in The Burren, this type of chemical breakdown is particularly effective. Percolating rainwater opens up structural weaknesses in the rock to form treacherous cracks that often intersect one another, thereby breaking the rock surface into numerous small blocks. Beneath the ground, the progressive decay and collapse of the limestone

Top– The Carboniferous Limestone cliffs of Kings Mountain rise above the Drumcliff River in Sligo. This view suggests how waste weathered from mountains may move downslope *en masse* to eventually reach the rivers that remove it towards the sea.
Above, left– Freeze-thaw action accounts for the angular rock debris littering the quartzite slopes of Croagh Patrick, Co. Mayo.
Above, right– Carbonation and solution at work on the Carboniferous Limestone in The Burren of north Clare.

can produce a complex of caverns, such as the Mitchelstown Caves in Co. Tipperary and the Marble Arch Caves in Co. Fermanagh. Where rainwater is held on the surface, small saucer-shaped depressions with scalloped rims are etched out by corrosion. One way or another, therefore, the limestone becomes riddled with cracks and cavities, the surface pock-marked with solution hollows and inevitably the land surface is lowered. This helps to explain why, with so much limestone, Ireland is largely a lowland country. Chemical weathering also has a profound influence on the landscape beyond the limestone areas. The granites of the Tullow basin in Co. Carlow and the Rosses in Donegal, for example, were lowered by chemical weathering. Indeed, with so many chemically incompetent rocks and so much percolating rainwater to serve as a vehicle for decay, it is hardly surprising that Ireland has so much lowland.

The only mechanical weathering process significantly to affect the Irish landscape is freeze-thaw action. Water that seeps into cracks in a rock by day may freeze at night, expanding its volume by 9 percent and thus exerting strong pressure on the surrounding rock. If the ice crystals melt the following morning, this pressure is released. However, if alternate freezing and thawing continues over several weeks and months, the rock will eventually yield to the accompanying shear stresses and rupture into angular fragments. Frequent fluctuations of temperature around freezing point occur in Irish uplands in winter. Accordingly, frost-shattered rock debris or scree litters the slopes of most mountains. Scree slopes are most conspicuous, however, on those mountains made up of rocks that are comparatively resistant to chemical weathering, namely sandstone and quartzite. Quartzite forms some of Ireland's steepest and most prominent mountains and cliffs, such as the Great Sugar Loaf near Dublin, The Twelve Pins in Connemara, Croagh Patrick south of Clew Bay and Errigal in Co. Donegal. The prominent cones of these mountains are often littered with accumulations of angular scree forming slopes up to 35°, the maximum angle of rest for such materials. The sandstone mountains in the south and west of Ireland are often similarly adorned.

The production of rock waste by chemical and mechanical weathering is but the first step in the sculpturing of the landscape, a fundamental prelude to erosion rather than an end in itself. In order to reach the rivers that form the main vehicles for waste removal, the waste must first make its way downslope. This it does under the pull of gravity, generally slowly, but sometimes catastrophically. Today, most soil and rock waste creeps almost imperceptibly downslope under its own weight, often with some lubrication from moisture and disturbance by frost action, soil organisms and animals. In this way, weathering can then attack the freshly exposed rocks and a slow but continuous supply of waste is ensured, a feature of much benefit to the development of healthy soils. Where such move-ment occurs on steep clay slopes, rock debris may creep and slip down-hill in waves, forming a series of little terraces across the slope. These terraces are probably accentuated by animals and, although mostly natural in origin, have been colourfully termed "sheepwalks" and "cowtours"

Under certain conditions, notably where dense permeable rocks form the crest of steep unstable cliffs or after heavy rains, large masses of both weathered and unweathered rock may flow or slide rapidly downhill into nearby valleys or, at the coast, into the sea. For example, massive landslides, some of which have rotated upwards as they slumped downhill, are found along the eastern edge of the Antrim plateau where the Cenozoic lava capping, its margins eroded earlier by glaciers and sapped by freeze-thaw action during the last cold stage, has collapsed towards the sea. Similarly massive slumps have sapped the steep-sided limestone plateaux of Sligo and Leitrim where, below vertical cliffs of the receding plateau edge, hillsides are often a confused welter of collapsed rock. One way or another, rock waste from the higher ground creeps, flows and slides downslope at speeds ranging from less than a centimetre a year to several kilometres an hour, to feed the rivers that are ultimately charged with removing this debris from the land to the sea.

Ireland is a damp country and nowhere is this better expressed than in its numerous rivers. Sometimes rivers can barely cope with the volume of water fed into them from the bogs and hillsides. Floods then spread across the valleys, and the major rivers, like the 370-kilometre long Shannon, broaden into elongated lakes. The persistent nature of the rainfall in Ireland ensures that streams rarely run dry. It is only on the most permeable materials, such as the Burren limestones with their many cracks and crevices, and the glacial sands and gravels of the Curragh, that surface streams are lacking. Nearly everywhere else after heavy rainfall, the land surface is glistening wet from thin sheets of water. But owing to the gentle quality of the rainfall and the large areas of gently sloping land, most water tends to percolate downward into the earth where it replenishes the ground water supply. It is from this latter source that the perennial streams derive most of their water and any fluctuation in the water table, the upper level of the saturated ground, is reflected in stream flow.

Many Irish streams have their sources in the bogs that cover so many hill sides. Bogs act as gigantic sponges, absorbing rainfall and melt water from the snow and then slowly releasing it downslope and into the underlying rocks. As soon as enough surface water accumulates to overcome friction, it begins to move downhill picking up pieces of soil and rock which in turn begin carving a small channel. Although the flow may be short-lived at first, drying up soon after the rain stops, with each rain the channel is deepened until the water stored beneath the ground from earlier rains is tapped, and a more continuous flow begins. Only in the very driest years will Irish rivers begin to dry up and even then the variety of soils and bogs from which the larger rivers derive their water is generally enough to maintain some flow.

In their mountain reaches, streams seethe with life, beauty and energy. Tumbling among rocks and boulders, they use most of their energy in overcoming turbulence and friction and have little left to erode their channels and remove rock particles. Rapids and foaming cascades are witnesses to the friction between the water and its uneven bed and banks.

The River Barrow meanders gracefully across the landscape of Co. Laois, contrasting with the straight lines of the man-made Grand Canal.

This photograph, taken in The Burren, shows clearly how the action of streams and rivers removes rock waste from the mountains and plains to the sea.

Sometimes, the stream course is broken spectacularly by a waterfall, perhaps where a rib of hard rock crosses the stream or where some legacy of glacial erosion has caused the valley to steepen suddenly, as in Glenmacnass and elsewhere along the flanks of the Wicklow Mountains. Farther downstream, the volume of water increases as tributaries contribute their share of rainfall and groundwater from an ever-increasing drainage area. As streams grow in size, the effects of turbulence and friction are reduced, velocity increases, and stream channels become wider and deeper. Towards their mouths, streams may appear to flow lazily through their floodplains but this is often no more than an illusion, the result of their size. Watching the swirls of the current from the parapet of a bridge, perhaps over the Blackwater above Youghal, soon shows how quickly and efficiently a very large volume of water flows to meet the sea.

If streams are gutters designed by nature to remove surplus water from the land, these gutters have a further role, namely that of removing rock waste from the mountains and plains to the sea. Some of this waste, comprising minerals derived from the chemical decay of rocks and dissolved in groundwater, is moved towards the sea while in solution within the water. This dissolved load is generally invisible but is reflected in the relative hardness of the water. Limestones and other carbonate-rich rocks commonly yield hard water, whereas sandstones will provide much softer water. The remaining rock waste to reach streams forms the solid load: boulders and cobbles are trundled along the stream bed, sometimes rolling more easily on a layer of smaller pebbles; pebbles in their turn may either roll or hop and skip downstream; sands may be carried in suspension near the bottom of the stream; and silts and clays, the finest particles, may be suspended in the water over long distances. During floods, nearly all the debris within a stream channel may be in motion, with large and small particles alike grinding away at one another and at the bed and banks of the stream. In this way, banks collapse, channels are scoured, valleys are widened and deepened and the rock waste is ground down until it reaches the sea as mostly fine material. Thus, when such large rivers as the Shannon, Barrow, Slaney and Blackwater reach the more tranquil waters of their estuaries, vast quantities of fine rock waste are available for deposition in the sloblands and for reworking by waves and currents along the coast.

Ireland's present coastline came into existence some 5,000 to 6,000 years ago at the close of the world-wide rise of sea level that accompanied the melting of the last ice sheets. Prior to this the sea was over 100 metres below its present level and large areas of the continental shelf around Ireland were exposed to rain and rivers and to colonization by land plants and animals, at least in those areas not covered by glacial ice. Rivers deepened their valleys to reach this low sea level, as shown by the deeply submerged channels cut into the bedrock to depths of 45 metres below sea level in the present Blackwater and Slaney estuaries and to 25 metres below sea level in the Barrow valley as far north as New Ross in Co.

Wexford. Thus, as the sea rose towards its present level, trees and other plants growing on the exposed continental shelf were drowned, forming the so-called submerged forests that lie beneath the sand of many modern beaches. The submerged forest that lies at low spring-tide level beneath the beach at Bray in Co. Wicklow has a radiocarbon age of 6,750 years before the present, presumably the date when the trees began to be overrun by the sea. The rising sea also flooded into the lower portions of most large river valleys, creating the highly indented coastline so typical of much of Ireland. In this way, Cork Harbour and other fine sheltered anchorages were produced.

The present coastline was not the first to occupy its position. Fragments of old seacliffs, abandoned shore platforms and cemented beach deposits found around the coast, especially in the south and east, show that sea level around Ireland was a few metres above the present shoreline during the last interglacial stage, between 130,000 and 70,000 years ago. Similar evidence from around the coast and the continental shelf shows that sea level rose and fell on several occasions during the Quaternary Period in response to the periodic decay and growth of the world's ice sheets. Thus it seems that the present Irish coastline may have some very ancient precursors. Even after the close of the last glacial stage and the accompanying rise of sea level, the relative level of land and sea did not immediately stabilize. The land which had been most heavily depressed beneath the glaciers, notably the area north of a line drawn from Dublin to Sligo, continued to rise slowly in response to the removal of that weight. Thus, coastal features that developed soon after the disappearance of the ice sheets were subsequently raised above the range of modern wave action. In this way, Howth, which for a short time had been an island in the postglacial sea, was linked to the mainland because the beach ridges around Sutton were raised slightly above sea level. Old beaches and cliffs stranded by this relatively late rise in land level are also found around Inishowen in Co. Donegal and along the coast of Antrim and Down.

Since the last rise in sea level, waves and currents have smoothed out many lesser irregularities around Ireland's submerged coastline. Headlands have been cliffed and, as these cliffs have retreated under wave attack, broad shore platforms have formed at their base. The coastline which faces the full force of powerful Atlantic breakers has acquired much wild and scenic grandeur. The 200 metre high Cliffs of Moher in Co. Clare, the lower but still sheer cliffs on Inishmore in the nearby Aran Islands and the Minaun Cliffs on Achill Island are three outstanding illustrations of the fury of wave attack. With their energy derived originally from the wind, the waves not only pummel the cliffs but also break down the resulting rock debris. This debris, together with the sediments brought down to the coast by rivers and such additional fragments as broken shells, is then moved by waves and currents until it comes to rest on the beach and the sea floor beyond. In Wexford and Kerry, some exceptionally fine beach spits and barrier beaches have been thrown across inlets by strong waves and currents. The zone from the foreshore to beyond the farthest line of breakers remains in a state of fairly continuous flux throughout the year, as sand is moved back and forth by the waves and sometimes moved strongly along the shore by wave-related currents. Above the foreshore, the wind helps to dry these beaches and blows the tiny particles inland to form sand dunes just beyond the reach of the waves. Such dunes change shape and location frequently until the sand is stabilized by the growth of Marram grass and other binding vegetation. Even then the vegetation cover is sometimes unable to prevent blowouts, namely hollows eroded by strong winds which can lead to refashioning of the dunes.

The action of the winds, waves and currents along the coast, and the work of weathering, mass movement and running water inland, are but the modern expression of the more-or-less continuous sculpturing to which the Irish landscape has been exposed since it first emerged from the sea. The land responds to these processes by changing its shape, very slowly to our eyes but with telling inevitability in the geological timescale.

This sand spit south of Strandhill has been constructed by waves and currents circulating around Sligo Bay since the last rise in sea level. Wind has subsequently blanketed the spit with sand dunes which the vegetation has some difficulty stabilizing.

A Barn Owl alights at its nest site to pass a small rodent to its mate. These white ghost-like birds of the night, once common and widespread in Ireland, are now scarce and declining – victims of poisoning of the food chain.

IRISH NATURE

Oscar Merne

S THE LAST Ice Age came to an end ten to twelve thousand years ago the basin of the Irish Sea filled, cutting Ireland off from Britain and the Continent. This early separation from mainland Europe and the warmer regions to the south had a profound effect on Ireland's flora and fauna. In the wake of the ice, animals and plants moved in to colonise the open ground, but in our case the barrier of the Irish Sea prevented many forms from reaching Ireland. Birds, with their power of flight, and marine fishes and mammals were not so hindered, but the terrestrial creatures and plants were. So, today, the visiting naturalist is often struck by the lack of diversity in Irish wildlife, though this lack is often compensated for by an abundance of many species living in a relatively unspoilt environment. Some of our natural areas have spectacular plant and animal communities.

Although Ireland is a small island, its geology, soils and climate have resulted in the formation of a wide variety of habitats, and in spite of the limitations to colonisation mentioned above, we probably have our fair share of plants and animals in these habitats. The seas around our coasts are shallow and are important spawning grounds for a variety of fishes — so much so that a number of species are in real danger of being over-exploited through our own fishing activities and those of fleets from a number of other European countries: the herring is a good example. The Irish shoreline is long (about two thousand miles) and its configuration varied. There are long stretches of sand and shingle beaches, shallow tidal bays and muddy estuaries, beetling rocky cliffs and islands large and small. These coastal areas support a rich and varied wildlife. Inland, much of the landscape has been tamed — forest clearance, drainage and agriculture have replaced the wilderness with a rather pleasant pastoral scene, especially in the more fertile lowland areas. So far we have escaped the worst excesses of prairie farming and our abundant and prolific hedgerows compensate to quite a large extent for the loss of most of our natural deciduous forests. They form many thousands of miles of linear woodland and support an abundance of wild flowers, shrubs, trees, small mammals, birds, insects and more. Although there has been considerable drainage activity, especially in the last century and the current one, we still have many varied lakes and ponds, rivers and marshes and other wetlands to support our aquatic and semi-aquatic flora and fauna. This is not to say we should be complacent, for serious water pollution has in recent times begun to manifest itself; and the wildlife which depends on extensive wetland areas is being forced to contract or to be displaced as drainage operations turn their wetland habitats into agricultural land. The sheltered bays and estuaries where fresh and salt water meet are particularly rich wildlife areas, but many of our larger towns and cities have been built up around these, and many are coming under increasing pressure from industrialisation and the attendant discharges of all kinds of unimaginable wastes into the waters, with dire effects on the local wildlife. In the more remote upland areas man-induced changes in the natural environment are perhaps not so evident. It is still possible to gaze over miles and miles of unspoilt mountain landscape — a combination of rolling moorland, rocky outcrops, screes, glacial valleys, peaks (few over three thousand feet), dark lakes, rushing streams — where the main artificial intrusions are the flocks of domestic sheep and the plantations of exotic conifers. In this chapter we will concentrate on a fairly small number of the most important natural habitats in Ireland and on the fauna and flora which inhabit them.

THE COAST

Ireland lies on the western edge of the European Continental Shelf and the seas surrounding our shores are mostly shallow: only in a couple of areas off the west coast does the hundred fathom line approach within thirty or forty miles. Inshore there is a narrow strip of water only five to ten fathoms deep, while in many of our bays and estuaries large expanses of sand or mud are exposed at low tides. In these shallow sea areas, coasts and inter-tidal zones we find a great variety of plant and animal life. Most of the plants are the marine algae or seaweeds and these come in a surprising variety of forms, from the long broad and leathery brown fronds with trunk-like stalks commonly seen on rocky coasts at extreme low tide, to the fine delicate cobweb-like green strands of the algal mats growing on the nutrient-rich mudflats of the estuaries. At the top limit of the tide's reach are the salt marshes, built on deposits of mud which have first been colonised by the pioneer fleshy plant *Salicornia* and then by a succession of other salt-tolerant species. At the dry-land end of the salt marshes the fine-leaved Red Fescue grass is the last species linking the typical salt marsh flora with the dry-land flora. In this zone there are often extensive blossomings of the attractive Sea Aster. Many of our largest salt marshes have been reclaimed from the sea in recent historical times by dyke-building, but new ones are constantly forming as silt accumulates in our sheltered bays and estuaries and is colonised by *Salicornia*. Fine examples of salt marshes can be seen in Dundalk Bay, at the North Bull Island in Dublin Bay, in Kerry at Castlemaine Harbour and Tralee Bay, on the Fergus Estuary in Co. Clare — to name but a few. A plant which is actively speeding up the formation of salt marshes around much of our coast is the rice grass, *Spartina townsendii*, introduced to Ireland about fifty years ago.

Another major coastal habitat type is the sand dune system which protects many of our coastal areas from being eroded by wave action. The fine sand particles, product of millions of years of the break-down of rocks by wear and tear and the elements, are deposited on our beaches by the tides. Above the high water mark the sand dries out and is then blown by the wind until trapped by debris or the stems of Marram grass. This plant grows strongly in fine loose sand and quickly stabilises it into sand dune ridges. In time other plants establish a foothold and a firm sward builds up which is characterised by a vegetation of short grasses and attractive flowering plants such as Sand Pansy, Wild Thyme, Bedstraw, Bird's Foot Trefoil and various vetches. In the damper hollows, or dune-slacks, small creeping willows establish themselves. Sand dune areas are particularly attractive to certain species of butterflies — Dark Green Fritillaries, Common Blues and Graylings, to mention but three of the more common species which are typical of this habitat. Here too Rabbits, and often Hares, are found, and with them one of their main predators, the Red Fox.

There are many fine sand dune areas around the Irish coast, including those at Dundrum Bay in Co. Down, much of the coast north of Dublin City and the North Bull Island in Dublin Bay, Brittas Bay in Co. Wicklow, the Wexford coast between Cahore Point and Rosslare Strand, Tramore in Co. Waterford, many of the sheltered bays on the south coast of Cork, Inch and Banna Strand in Co. Kerry, Lahinch in Co. Clare, many of the bays in west Galway and Mayo and much of the coast between Sligo and Ballyshannon, while in Donegal there are a considerable number of sand dune areas right around the coast to Doagh Isle on Inishowen. Sand dunes attract people in fine summer weather and unfortunately some areas close to population centres are subjected to too much human pressure: the fragile covering of vegetation is quickly broken down and the dunes become unstable. In some areas the sand is blown inland to swamp good agricultural land; in others coastal erosion follows the breakdown of the dune barrier.

The shallow seas, especially on the north, east and south coasts, have important commercial fisheries. The main species caught are Cod, Whiting, Haddock, bottom-feeding (demersal) flat-fish such as Plaice and Dabs and surface-living (pelagic) fish such as Herring and Mackerel. Prawns are also caught in abundance off the east coast, while all along the rocky shores and off-shore reefs there are lobsters, Edible Crabs and crayfish. Other commercially-fished sea creatures include shellfish such as scallops, oysters, mussels and cockles. In addition to the species mentioned above there is a host of other, "non-commercial" fish, crustaceans, shellfish and various "lower" invertebrates right down to the microscopic organisms which form the first link in the food-chain of life in the sea. Many of the larger fish are cannibalistic, and they in turn are preyed upon by man and carnivorous fish such as sharks and by marine mammals — whales, dolphins, porpoises and seals. Some of the largest of these animals, however, such as the Basking Shark and some of the whales feed not on large fish but on vast quantities of tiny plankton and other small marine organisms. Whales are not often seen in Irish waters (though individuals or small schools are sometimes stranded on our beaches), but dolphins and porpoises are quite numerous, especially off the southwest coast. Basking Sharks are sometimes seen with snout, dorsal fin and tail sticking out of the water (giving a good indication of their immense size!), but they are quite harmless. At one time they were commercially fished on the west coast, especially around Achill Island, but nowadays they are only occasionally hunted by visiting Norwegian harpooners.

In Ireland there are two species of seal, the Common or Harbour Seal and the Atlantic or Grey Seal. Of the two the latter is by far the more numerous and in some places a hundred or more can be found hauled out on rocky islets, reefs or boulder beaches. The Common Seal is found more in sheltered waters and often hauls out on sandbanks. Large marine turtles occasionally reach our shores, borne by the warm waters of the Gulf Stream current.

Few of the creatures of the coast mentioned so far make their presence known to the casual observer: most of the fish are not seen until they lie in rows on a cold slab in a fish-monger's shop; the cetaceans (whales, porpoises, dolphins) are usually encountered by chance sightings from boats or headlands; and the seals are usually shy because they are harassed by fishermen whose nets and catches they sometimes damage. But one group of seaside creatures — the seabirds — are ever present and visible to even the most unobservant. The true seabirds are limited enough as to variety, but some species are extremely abundant, and for a few Ireland is the headquarters of their North Atlantic populations. The seabirds which occur around our coasts are a mixture of native breeding species and birds of passage. The latter group includes such ocean wanderers as the Great Shearwater, which breeds only in the Tristan da Cunha group of islands in the South Atlantic, half-way between southern Africa and South America, and which, outside its breeding season, performs a great circular migration around the South and North Atlantic, passing southwards off our west coast in autumn. The prominent headlands of the West and Southwest, and especially Cape Clear Island, are the best vantage points from which to see this powerful seabird. Another regular Antipodean visitor is the related Sooty Shearwater, while various rare shearwaters, petrels, albatrosses, frigatebirds, skuas, gulls, terns and auks from far-flung areas of the Arctic, Antarctic and North and South Atlantic Oceans, may be seen from time to time off our coasts. Ireland's position, butting into the Atlantic at the western fringe of Europe, makes it an ideal

Top– The Grey Seal is found all round the rocky coasts of Ireland. Their numbers have been grossly exaggerated by some who regard them as a serious fishing competitor. *Above, left–* The Gannet, a magnificent seabird with a seven foot wing-span. There are only three breeding colonies, one of which contains 20,000 pairs. *Above, right–* A pair of penguin-like Guillemots occupy a small ledge on a sheer sea cliff. A single egg is laid on the bare rock.

country from which to observe the oceanic passage of these birds, in their hundreds of thousands or their ones or twos, according to species.

In addition to the ocean wanderers we have large breeding populations of seabirds, numbering twenty-one species. Some of the gulls and terns form their breeding colonies both inland (usually on lake islands) and on the coast, but it is on the coastal headlands and islands that one finds the most spectacular assemblages. Colonial seabirds are extremely gregarious and pack together in dense hordes, often with just a few inches separating one sitting bird from its neighbours. Cliff-nesting Guillemots and Kittiwakes are often particularly closely packed, crowding every available rocky ledge. Their colonies can number thousands of pairs — in the case of the Guillemot there are several Irish colonies which have over ten thousand pairs. Some of the best Irish seabird colonies, for these and other species, include Rathlin Island in Co. Antrim, Lambay Island in Co. Dublin, the Saltee Islands in Co. Wexford, the Old Head of Kinsale in Co. Cork, the Skelligs and outer Blaskets in Co. Kerry, the Cliffs of Moher in Co. Clare, the north Mayo cliffs and Horn Head in Co. Donegal. Two nocturnal species of seabird, the Manx Shearwater and Storm Petrel, are found on islands off the west coast of Ireland in numbers equalling or exceeding those found anywhere else in the world. Puffin Island, off the Kerry coast has an underground colony of over ten thousand pairs of Manx Shearwaters: a visit in daytime gives little indication of their presence and one would be forgiven for thinking the island was riddled with Rabbit burrows. But at about half-past eleven on a dark summer's night the air becomes alive with the weird crowing calls of a myriad of Manx Shearwaters as they return from fishing trips to the Bay of Biscay in pursuit of the shoals of sardines and sprats. Similarly, the much tinier Storm Petrels (frail-looking swallow-sized seabirds with fluttering flight) flit in from the sea in the dark of the night to their nesting places in crevices in shattered rocks or old stone walls. They have some huge colonies in a chain of small islands from Kerry to Donegal.

Off the Kerry coast lie the two Skelligs, jagged mountain-tops rising precipitously from the Atlantic. On the smaller rock is a colony of 20,000 pairs of Gannets, magnificent white seabirds with black-tipped wings spanning seven feet. This is one of the largest colonies in the world and there are only two other Irish nesting sites — both much smaller — on the remote Bull Rock off west Cork and on Great Saltee off the Wexford coast. Besides the Gannets, the Skelligs hold large numbers of many of the other cliff-nesting seabirds — Fulmars, Storm Petrels, Shags, Kittiwakes, Razorbills, Guillemots and Puffins.

The tern family, of which five species nest in Ireland, shun the rocky islands and cliffs and nest instead on small low islands (of sand, shingle or covered with short vegetation) in sheltered bays, estuaries, coastal lagoons and, in the case of the Common and Arctic Terns, in inland lakes. These attractive seabirds, in size like small gulls and in shape like swallows, are summer visitors to our shores. They are here from late March or April until September or early October and while here feed off shoals of Sand

Eels, sprats, the fry of various other fish and occasionally crustaceans. Unfortunately, their numbers have declined seriously in recent decades, for reasons both known and unknown. The smallest of the five Irish species, the Little Tern, was probably never very abundant, but with the growing recreational use of our beaches, the nesting birds are increasingly disturbed or have their eggs or young trampled underfoot. The very camouflage which is so effective at protecting the eggs and young from natural predators (such as gulls, crows and foxes) results in them being inadvertently stood upon. Consequently their numbers have declined as human pressure has increased on the beaches which are the Little Tern's favourite nesting places. There are probably fewer than three hundred pairs in Ireland now. Another species which has declined dramatically in Ireland — indeed throughout its European range — is the Roseate Tern. This is particularly unfortunate as the total European population probably never exceeded 4,000 pairs during this century, of which over half were found in Ireland. Indeed, the largest Roseate Tern colony was situated on Tern Island in Wexford Harbour, where, in the 1960s, up to 2,000 pairs nested. This island, which was really just a small sandbank with a dune ridge of Lyme Grass, was eroded away to nothing by winter storms, and the terns were forced to move elsewhere: so far alternative nesting places (if any) have not been located. In addition to problems on their breeding grounds, the Irish terns face other risks in their wintering grounds on the west coast of Africa including the trapping of large numbers for food especially by native peoples along the coast of the Gulf of Guinea.

The populations of the other seabirds however, are mainly in a healthy state. Fulmars which first nested in Ireland in the early years of this century have increased and spread to all suitable cliff sites; Gannets, once reduced to near extinction in Ireland by the human harvesting of their eggs and young, have recovered admirably since this practice died out; the gulls have benefited from man's wastefulness by scavenging at rubbish dumps, meat factories, sewage outfalls and such like, they are now never short of food and no longer are the populations controlled by winter starvation. Some of the auks (Razorbills, Guillemots and Puffins), however, give cause for concern. They spend most of their lives swimming on the sea and seem to be particularly vulnerable to oil spills. Tens of thousands die each year in series of "minor" spills which never hit the headlines, while single major incidents like the wrecking of the *Torrey Canyon* and the *Amoco Cadiz* can kill five or ten thousand birds. The auks are also susceptible to being entangled in almost invisible drift nets and large numbers are drowned this way — both on our coasts near the breeding colonies and in the wintering areas around Spain and Portugal. Many are also known to be carrying abnormally high levels of heavy metals and synthetic chemical residues in their body fat, which are potentially dangerous if the birds are subjected to stress caused by food shortages, stormy weather, feather moult and so on. While man's discharges of offal and sewage into the estuaries and coastal seas may benefit some birds, the spilling of oil and industrial wastes is a serious

The Rook (in flight) is probably trying to steal a morsel from the young Herring Gull, which in turn has probably picked up some edible rubbish thrown down by someone who can't read.

threat to others. In many cases the dead seabirds on the beaches are simply tangible evidence that the whole marine environment has been insidiously or grossly polluted by man's carelessness.

In addition to the true seabirds another major group of birds is found on the coast. These are the waterfowl — ducks, geese, swans and waders — but as they also inhabit the inland wetlands, they will be mentioned in the next section on wetland habitats.

THE WETLANDS

Wetlands, with which Ireland is well endowed, provide extremely varied habitats. The definition covers a multitude of different wet habitats including ponds, lakes, rivers, marshes, callows, fens, bogs, turloughs, swamps, canals, gravel-pits, reservoirs, estuaries, sheltered tidal bays and so on. Because the definition covers such a broad range of habitats, one would expect to find an extremely diverse flora and fauna associated with it, and indeed such is the case.

Ponds are everywhere in Ireland. Many are natural and have formed wherever hollows occur where water collects faster than it drains away in streams or through permeable soils or underlying rocks. There are also many man-made ponds — the result of the removal of clay or gravel for building purposes, watering places for livestock, ornamental waters in big estates and parks. Some ponds are rather sterile, such as the black corrie lakes gouged out of the mountain sides by ice thousands of years ago, or the peat-stained bog pools which dot our very extensive areas of blanket peat. The blanket bog area between Roundstone and Clifden in Connemara contains almost more ponds than peat. Such ponds support little flora or fauna as they are acidic and lack the nutrients on which plants grow. One might be lucky and find some which contain Brown Trout, but more often than not even these are stunted by lack of a sufficient diet. However, many of our ponds, especially in the richer lowland regions and in areas where limestone is the predominant rock, are rich in plant and animal life. Algae of various kinds float about in midwater or on the surface, while others such as *Chara* grow from the bottom. Water lillies and pondweeds such as *Potomageton* root in the mud at the bottom and grow to the surface. Closer to the edge where the water is shallower, *Phragmites* reeds and bullrushes grow tall above the water and sway and rustle in the breeze. Along the fringes various sedges, bur-reeds and other marsh plants grow in profusion, providing they are not heavily grazed by livestock.

Ponds are really small lakes — the bigger they get the more likely will they be called lakes, and apart from size the main differences are that lakes are often deeper (at least in the middle) and the edge vegetation in them is often exposed to much more severe wave-action. Lakes, too, often have large rivers flowing into them and out again at the other end. Ponds, because of their small size and their relatively sheltered waters, often have high densities of both flora and fauna. The vegetation supports a myriad of small invertebrates; these in turn support larger, predatory invertebrates such as the larvae of dragon-flies; the aquatic insects and other invertebrates are fed on by the various fresh-water fish which inhabit our ponds and lakes — some fish, such as the introduced coarse fish, also feed on some of the water plants; large fish, and especially the predatory Pike, feed on the smaller fish; Otters make their holts by rivers and lakes and feed on Eels, Trout and the other fish which abound in our fresh-waters. Then there are the water-birds which nest in the reed-beds, feed along the edges or in the shallows or swim and dive in search of animal or vegetable food. Mallard, Moorhens, Coots, grebes, Grey Herons, Mute Swans, Black-headed Gulls and one or two others are the most common species frequenting our lakes and ponds throughout the year. Other species visit these and the other wetlands during the migration times and in the winter months. Many of our small ponds provide spawning places for our only two common amphibians, the Common Newt and the Common Frog, while the third Irish amphibian is confined to a few ponds on the low-lying sandy shores either side of the Dingle Peninsula in Kerry: this is the Natterjack Toad. Of the larger Irish lakes the most important for water-fowl and other wildlife are Loughs Neagh and Beg in the North, the lime-stone lakes around Mullingar in Co. Westmeath, Loughs Ree and Derg on the Shannon, Lough Corrib in Co. Galway, Lough Gara on the borders of Roscommon and Sligo and Lough Oughter in Co. Cavan.

The flora and fauna of our rivers and streams depends very much on the speed of water flow. Only a limited number of plants and animals can live in fast-flowing mountain streams and torrents, simply because the force of the water threatens to sweep them away. Mosses and long green waving fronds of algae attach themselves to the rocks and stones and provide some shelter for aquatic larvae and other small creatures. Brown Trout are well able to make headway against strong currents, while Dippers (in Ireland there is a distinct sub-species) plunge from rocky perches into the fast-flowing waters to creep along the bottom searching for Caddis-fly larvae and other morsels. Grey Wagtails are common along the courses of the fast-flowing rivers and streams. Some of the smaller Irish rivers run straight from their mountain sources to the nearby sea, but others meander along leisurely courses across the plains and lowlands of Ireland. The greatest of all our rivers is the Shannon which flows 240 miles from source to sea and which receives a number of major tributaries along the way: the Boyle, Inny, Suck, Brosna to name but a few. Other important river systems are those of the Bann, the Boyne, the Slaney, the Barrow, Nore and Suir, the Munster Blackwater, the Lee, the Moy, the Erne and the Foyle. Where the rivers run slowly their vegetation and animal life is often similar to those of the lakes, but a number of rivers are prone to winter flooding and consequently have extensive alluvial flood plains. These usually have short swards of grasses and other plants which are tolerant of periodic immersion, and these flood areas are usually known as callows. When covered in shallow water the callows are extremely attractive to large numbers of wintering wildfowl and waders. The callows of the River Shannon between Loughs Ree and Derg, together with the

This Red Fox, driven onto the open ice by hunger must be sorely tempted by the sight of so much food. A swan could provide fifteen pounds of meat and they are occasionally killed by foxes.

Left– A rare view of the Otter, a shy and scarce aquatic mammal. Otters are found in many of our streams, rivers and lakes and also in sheltered rocky bays on the coast.

Left– A blue, orange and white jewel of our unpolluted rivers and canals, Kingfishers are quite widespread but often overlooked except by fishermen who spend long hours by the river banks.

Above– This tiny frog, hitching a ride on a leaf, was probably a tadpole not long before the photograph was taken. When full-grown it will be about ten times the size.

adjoining callows of the Rivers Suck and Little Brosna, cover a vast area which in winter supports hundreds of thousands of ducks, geese, wild swans, plovers and other water-birds. A number of other rivers have important callows, especially the Suir, the Munster Blackwater and the Leinster Blackwater — a tributary of the Boyne.

The limestone plains of east Galway and parts of north Clare and south Roscommon have a uniquely Irish type of wetland — the turlough. Turloughs are lakes or ponds which appear during the winter months when rainfall causes the ground water level to rise and flood the turloughs through cracks, fissures and "swallow-holes" in the underlying limestone. In spring the water table falls and the turloughs dry out, leaving the flat grassy bottoms exposed for a few months. The typical vegetation is composed of Creeping Bent Grass, Silverweed and other plants tolerant of prolonged flooding and heavy grazing. Though the species diversity is usually low, the turlough beds are fertile and produce an abundance of plants which are grazed in summer by domestic livestock, in winter by Wigeon, Whooper and Bewick's Swans and other grazing wildfowl. There are very often outcropping limestone boulders in the beds of the turloughs and these usually have a lush skirting of dark green moss known as *Cinclidotus fontinalis.* Because of the complete change from lake to dry pasture between winter and summer the animal life of turloughs is almost non-existent, for few creatures can withstand such extremes of environment. An interesting creature which is found in Ireland only in the turloughs is the Fairy Shrimp which survives the dry periods in the egg form, hatching out in abundance with the first flooding.

The fresh water wetlands cannot be left without mentioning the bogs, which cover such a large proportion of the surface of Ireland. There are two main types, raised bogs which are found mainly in the central plain and blanket bogs which clothe most of our mountains, especially in the West. The raised bogs were formed through the slow processes of plant succession, starting with the gradual filling in of shallow limestone lakes with aquatic vegetation and its decaying remains. After a period the waters became completely choked up and the lakes became reed swamps, then fens and finally raised bogs. These bogs are slowly self-perpetuating as the typical bog vegetation of Sphagnum mosses, Bog Cotton, dwarf willow shrubs, heathers and so on, die and decompose and add layers to those already underneath. Many of the bogs are twenty to thirty feet deep, and as about one-seventh of Ireland is covered with peat bogs we have an abundant natural fuel resource. The blanket bogs missed out on the early stages of development of the raised bogs, being formed directly on the mountains where high rainfall favoured the growth of the mosses and other plants from which the peat is formed. Although the raised bogs are built up on a limestone base, they and the blanket bogs are very acidic. Consequently the vegetation grows extremely slowly. Growth is further hampered by the exposure to the elements to which most of the bogs are subjected. They are inhospitable places but they do harbour some attractive small plants such as Sundews and Marsh Andromeda. The beautiful day-flying Emperor Moth is a common inhabitant of Irish bogs, while one of our scarcer butterflies, the Large Heath, is largely confined to boglands. Curlews nest commonly as do Meadow Pipits, while the small Irish breeding population of Golden Plovers is found on the rolling moors of the West and Northwest.

Finally, there are the coastal wetlands including the salt-marshes, mud-flats and shallow sea bays already mentioned. Also in the coastal zone are a number of brackish lagoons which contain an interesting flora and fauna. These lagoons have usually been formed when shallow bays have been cut off from the sea by bars of sand or shingle. They are fed by rain-water and small streams and also by seepage of sea-water which makes them slightly saline. Most are shallow and have a rich growth of aquatic plants such as the emergent *Potomageton* and *Ruppia* and many have edges fringed with Phragmites reeds. Lack of rainfall in summer, together with the reduced inflow of stream water and increased evaporation, results in a lowering of the water levels and often banks of sand or mud are exposed during the summer and autumn. In such conditions the coastal lagoons seem to be particularly attractive to some of the rarer species of shore-birds: lagoons at Akeragh in Co. Kerry, Ballycotton in Co. Cork and Lady's Island in Co. Wexford provide resting and feeding haunts for tired transatlantic waders each autumn, and ornithologists from all over Europe join the Irish ones in watching these rare American visitors.

Irish wetlands are a great natural resource, not always appreciated by many, for there are constant attempts to drain them. Drainage resulting in the winning of good agricultural land is, of course, most desirable, but unfortunately a number of drainage schemes have produced little or no gain in agricultural land and have instead destroyed a number of areas of high amenity and aesthetic or scientific value. Wetlands are reservoirs from which we draw drinking water for ourselves and our livestock; our expanding industries require increasing quantities of pure water; our fish need clean waters and many of these are an important asset for tourist anglers as well as our own fishermen; increasingly we are recognising the importance of our waters for recreation — for swimming, boating, water-skiing and so on; and our wetlands are among the last wilderness areas left to us and to our wildlife. We have a responsibility to manage our wet-lands wisely: it is in our own best interests to do so, and future generations will be grateful if we accept this responsibility.

Our wetlands are important not only to us and our native flora and fauna: they are vital to the very existence of hundreds of thousands of migratory waterfowl which seek winter refuge in the relatively mild climate of Ireland. Each autumn and early winter ducks, geese, swans and shore-birds stream into Ireland from breeding grounds as far away as Greenland and Arctic islands of central Canada, from Iceland and the Faeroes, from Scotland and Scandinavia, from central Europe and the wastes of Arctic Russia and Siberia. For thousands of years they have been following their traditional flyways from the northwest and the northeast to the rich wetlands of Ireland. Surrounded by the sea and under the warming influence of the Gulf Stream our winter climate is temperate and our inland wetlands seldom freeze; our tidal shores hardly ever. And so the migratory flocks can always find open water and ice-free feeding places.

Their numbers and diversity are impressive enough, but for several species Ireland is a particularly important wintering place. No less than three-quarters of the world's Greenland White-fronted Geese come to our bogs, callows, turloughs and salt-marshes. Their main haunt is the Wexford Slobs. Practically all the Pale-bellied Brent Geese which come to Europe from breeding grounds in the high Arctic of Greenland and Canada make Ireland their wintering home: they feed mainly on the "fields" of *Zostera* and *Enteromorpha* between the tides. From Siberia come the small wild Bewick's Swans: of the total European wintering population of 9,000 birds, no less than 2,000 come to Irish wetlands — more when Europe freezes. One could go on cataloguing migratory waterfowl which find in the wetlands of Ireland just the right combination of food, water and security to ensure survival. It goes without saying that if our wetlands are lost through careless mismanagement, we will also lose forever the opportunity of seeing thousands of waterfowl flying over our marshes and estuaries.

TERRESTRIAL HABITATS

Little has been said about the terrestrial habitats and their flora and fauna. This is because there are few dramatic examples of land animals or plants or natural areas which are unique to Ireland. Reference has already been made to the fact that many land creatures were unable to colonise this country because of the flooding of the Irish Sea soon after the last Ice Age. Thus we have no land reptiles except the Common Lizard. Many of our mammals have been introduced by man, mainly since the coming of the Normans in the twelfth century, or in much more recent times. House Mice probably came with man in prehistoric times, but the Brown Rat is a much more recent arrival and probably even less welcome. Brown Hares were also introduced, deliberately, as were Grey Squirrels and Sika Deer in the last century. The only Irish vole, the Bank Vole, was discovered in Kerry and Limerick as recently as 1964 and has since spread to adjoining counties. This species was almost certainly introduced too. On the debit side the Giant Irish Deer died out long ago, while Wild Boars and Wolves were exterminated by hunting in more recent times: the last Wolf was killed in the eighteenth century. Bears, too, are part of our lost fauna. When all these mammals are discounted we are left with very few natives: Pine Martens, Stoats (contrary to popular belief, there are no Weasels in Ireland), Wood Mice, Red Deer, Irish Hares, Badgers, Red Foxes, Hedgehogs, Pygmy Shrews, Red Squirrels, a few species of bats and one or two other mammals are all that are left. Most of our woodland, too, is artificial and composed of introduced exotic species. Nearly all the native woodland was cleared by man — first by fire to create pasture and later by

Top— This fine panoramic view of the Glen of Aherlow by the Galty Mountains in Co. Tipperary is a good example of the varied landscape: high mountains and moors, flanked by conifer plantations, and rich pastures criss-crossed by prolific hedgerows and small areas of woodland.

Right— A young Badger peeps tentatively out of its earthen set to catch the reflection of the photographer's flash in its eyes.

felling for charcoal smelting, ship-building, fuel and many other purposes. By the end of the last century almost all the woodland had disappeared and during this century there has been increasing afforestation with quick-growing coniferous soft-woods, particularly spruces from western North America. A few natural oak-woods survived, notably the extensive ones in the Killarney area. Another remnant of bygone times is the hazel-scrub of the limestone pavement areas of Clare and south-east Galway. This brings us to one of the few remaining outstanding natural habitats not mentioned before.

In the northwest corner of Co. Clare is a remarkable 100 square mile area known as The Burren. Here the limestone rock has been pushed up, in places to 1,000 feet above sea level, into a series of strangely shaped plateaux which at a distance look like massive and ancient man-made steps. It is a bleak and beautiful area, the like of which is found nowhere else in Europe outside the Karst areas of Dalmatia in Yugoslavia. The plateaux are virtually bare of vegetation but on close examination one finds that the limestone has been weathered into myriad squares and rectangles separated from each other by narrow clefts and crevices. Sheltered in the fissures and nourished by the rich water-laden humus which has slowly collected over the ages, are a great variety of small plants. Many are rare or absent elsewhere in Ireland and even in much of Europe, while others are found more typically in Alpine or Arctic regions.

In addition to the strange and varied vegetation of the limestone cracks, areas of The Burren are carpeted with rare flowers such as the delicate Mountain Avens with their eight creamy petals which give them their Latin name *octopetala*. The unbelievably blue Spring Gentian is also found in abundance. These and other flowers of high mountains and high latitudes grow in The Burren right down to where the sea spray from the Atlantic drenches the western edge in the area of Black Head. One of the peculiarities of the flora of The Burren is that plants which normally grow in much more southerly regions, in Iberia and the Mediterranean, are also found there. So great is the mixture that botanists from far and wide come to see the extraordinary spectacle. The Burren is not only a botanist's paradise, it is also a place of pilgrimage for the entomologist, more especially the lepidopterist. Many species of butterfly and moth occur here which are rare elsewhere in Ireland. The Pearl Bordered Fritillary butterfly is common in The Burren but absent from the rest of Ireland and the Transparent Burnet and Burren Green, both moths, are virtually confined to this limestone region. It is likely that further study would produce a list of very interesting varieties of other insects too. Between the limestone plateaux where soil has accumulated, ancient "woods" of hazel and stunted oak grow. Unfortunately, land clearance is taking its toll and this interesting vegetation is steadily disappearing. Grazing animals are also speeding up the disappearance of this natural vegetation by preventing the regeneration of the hazel scrub. Plans are afoot, however, to establish a National Park in The Burren and perhaps this will help preserve the rich vegetation of the area.

The strange physical structure of the place and its rare and varied plants and insects are not the only interesting features: The Burren has a rich assemblage of man-made structures ranging from megalithic tombs to iron-age forts, early Christian churches, round towers and Norman castles. Underground massive caves have been dissolved out of the limestone by rainwater seeping down from the surface through the millions of cracks which criss-cross the rock pavements. Birds and animals on The Burren are scarce. The environment is too hostile for them: the plant life, which is seldom more than a few centimetres high, simply does not supply sufficient cover. However, one should be watchful for traces of the rare Pine Marten which slinks about quietly in the tangled hazel scrub. And right in the centre of The Burren is a depression which becomes Lough Carron in winter when it is often full of water. It attracts good numbers of ducks, Whooper Swans and occasionally, White-fronted Geese. At its eastern edge The Burren falls away sharply to become a low, flat limestone plain running south from Kinvarra towards Ennis. Here there are numerous lakes and turloughs interspersed with scrub woodland and fens. In these areas there is a much greater variety of water-birds and others. Just to the southwest of The Burren stretch the great Cliffs of Moher, mentioned earlier, where large colonies of breeding seabirds may be viewed from the top of the 500 foot precipice. If one were to recommend a single area in Ireland which would be of profound interest to the all-round naturalist, it would be difficult to think of a better place than The Burren and its adjacent lands and sea-coast.

Hedgehogs are charming little mammals that browse in long vegetation. They are quite common throughout Ireland and, sadly, many are squashed by cars.

Opposite– One view of The Burren and its solution-cracked limestone and numerous ancient man-made structures.

The passage grave at Knowth, Co. Meath.

FROM EARLIEST TIMES

Joseph Raftery

HE FULL STORY of a community's past can never be recovered since so much of it dies with the minds in which it is conceived. What can be recovered comes from a number of sources. For preliterate times, archaeology alone, assisted by the relevant natural sciences, can be used. For later periods when writing was known and could be used to compile documents archaeology, the natural sciences and written records are all available to tell us something of our past. Archaeology is the study of man through his artefacts, but the artefacts alone are not enough. We must know something of their stratigraphy or the way they are deposited in the earth, their associations and distribution over the land and above all — and this is the essence of our work — we must be able to logically deduce what purposes they might have served, what social organisation they might have supported and with what religious, philosophical or moral beliefs they might have been associated. Because the inferences that can be drawn from recorded archaeological facts are extremely limited, much is lost to us forever. What, for instance, can we say of the poetry or music of those eras before men learned to put their thoughts on paper or parchment? And even when men could write, how much has been lost because they failed to describe in detail the things which they considered commonplace?

For all these reasons we must realise from the beginning that the story of early Ireland is far from complete. We sometimes think that we know more than we do, but any critical appraisal of the sum of real facts available to us gives, more than anything else, an indication of the amount of continuing research before us. The situation is not much better in later, text-aided times, that is, in Ireland after 500 A.D. For written manuscripts are not always specific and even where they are specific it is difficult if not impossible to decide to which century they refer. It is frequently difficult to tell precisely when a text was written down and it is rarely clear whether the events, things or social organisation described are contemporary or obsolete and taken simply from folk memory or else copied from earlier texts. Thus, even literary sources in early Ireland must be used with great caution.

Certain broad assumptions, however, are admissible. One, based on the experience of history, is that the psychology of man changes little and that in general terms social patterns tend to repeat themselves. We can assume then that individuals always varied and that some men were at all times superior to others — some were rulers and others acceptors of rule. There seems no reason to believe that this was not the case for Ireland too. All the evidence suggests that from as early as the New Stone Age five thousand years ago, and perhaps even earlier, Irish society was rural, familial, socially graded and aristocratic. This last sentence is of course, of far-reaching import and suggests a further fundamental assumption. Namely, that from the earliest times there has been continuity of population in Ireland. It used to be fashionable to talk of invasions; invasions were invoked to account for every technological change in the culture of the land. But what evidence is there in the archaeological record to indicate that such invasions took place? The exact criteria by which the intrusion of extraneous peoples may be assessed are extremely difficult to define. How can one decide what are "proofs" of invasion or immigration, of commercial contacts or of political or cultural influences? For later times, written sources are of help but the interpretation of the archaeological record must also be unequivocal.

A word must be said about chronology for such is the nature of man that events must always be put within a time-scale. At first, dating was based on correlations between objects in connected areas all of which were dependent upon dates derived from written documents, especially those of Egypt. While this method is still used, in more modern times greater precision in dating has been made possible by the use of various scientific methods such as radiocarbon dating and pollen analysis. Individual objects made of organic materials and dated by the radiocarbon or Carbon 14 method, for instance, will themselves, when found with other objects, date those objects. In this way a chain of dates is constructed which provides a framework into which all objects and cultures can ideally be fitted.

There is one aspect of chronology about which we in Ireland should exercise caution. This is the concept known as "time lag". It depends for its efficacy on geographical distances and works something like this: an idea, technique or object originating in, say, Central Europe will spread from its centre of origin, taking longer and longer to reach further distances. Thus, it may move westwards, cross the Straits of Dover and establish itself in southern Britain. Because travel must have been slow in ancient times, an idea took a long time to reach Scotland or Wales and appreciably longer to reach Ireland. Indeed, according to this theory it is possible to imagine groups of objects arriving in Ireland after they had died out in their homeland! But this theory fails to take into account the importance of sea routes which brought and kept Ireland in relatively close and rapid contact with the whole of Atlantic Europe. Indeed, in the case of some ideas such as the introduction of metallurgy into Ireland, it is possible to argue for a somewhat earlier implantation here of certain aspects than in Britain.

We do not yet know exactly when man first set foot on what was later to become the island of Ireland. One or two isolated objects of Palaeolithic or Old Stone Age date suggest the possibility of a lost or strayed early hunter, but there is no evidence that man had penetrated in any numbers so far west during those millennia when people lived in caves on the Continent and when the massive ice sheets of the great Ice Age were in retreat. The earliest known site in Ireland on which men lived and worked is at Mount Sandel on the River Bann in Co. Derry. This has been dated by Carbon 14 to roughly nine thousand years ago, to a period known as the Middle Stone Age or the Mesolithic. At several other sites in the northeast of Ireland such as Toome, Newferry and Cushendun in Co. Antrim, assemblages of material of Mesolithic character have come to light. With the exception of groupings of holes for upright wooden posts at Mount Sandel, no certain indication of the presence of domestic structures has been recorded. Indeed, several of the known Mesolithic sites are located on raised beaches along the Antrim coast. They are stratified in such a way as to suggest that the objects we now find have simply been washed up on to the beaches.

Vast quantities of artefacts have come to light. The bulk of them are made of flint, a very hard stone found in Ireland chiefly in Co. Antrim but elsewhere as stray nodules in soils carried and spread by the glaciers. The number of types of artefacts is limited. Most objects are made from flakes and were used for cutting or scraping; roughly chipped axeheads are also well-known and there are crude heavy objects which might have been used as choppers. Abundant pointed blades with chipped tangs which when mounted on the ends of wooden shafts might have been used in the chase have also been found. In addition to stone objects, a few cut pieces of timber of unknown function have been found at the Toome site and a very small number of bone points are also recorded as at Rough Island, Co. Down and Rockmarshall, Co. Louth.

Though a great number of individual artefacts have come down to us from Mesolithic times in Ireland, it is virtually impossible to deduce with any degree of certainty the precise functions they had. On negative grounds, we can say that the Mesolithic people of Ireland had no pottery and no knowledge of agriculture; we assume that they had no domesticated animals. We are unable to say whether or not they wove cloth from animal or vegetable fibres or made baskets or fish-traps. In fact, it can be stated that of these earliest Irishmen we as yet know virtually nothing. Most of their material culture, their social organisation and their modes of thought elude us.

By analogy we may assume that these folk were neither pastoralists nor agriculturalists but rather that they were hunters, fowlers, fishermen and

Excavations in progress on the Mesolithic site at Mount Sandel, Co. Derry. The huts, whose former existence is indicated by arcs of post-holes, were about six metres across and date from between 7,000 and 6,500 B.C. They constitute the earliest structures yet discovered in the British Isles.

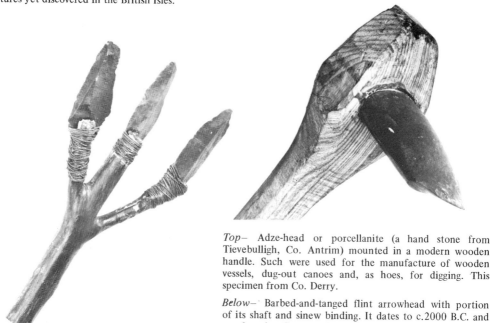

Top— Adze-head or porcellanite (a hand stone from Tievebulligh, Co. Antrim) mounted in a modern wooden handle. Such were used for the manufacture of wooden vessels, dug-out canoes and, as hoes, for digging. This specimen from Co. Derry.

Below— Barbed-and-tanged flint arrowhead with portion of its shaft and sinew binding. It dates to c.2000 B.C. and was found at Gortrea, Co. Galway.

Above— Simple, painted beades of flint or chest called Bann flakes were in widespread use in Ireland in Stone Age times. Their purpose is not known but, as most come from river or lake sites, it is presumed that they were used in connection with fishing. Here three are mounted on a three-pronged fork to make a fishing-spear. The reconstruction is modern and imaginative; the flakes were found on the shores of Lough Gara, Co. Sligo.

gatherers. Most of the Irish Mesolithic sites known to us are found near bodies of water — on lake shores and along the sandy coasts. It is, thus, reasonable to assume that fish played a large part in the diet of these early people. They also hunted but we have as yet no way of knowing what the main animals of the chase were, exactly how large the animal population was or what area would have had to be covered to ensure a sufficiency of food. Game would presumably have been limited in quantity because, as pollen analysis demonstrates, the country was heavily wooded at the time and this would have militated against the development of large herds of animals. Roots, wild fruits and berries, nuts, herbs and the like would have supplemented the diet. It is not necessary, however, to think in terms of a shifting, nomadic population. It is highly likely that Mesolithic Irishmen had fixed centres, homesteads of a sort, from which they sallied forth in their search for food. And this search may not have been as time-consuming nor as arduous as some would like to believe. Cultural anthropologists have demonstrated that as little as three hours per man per day is all that is required for modern hunter-gatherers to provide adequate sustenance for themselves and their communities. There may even have been a surplus beyond subsistence which would have allowed some degree of specialisation such as flint-knapping — and certainly, there must have been adequate time for rest and leisure activities.

We know nothing of the houses of our Mesolithic people apart from the few post-holes at Mount Sandel. So far no Mesolithic burial has come to light. We do know, however, that Mesolithic man in Ireland was not, as was previously believed, confined solely to the coasts of the Northeast. Traces of his activities have been found in the Midlands (at Lough Derravaragh, Co. Westmeath; Lough Kinale, Co. Longford; and Lough Sheelin, Co. Cavan) and in the west of Ireland (at Lough Allen and Lough Scur, Co. Leitrim; Croghan Lake, Co. Roscommon; Lough Gara, Co. Sligo; and elsewhere). A few objects of Mesolithic type found at Lough Gur, Co. Limerick suggest that by about 3,500 B.C., Mesolithic man may have penetrated far to the south in Ireland. Outside counties Derry, Antrim and Down chert — a dark, flint-like stone found in limestone formations — was the main material used in tool-making.

Not only do we know little of the way of life of Mesolithic man when he reached Ireland, we as yet do not know from where he came. Implements similar to some of those recorded in Ireland have been found for the same period around the Baltic Sea and especially in Denmark; similar objects occur on English and Scottish sites and it may be that these people came to us ultimately from the Baltic by way of England, reaching Ireland over a very narrow channel which had but recently cut this island off from the mainland of Europe.

The general conditions outlined above continued in Ireland for about three thousand years until they were supplanted around 3,600 B.C. by an agricultural system the origins of which are as yet uncertain. Instead of depending entirely on natural food-production, man was now able to control to some extent the rate of plant and animal reproduction. At no stage in our long history, however, was hunting and gathering ignored entirely. Indeed, much of our early literature concerns the delights of hunting and the joy and comforts provided by meat and various animal by-products.

To this new period, the names New Stone Age or Neolithic have been given. Although they are terms without real significance, they are sanctioned by long usage and may be retained for convenience. In this period, there were technological improvements and cultural innovations. Men now learned how to polish stone for the production of axeheads and fishspears — long, slender, tapering blades of slate. Ways of producing fine secondary flaking of flint implements by pressure and the knowledge of pottery making were added to their craft repertoire. Above all, as already pointed out, they became agriculturalists and pastoralists — Ireland's first farmers and stock raisers.

How all this came about is by no means clear. When studying the limited remains of the past, there is a strong tendency to run events together and to look on a period, in this case fifteen hundred years or more, as if it were compressed into the life-span of a single man. Did the knowledge of making improved stone implements come first? At what stage did pottery become known? Were they contemporary with or did they precede the introduction of agriculture? The answers to these and many other questions remain targets of future research. We do know that the introduction of agriculture gave a new dimension to living. From excavations currently in progress under peat bogs in Co. Mayo, we know that Neolithic men there and presumably elsewhere in Ireland tilled relatively large areas of land on the ridge-and-furrow or lazy-bed principle. It is not known what crops were cultivated but the presence of saddle querns — dished oval stones — suggests that grain of some variety may have been grown. Dry-stone walls indicate fencing or marks of division and one possible, though not certain, interpretation would be the existence of private property. One of our problems is to decide how extensive the cultivation of crops in Ireland was, especially at the beginning. Further survey is required to indicate what areas, if any, might have continued in the old way. Nor do we know to what extent the population was supported by the produce of the fields or to what extent their diet had to be supplemented.

A few sites, such as Lough Gur in Co. Limerick, show that houses were both round and rectangular in plan. They were built of stout upright posts. These may have been connected with woven twigs or wattle and plastered with mud but solid evidence for this and for the method and materials of roofing still eludes us. Nor do we know whether houses were isolated or clustered in village groupings. In each house the remains of a hearth where wood fires had been burnt were found. Here cooking was done, possibly in new-fangled pottery containers, corn was ground, and animals were slaughtered. Water could have been boiled in leather vessels or in caulked, wood-lined pits where fire-red stones were thrown in to bring the liquid to the required temperature.

Left— The earliest known piece of basketry in Ireland. Dating to about 2500 B.C., it was found at Twyford, Co. Westmeath.

Top— Reconstructed hand made pottery vessel called a "Beaker". Such are frequently found in graves but also served domestic purpose. This specimen comes from Grange, Lough Gur, Co. Limerick, and dates to about 1800 B.C.

Right— Handmade pottery vessel called a "Food Vessel". It was found at Rackavra, Co. Westmeath. Such bowls were highly decorated all over their faces and are commonly found in graves of the Bronze Age between about 2000 and 1000 B.C.

The animals — whether domestic or wild — had an economical value beyond the simple provision of protein in the diet. Their skins were used for shoes of a sort and, presumably, for the production of garments and bed coverings; sinews could have been used for sewing and thonging; the bone structure — including the antlers of deer — for the manufacture of a wide variety of everyday objects such as points and needles, harpoons for fishing and pointed tips for spears, javelins and arrows; shoulder blades of large animals could have been adapted as shovels and some might have served as digging implements.

The pottery of the period is characteristic. Some plain, flat-bottomed vessels were formerly ascribed to this period but this is no longer certain. The bulk of the known wares are round-bottomed; some are plain with short necks and rolled rims, others are small round bowls, heavily decorated with deeply-marked patterns. The best of these come from the burial sites of the Neolithic. Because of the intensive work done on burials over the past quarter of a century, it is probably true to say that we know more of man's life through death customs in Neolithic Ireland than through the actual remains of the living. Burials were of two main types: single graves and great stone vaults. The single graves were stone-lined and sometimes quite small. Occasionally they were made of side stones of large, almost megalithic proportions. The bodies in these were unburned and were usually accompanied by a decorated pottery bowl and occasionally, as at Linkardstown, Co. Carlow, by a polished stone axehead as well. These single graves or cists, as they are known to archaeologists, were usually covered by a mound of earth and stone. Sometimes the mound was very low, as at Ballintruer More, Co. Wicklow; sometimes it was quite high, as at Baunogenasraid, Co. Carlow. The Neolithic tombs made of very large stone blocks are known as megaliths, from the Greek words signifying "large stone". In Ireland there are four major varieties: passage graves, court cairns, dolmens and wedge graves. The most impressive are the great passage graves in the Boyne Valley, at New Grange, Knowth and Dowth. (Although we cannot yet say what length of time intervened between the erection of each, it seems reasonable to assume that they were not contemporary.) The passage grave, as the name implies, comprises a long passage leading to a central chamber off which smaller side-chambers open. It is not known whether such tombs were erected for the disposal of one important personage or whether they were family vaults used over a period. The other types of large stone tombs — the court cairns, wedges and dolmens — would appear to have been used once only and then sealed. How these imposing monuments are to be dated in relation to each other is as yet uncertain.

The existence in the same general period of small cists and massive megalithic tombs does suggest some form of social differentiation and thus by projection, a hierarchical social structure. The organisation of the labour required for the construction of megaliths argues in a similar way, though one must not overlook the *meitheal* system known down to modern times in the Irish countryside, where neighbours gather together

Above— Interior of the passage grave of Newgrange, Co. Meath, showing one of the motifs incised into the surface of the stones.

Ballykeel Dolmen, Co. Armagh.

and voluntarily pool their work to produce what a single person alone could not. In such a system all participants would be equal, though greater knowledge or expertise on the part of any individual would be recognised.

There are no markings or ornament of any sort on the stones forming the tombs of three of the four groups mentioned above. In contrast, the passage graves are distinguished not only by their architectonic form but by a wide range of designs incised or pecked into the surfaces of the stones, both inside and outside the tombs. These motifs comprise zig-zag lines, lozenges and triangles as well as curvilinear patterns including rounded zig-zags, circles with central dots and circles with rays projecting from their edges. It is not clear what interpretation should be given to this body of art: it may be merely decorative or it may have had some religious or ritual significance. Certainly it is significant that ornament, if such it may be called, is found on this one group of grave monuments only and that similar ornamentation has been found on tombs of like construction outside the country, especially in Brittany.

The passage grave is of the *tholos/dromos* variety. Such graves are found from Greece in the east, across the Mediterranean to Iberia, in Brittany, in parts of Britain and in Ireland. Megaliths in general have a wide distribution in Europe and much thought has been given to the interpretation of this phenomenon. It is interesting to note that in each area, the objects found in the local tombs are those of the regions in which the tombs were erected. It would appear, therefore, that one should consider the implantation of an idea in all the different districts rather than envisage, as some have done, the wholesale movements of people. The idea implanted may have been religious; it may have been an architectural concept alone; it may have been a combination of both. Whatever the true explanation may be, it seems reasonable to conclude from the facts available that Ireland almost five thousand years ago was in close contact with the rest of Europe, especially western and mediterranean Europe and that, in consequence, Ireland must have shared in developments of thought and technology taking place outside her shores.

Foremost amongst such developments was the discovery of the uses to which metal could be put. The conditions for the exploitation of this knowledge were already present in Ireland. Hunting and fishing went hand in hand with pastoralism and the tilling of the land. Although we know that men lived in communities in pre-agricultural times, the new life-cycle would have bound men more securely to one place. Specialisation and commercial operations with far-reaching organisation are also evident during the New Stone Age. For instance, axe-factories are standard for Neolithic Europe and in Ireland one at Tievebulliagh in Co. Antrim, is of special significance. Here there are large deposits of a hard stone called porcellanite and from it axeheads and adzeheads used for tree-felling, carpentry and possibly digging the land were produced in large numbers. From this centre they were traded to many parts of Ireland and exported in quantity to Britain. Thus, we have, by 2,000 B.C. a stable agricultural society with considerable organisational abilities as evidenced by great megaliths on the one hand and by systematised trading on the other. It was, furthermore, a rural community with aesthetic tendencies and religious concepts. This is the people to which a knowledge of metal came. The name given to the period of earliest metal-using in Ireland is the Bronze Age.

Ireland is rich in ores of copper, especially in the southern part of the country, and it was not long before this metal was being used in a big way. Native copper, that is, copper in the metallic state, cannot have been available to our earliest bronze-smiths. Instead the ores had to be located and identified; then they had to be mined in the opencast manner or as is seen at Mount Gabriel in Co. Cork by driving tunnels or adits into the sheer rock face. All this argues for considerable knowledge. Even further knowledge is necessary for the smelting of the ores so that usable metal is produced. From where did this knowledge come? The answer is, at the moment we do not know. It has been suggested that a knowledge of metalworking was brought to Ireland by a people known as the Beaker Folk, so called from the gracefully decorated hand-made pottery vessels found in their graves. There is little evidence, however, for this view. A handful of knowledgeable miners or metalworkers would have been sufficient to teach what was necessary, especially when Ireland would appear to have been in full communion with the rest of continental Europe. Innovations of great importance such as the knowledge of metal-working would not have passed her by.

Although we do not yet know clearly how metallurgical processes were organised in the country, it may be assumed that they were not in the hands of simple farmers. A skilled specialist class must have developed quickly. (Indeed, to judge by later Irish literature, it would seem that the smith, the craftsman, the artificer, always had a special and specialised status within Irish society.) We have to imagine what went on: how prospectors located the sites of ores; how, by pounding with heavy stone mauls after large fires had cracked the rock face, tunnels were gradually pushed forward; how the great ore lumps were carried away, loaded, perhaps, in panniers on the backs of beasts of burden — most likely oxen or horses — or on block-wheel or wheelless carts and were brought to the smelting places. The ore does not appear to have been smelted at the mines and no early smelting place has so far been identified. When the copper had been produced from its ore it was cast, at first in an open stone mould. The earliest objects made were flat axeheads which were hammered to give sharp cutting-edges; small daggers and knives were also made.

Gold was also a metal used extensively in early Ireland. The earliest objects were collar-like pieces made of a very thin beaten metal, and called lunulae from their crescentic shape. They were decorated with rectilinear patterns on their pointed terminals and along the borders of the wide portion between. Apart from some small decorated plaques of gold said to have been found on a body in a cave at Castlemartyr, Co. Cork, no other objects of gold have ever been found with a burial in Ireland. As a result it is not possible to say whether early objects made of gold were worn or, if so, whether by men or women. How they might have been worn is again uncertain. They might, of course, have been cult objects or might have ornamented houses or been used as media of exchange. Lunulae are important for another reason also, for they were exported to Britain, France, Germany and Luxembourg and were imitated in Denmark. What came back in return for these exports is unknown. Another early group of gold objects are those called, probably mistakenly, "sun discs". These are thin roundels of beaten gold with a lightly raised cruciform design and two tiny perforations in the centre. They are normally found in pairs, and it is thought that they were used to adorn garments, being attached through the holes to either side of the breast. Similar discs are found in the Iberian Peninsula which indicates the continuing existence and use of the Atlantic Sea Route from the Mediterranean in the south to the Baltic in the north. This route was in common use before the transcontinental amber routes were opened up about 1,000 B.C. Ireland enjoyed a favourable half-way position on this route and so was able to give and receive more from both south and north.

Flint, stone, bone and wood continued to be used for a variety of everyday purposes throughout the Bronze Age. Life probably continued largely unchanged: people hunted, fished and farmed as before but, with metal tools, somewhat more efficiently. It may be that megaliths were still built but now in ever-decreasing numbers. The dead were now buried crouched in stone-lined graves or interred as cremations in pits or cists. Normally, each body was accompanied by a small hand-made pottery vessel called a food vessel; cremated bones were contained in larger cinerary urns of which there are several varieties.

About 1,000 B.C. changes in the life-style of the Irish began to be apparent. The climate began slowly to deteriorate but, to judge from an examination of pollen grains in ancient bog deposits, agriculture seems to have intensified rather than slackened. There were great changes also in technology and in art. Implements and tools were now made exclusively of bronze, an alloy of copper and tin; they were cast in two-piece moulds of stone or clay. The socket was introduced and a new and highly sophisticated method of casting, the waste wax process, was adopted. Now, for the first time clear evidence of martial affairs is provided by the existence of long, graceful, flange-hilted swords of bronze, by socketed spearheads in several varieties and by circular shields of leather, wood or sheet bronze. Socketed hammers and chisels and small anvils and saws indicate the work of craftsmen; socketed sickles of bronze must have lightened the task of gleaning corn. The production of sheet bronze assumed an important role and large round-bottomed cauldrons, made of wide sheets of thin metal riveted together, and hung by a pair of suspension handles, were masterpieces of the bronzesmith's art.

All the new weapons, tools and techniques imply considerable wealth and, as a result, a comfortable standard of living. This is further stressed by the great wealth of the country in gold. Whether this was of Irish origin

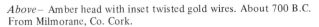

Above– Amber head with inset twisted gold wires. About 700 B.C. From Milmorane, Co. Cork.

Top right– Flat axeheads of bronze were frequently ornamented on both faces and on the narrow edges.

Right– In the later portion of the Bronze Age, after about 1000 B.C., the socket was introduced. Here it is used for axeheads of bronze.

Below– Ireland achieved a high degree of excellence in the production of objects of sheet bronze in the late Bronze Age, such as this fine cauldron from Castlederg, Co. Tyrone, dating to about 700 B.C.

or imported is still a matter of debate but the objects fashioned from it display an astonishing virtuosity both in form and applied ornament. There were finely made objects resembling the earlier lunulae in shape but with raised ridges and simulated torcs to decorate them and with ornamented discs sewn to the terminals with fine gold wire. Were these collars or gorgets, worn on the breast? We do not know. There were also double-conical objects, thought to have been hair pendants, made of hundreds of very fine wires sweated together. The wires themselves were made of thin strips of gold twisted closely along their lengths. There were heavy gold bracelets with conical terminals and large and small objects known, but without any great reason, as dress-fasteners.

In addition to the great wealth of gold, large bracelets of pure tin were also worn. Connections with northern Europe and the Baltic are indicated by a considerable wealth in imported amber beads, some of them decorated with twisted gold wire. The presence of so much affluence argues in favour of a highly-developed agricultural and pastoral system which could produce a sufficient surplus of food to support specialist classes within the community. Whether these specialists were attached to local groups or whether they were itinerant is not known; possibly the latter, as this would explain the uniformity in object and ornamentation throughout the country during the later centuries of the Bronze Age.

The amount of information available to us about the living conditions of Bronze Age man is limited. We know that some lived on small artificial islands built in shallow waters on lake-shores; on one there was a rectangular house but so few traces of houses remain on these crannogs, as the artificial islands are called, that we do not know what they were like in general. The people of the time may also have lived in some equivalent of the rath or ring-fort and it is now becoming clear, especially from excavations at Rathgall, Co. Wicklow, that we may have to revise our ideas about early times in Ireland and consider the possibility of the existence in the country of small townships with something approaching village organisation and economy. It is a peculiar thing that there is great uncertainty as to how the Irish of the period 1,000 B.C. to 300 B.C. disposed of their dead: no burial of the period has as yet been identified apart from a few cremations in pits and urns at Rathgall.

Somewhere about the beginning of the last millennium B.C. on the Continent a new metal, iron, began to replace bronze and stone in the manufacture of everyday things such as knives, axes, sickles, billhooks, swords, and spears. But it was not until about 500 B.C. or slightly later that knowledge of working iron reached this country. We see it at first tentatively when socketed axeheads of iron began to imitate their bronze forerunners; then, as on the crannog of Rathtinaun in Lough Gara, Co. Sligo, we find iron pins (of a variety called "swan's neck" because of their shape) associated with material normal to the Bronze Age culture. We may interpret this evidence, meagre though it is, as indicating commercial and cultural contacts between Ireland and mainland Europe. It would stretch inference too far, however, to postulate the intrusion or invasion of immigrant groups.

What happened in the centuries after about 500 B.C. down to the birth of Christ and later, the period known as the Early Iron Age? During this time there would appear to have been a change in the expression of affluence: the great wealth of gold of the preceding Bronze Age abated strikingly and hardly more than a dozen pieces of this metal are recorded for the long centuries of the Iron Age, but considerable wealth of another sort took its place. This was in the form of decorative bronzes. Indeed, it is by such objects that the Iron Age in Ireland is mainly identified. Bronze was no longer the metal of everyday things. It became instead the medium of adornment. The brooches, the pins, were all of bronze; so too were the finely ornamented sword scabbards, the spearbutts used in parade. The remains of ceremonial head gear, such as the so-called Petric Crown, the horsebits, the round discs, all of bronze, were beautifully ornamented.

From archaeology we know little of the ordinary objects of life. There are a few triangular iron knives, bone spindle-whorls and combs and an axehead or two. In general, however, it must be said that archaeology alone would give but a shadowy picture of life in the Ireland during the Iron Age. The people were agriculturalists producing grain crops as indicated by decorated beehive-shaped querns or grinding stones. Quantities of animal bones show that they also had a wide variety of domesticated animals, though preponderantly cattle, and that they also indulged in hunting. Some lived in small raths or ring forts and some in crannogs, some may have lived in larger groupings in hill forts. They practised cremation and deposited the burnt remains in small pits in mounds, as at Carrowjames, Co. Mayo where the bones were accompanied by glass beads and bronze rings. They may also in some areas have buried unburnt bodies extended in long, stone-lined graves.

We cannot be certain who the people of the Iron Age in Ireland were. The ornamentation they used is of a type known as La Tène, named after a type-site in Switzerland. The people who developed the La Tène culture were widespread in Europe and are known to have been Celtic-speaking. From a centre located somewhere about the head-waters of the Rhine and the Danube their particular and characteristic culture spread eastwards, west and south. In Ireland, however, it must be noted that, though La Tène art motives were well-known and were applied to a large variety of objects, the objects themselves are of types unknown outside Ireland or are local adaptations of continental forms. From this it seems fair to conclude that it was not a movement of people into Ireland that resulted in the change from the culture of Bronze Age times to that of the Iron Age. Once again, it seems more likely that a spread of ideas, an adoption and adaptation by the indigenous population of foreign concepts, took place. We cannot, of course, know exactly what prompted the adoption of these ideas but such changes appear to be inherent in the historical processes which lead to the cultural development of mankind.

The Irish of the Early Iron Age did not know how to write but it has been suggested that some writings of later centuries, especially the epic

Right— Decorated sheet bronze object thought to have been portion of a ceremonial crown. Its find-place is not known. Probably 1st century, A.D.

Below— Cast bronze buckle from the royal crannog of Lagore, near Dunshaughlin, Co. Meath Mid 7th century, A.D.

Bottom— Side view of bronze ring-brooch of the 4th or 5th century, A.D. There are, in red enamel, insets of what is called millefiori glass. From Castledermot, Co. Kildare.

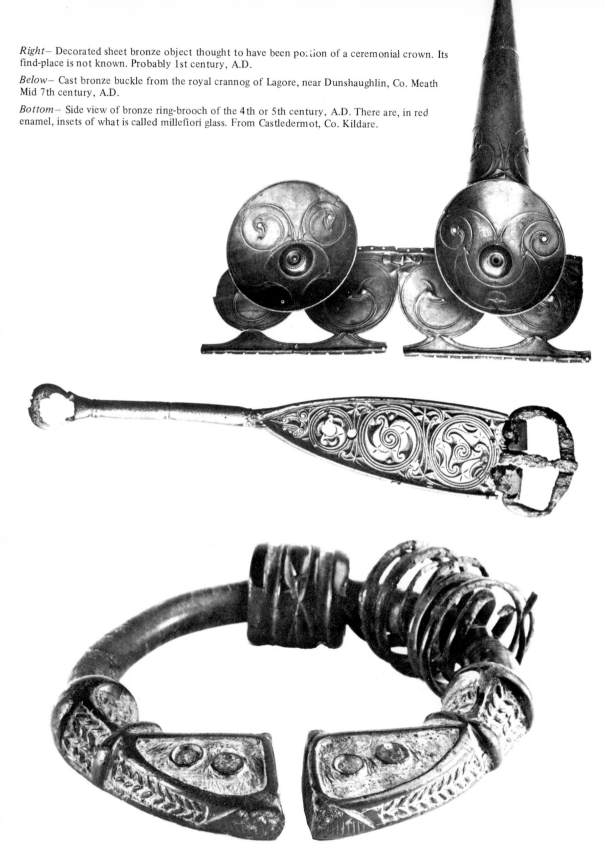

tale known as *Táin Bó Cuailgne,* may contain within them details of the earlier period which had been retained and transmitted through folk memory. It is not clear to what extent such a claim can be substantiated but if only partly true and if the precise Iron Age details could be isolated with certainty, this literature would be an invaluable aid to the meagre archaeological record.

As time went on and Celtic La Tène influences waned on the Continent with the rise of Roman power, Ireland was again subjected to change. Indeed, a study of the material suggests the existence of what may almost be called a Romanising period in this island. Contacts with Roman Britain and Gaul were close and what was happening in those areas affected Ireland too. A knowledge of writing in the form of the cryptic Ogham alphabet, based on the Latin, was introduced and from the fourth century A.D. onwards new religions and philosophical concepts in the form of Christianity began to infiltrate the land. By about 400 A.D. a considerable body of Christians lived in Ireland, especially in southern regions. It was to organise them properly in communion with Rome that a special envoy, Ireland's first bishop, was sent by Pope Celestine in 431 A.D. The question of the formal organisation of the Christian church in Ireland has given rise to much historical controversy; but leaving the controversy aside it can be seen that one great name has come out of it all, that of Saint Patrick, Ireland's patron saint. We also know that although the church was at first organised on a diocesan basis in the Roman manner, it soon changed to a monastic organisation which suited Irish social organisation and temperament better.

The Church and the contacts it established led to great developments in Ireland, especially in the field of applied art. Books and utensils were required for religious purposes; the former were elaborately ornamented copies of the Gospels in Latin. Volumes such as the Books of Durrow and Kells have remained to us as proof of the spiritual fervour of the people of Early Christian Ireland. Sacred objects such as the Ardagh Chalice have come down to us as proof of the fantastic technical skills of the craftsmen of the time: here we see and enjoy, almost with sensuous pleasure, the interplay of gold and silver and red and blue enamels and amber and rock crystal, we follow the intricate details of geometric interlacing and bird and animal patterns executed in a bewildering variety of gold wire filigree. Granulation, too, was used extensively. Combined with the animal interlacing patterns which must have come to us from a Germanic background were motives such as chip-carving from the Roman world and spirals, scrolls and trumpet patterns from ancient pagan Ireland. Not only was such ornament applied lavishly to objects for religious purposes, but it was also used extensively on profane objects. There is, for instance, the incomparable Tara Brooch with its rich ornament of gold on the front and its equally elaborate patterns on the back where ornamentation would not normally be seen. This, indeed, points to something unusual in the Irish of the time — a desire for completion and perfection. We see it in manuscripts, on reliquaries, on brooches and on many other objects.

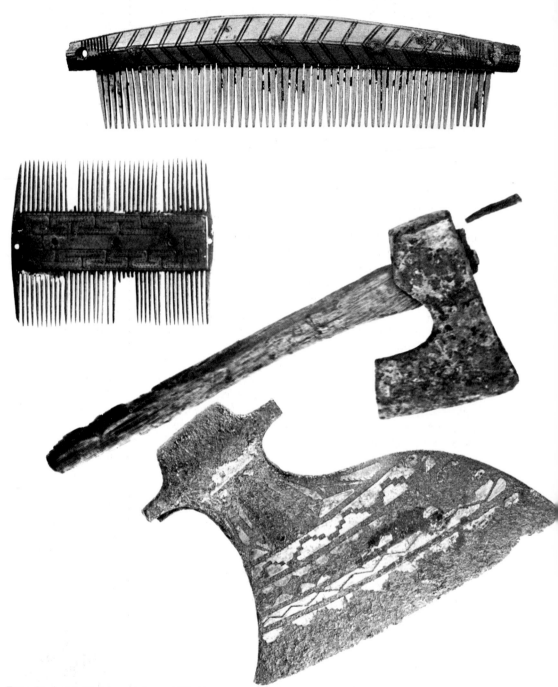

Top– Single-sided bone comb from old Dublin.

Left– Two-sided bone comb of the early Christian Period from Lagore, Co. Meath.

Centre– Iron axe from the Curlew Mountains, Co. Roscommon.

Above– Iron battle-axe with appliqué silver decoration. From Co. Donegal. Such were used by the Scots mercenary forces called *Gallóglaigh* or "Gallowglasses".

Opposite page– Flesh hook discovered in Co. Antrim.

This feeling of spirituality also arises from the beautiful nature poetry left to us, simple but stirring lays composed in Irish.

People then lived in ring forts and in crannogs — the homesteads of the farmers of the time. They dressed in the standard garments of *léine* (a long robe), *brat* (a cloak) and leather shoes which were often decorated. Their garments had many colours: rank, it is said, was indicated by such colours. Personal ornament in the form of brooches, beads, ornamental buckles, and so on was common. The men of the crannogs and forts worshipped in local churches made mainly of wood but sometimes of stone, prayed at stone crosses with carved panels of Biblical scenes and finally rested, extended on their backs, in churchyards within the monastic enclosures.

Early Christian Ireland was wealthy, especially the Church. In the churches were treasures of all sorts, ecclesiastical and lay, since they were used as secure storehouses for crops, grain and other personal goods. Irish missionaries went far afield, and with them the knowledge of what booty there might be in Ireland reached the Vikings of the north who were beginning their adventurous voyages of conquest and plunder. From 795 A.D. onwards they raided Ireland, concentrating on the wealthy monastic centres. The Irish built round towers as a form of protection against them, but gradually the Norsemen began to establish small settlements, engage in commercial enterprises and meet and intermarry with the native Irish. One of the towns they established — Dublin — was founded in 841 A.D.

It was the Vikings who first gave Ireland towns in the modern sense. It was also they who introduced coinage, improved ship-building techniques and introduced new art styles which were taken up with enthusiasm by Irish artificers. But although the Norsemen exercised a strong influence on parts of the country, it was not long before they began to be absorbed into the local population. The exact location of the first Viking settlement in Dublin is as yet uncertain, but it was probably somewhere in the area of Dublin Castle. From this, the town spread westwards and northwards towards the River Liffey and, a century after its foundation, it may be said to have been Hiberno-Norse rather than pure Viking. Cork, Limerick, Waterford, and Wexford were similarly townships established by Viking settlers who were gradually absorbed. For several centuries a Hiberno-Norse population held a position of distinction along areas of the Irish coast. This position of importance ended with the intrusion, late in the twelfth century, of Norman adventurers. With this movement Ireland's history changed radically.

Above– The River Liffey, Dublin with its distinctive quay-side buildings.

Left– This stone Victorian lion's head comes from a gateway in Ballsbridge, Dublin.

FIVE CITIES

Patrick Shaffrey

THE EXPLOSION OF the cities is a feature of modern society. For many years, their growth has been equated with greater prosperity and better standards of living. Today, however, this view is being increasingly challenged. The reality is that the growth of cities has generally been accompanied by a decline in the quality of the environment together with the problems of unemployment, poverty and vandalism. The city itself is a paradox — most of the great ideas in art, literature, philosophy, and music originated in the cities. On the other hand, it breeds loneliness, corruption and crime. A person could be more alone on O'Connell Bridge in Dublin than on a quiet bay in the west of Ireland. The size of a city is also a relative thing. It can be argued that Dublin is too large compared to the rest of Ireland, even though by world standards it is still a comparatively small city.

The ideal settlement would, of course, be one where there was an environment which combined the liberalism of the city with the friendliness and personal contacts of the small village. This balance was achieved in the Greek city states, the Renaissance cities of Tuscany and the American cities of the eighteenth century.

In Ireland recent economic progress has, as in other countries, been marked by the growth of its cities. They are still relatively small, particularly with regard to their scale and form. The development of Irish cities followed the overall development of the country with a period of rapid expansion in the eighteenth and early nineteenth century, and then stagnation and decline. The architectural charm and quality of this great period of town building can still be seen in them despite the many insensitivities of recent years.

The exception to the above pattern is, of course, Belfast, whose major period of expansion occurred after 1850. Northeast Ulster was the only part of Ireland to be seriously involved in the first Industrial Revolution, and Belfast was the centre of this activity. Its population grew in a relatively short period from a small town of thirty thousand to a large metropolis of nearly half a million.

Like settlements everywhere, Irish cities all have individual character-istics, influenced by their historical, social and economic development. This essay, however, deals principally with their visual qualities and how these have been affected by recent economic development. The significant elements which influence the visual character of cities are not so much the qualities of individual buildings, but the atmosphere, scale and sense of place formed by the relationship of buildings and groups of buildings to each other, and the relationship of the city as a whole to its natural environment. It is when this overall atmosphere within the city is eroded and the balance between the city and its natural setting is ignored, that its visual qualities begin to decline.

It has been said of the Irish that as a nation we are highly articulate in a literary sense but visually blind. A cliché perhaps and like all clichés not quite true. We are not quite as literate as we would like to think, and the architectural character of our cities and towns, particularly the older areas, gives lie to the argument that we have no visual sense. Yet, somehow, this inherent sense of place and visual identity has been ignored in recent times. The development of even the smallest villages has been more influenced by the "Sunset Boulevard" ethic (individual buildings unrelated to their surroundings, large neon signs) than any "Irish sense" of identity and place. All this has happened in the last decade or so, despite the presence of a comprehensive planning system. Unfortunately, architecture in Ireland was never considered as intrinsic a part of the nation's identity as language, music and literature. In the view of many politicians and decision-makers, our architectural heritage was somehow part of our colonial past and therefore never really respected for its true value.

While language, and to a lesser extent music, have been identified with one or the other political tradition in Ireland, our architectural heritage is common to both North and South. Perhaps a greater awareness of the merits of Irish architecture and townscapes, their common expression North and South, will provide one of the bridges by which people all over the island will get to know and respect each other better and, in the process, ensure that the unique qualities of Irish cities are enhanced and developed.

A special word about the Northern cities. For the past ten years, the Troubles have gravely affected them both physically and socially. Yet, despite all the problems created by civil unrest, the people still endeavour to go about their business and partake of their recreational, social and cultural interests. Concern is still being expressed about the effect of road plans on city communities and about the loss of good buildings and townscapes. Perhaps this is because there is a greater appreciation and concern for architecture in the North than the South. The tremendous work by the ever enthusiastic Ulster Architectural Heritage Society in producing comprehensive architectural surveys of the cities and towns in the North has not yet been followed to any great extent in the other provinces. Irish cities are now undergoing another period of great change. This is taking place, as in other European countries, against a background of increasing community concern for the environment.

DUBLIN – THE CAPITAL OF IRELAND

The three great Georgian cities in these islands are Dublin, Edinburgh and Bath. Prominence of stone in Edinburgh and Bath gives these cities a robust character which is not to be found in Dublin. Georgian Dublin is essentially a brick city. Its essential character comes from the pleasant relationship of streets and squares laid out on a rectilinear pattern. Unlike both Edinburgh and Bath, there are no dramatic topographical features in the city centre. Therefore, its architectural character tends to be more restrained and self-effacing and, as a result, more fragile. Arguably also, it has suffered more damage over the last decade than either Edinburgh or Bath.

Dublin is now, of course, one of Europe's capital cities and has always benefited from the many famous literary figures associated with it. Its real international significance, however, rests on the physical beauty of its central area, the foundations of which were laid in the eighteenth century when Dublin was the second city in the empire and perhaps a more important city in the European context than it is today. It is not a great centre of international finance or politics.

Dublin, however, is more than just a Georgian city. Its foundations go back over a thousand years. It was established by the Vikings in the ninth century, and the street patterns laid down then formed the basis for the later medieval city. Recent archaeological excavations have thrown into sharp relief the international significance of Viking Dublin. Unfortunately, as is so often the case, these findings have been accompanied by controversy – between those people who would wish to see the excavations preserved in their original locations and the city fathers who are anxious to proceed with the building of the new City Hall. Like many such controversies, it has ended in compromise; the excavations are continuing for the present, but the City Hall is also being built on the same site. Other considerations have also affected this important municipal project. The position of the buildings was changed to allow a full view of Christ Church Cathedral – a building never really intended to be seen in full view and whose main interest comes from its profile seen in relationship to the other small buildings, grouped around it. The City Hall will now be much closer to the river and its mass and height may very well have a detrimental effect on the character of the quays. The results to date have been greeted with widespread unhappiness.

Much of the material from Viking Dublin can now be seen in the National Museum. There are few tangible remains of Medieval Dublin except scattered fragments of the city walls. The two cathedrals, St.

Top, left– A view of the front of the General Post Office, O'Connell Street, Dublin.

Top, centre– A portion of the interior of the Bank of Ireland, former House of Parliament, Dublin.

Above– One of the many fan-lights which adorn Dublin's Georgian doorways.

Far left– View of College Green, Dublin with the Bank of Ireland on the left and Trinity College on the right. Although photographed at the turn of the century, this view remains remarkably unchanged today.

Left– Trinity College, Dublin, founded in 1591.

Patrick's and Christ Church, have been greatly altered through the centuries and were extensively rebuilt in the nineteenth century. In the sixteenth century, the city spread out beyond its medieval core with the establishment of Trinity College. Following the troubles of the seventeenth century, came the development of Georgian Dublin as we know it today, eventually culminating in the fine squares and streets, particularly Merrion and Fitzwilliam Squares, in the south side of the city. The development of Georgian Dublin began, however, on the north side with Henrietta Street, Dominick Street and that magnificent urban space — Mountjoy Square. These fine streets and individual buildings have been in a continual state of decline for over one hundred years. The pace of development in Dublin slackened off after the Act of Union in 1800, but the Georgian influence remained. Many suburban streets have a distinctive Georgian character, particularly in Rathmines and Rathgar, although in some instances they were built towards the end of the nineteenth century.

The river Liffey, or Anna Livia as it is known in the literary sense, flows through the centre of Dublin. Like the city, it is small in scale and more intimate when compared with the Thames and the Seine but, unfortunately, no less polluted. The quays are one of the most significant architectural areas in the city, containing not only important buildings like the Custom House and the Four Courts but a number of interesting churches and terraces facing on to the river. Part of Dublin's essential character can be observed by a walk along the Liffey — a city of quite small domestic scale with only the spires and domes of the churches and public buildings breaking the skyline.

Dublin has been spared the rash of high buildings which disfigure so many other European cities. Unfortunately a number were allowed along the quays and their very presence should be a warning as to how the entire character of the city can be changed by wrongly located high buildings. Despite these, however, the riverside retains to a large extent its intimate scale and character and its importance is being increasingly appreciated by ordinary citizens. As in so many other cities, the river forms a psychological as well as a physical dividing line. For many years now, it has been difficult to secure redevelopment or renewal on the north side and here the classic problems of the inner city are most acute — unemployment, declining population base, poor social facilities and large areas of dereliction. At the same time relatively good buildings are being demolished in other parts of the city. This is a major problem facing Dublin which must be overcome by some means or other, perhaps a ban on public offices on the south side.

Dublin, however, is more than a pleasant man-made creation. It is blessed with natural advantages as well. The city has developed around Dublin Bay in a sensitive fashion, from the hill of Howth on the north side to Killiney and Bray on the south. Until recently, most Dubliners lived within five or six miles of the sea, and the joy of the seaside, in particular Sandymount strand in the south and Dollymount strand and

Bull Island in the north, is part of their social heritage.

Bull Island, an artificial island created by the extension of Dublin Port in the nineteenth century, is now not only an important recreational area but also a bird sanctuary of international significance. Indeed, Dublin is unique among major cities in having such an important natural and scientific resource within a few miles of its centre. By far the most dramatic entrance into Dublin is by sea. Arriving by boat, a panoramic view of the city with the Dublin mountains behind is obtained making it one of the most dramatically situated of European cities. Although the development of the port in the nineteenth century brought with it the benefits of Bull Island, its expansion plans in recent years have aroused considerable controversy — not least the proposal to build an oil refinery in Dublin Bay. This aroused tremendous opposition, and the planning enquiry had the emotion-charged atmosphere of a major dramatic or political event rather than a sober assessment of a planning proposal. The proposal like many others was, of course, speculative. Permission was refused, and most Dubliners hope that the idea is now dead.

The mountains are also an important visual element in the city. One is aware of their proximity in many parts of the city centre. In Fitzwilliam Street — that great Georgian thoroughfare — the mountains appear at times to be so close that one could touch them.

There is also another Dublin away from the Georgian city, the bay and the mountains. As in other cities, it is not only the great architecture that gives Dublin its character but the many smaller buildings and streets that impart the scale and atmosphere of a small town. There are many areas of small single and two-storey houses built mainly in brick that have an elegance not usually associated with nineteenth century domestic housing. Dublin, in one sense, is a collection of villages. Over the years, with the expansion of the city, many outlying villages have been incorporated within it. These, however, have retained the intrinsic quality of villages — a variety of land uses, a mixture of building types, a concentration of shops, churches and social facilities, and strong community groups concerned for the preservation and conservation of all that is best in their areas. The Dublin villages vary greatly in character, from the ancient village of Ringsend where Cromwell landed to the riverside village of Chapelizod in the west and the thriving fishing port of Howth in the north. South of the city, there is the graceful elegance of Dun Laoghaire and the charm and intimacy of Dalkey.

Dun Laoghaire, or Kingstown as it was formerly called, developed considerably following the establishment of the Dublin–Kingstown railway in the 1840s. Architecturally it is one of the most important boroughs in the country and is arguably one of the best examples of a Regency town in these islands. It has fine elegant terraces and handsome individual villas, executed mainly in stucco work, many of which are now being repainted. It retains much of the atmosphere of the Victorian seaside — a good promenade, wide open spaces and large hotels and guest houses, some now being converted rather insensitively to other uses. It has a magnificent harbour designed by John Rennie and constructed of Dublin granite brought down from the nearby mountains. It was one of the great engineering feats of the nineteenth century. The harbour, however, was never a commercial success although it is now the principal ferry port in the South.

It is expected that by the turn of the century, there will be over a million people living in the Dublin area. With the growth of white collar jobs and mechanisation in agriculture, people have been flooding into Dublin from all over the country. This rate of expansion compares with the growth of Belfast in the late nineteenth century. The basis for the physical expansion that has of necessity accompanied this population change is a plan prepared in the 1960s known as "The Wright Plan". Conceived in the days of cheap energy, it unfortunately ignored the environmental possibilities of the coastline and the only major suburban railway line which ran along it. As a result, the city is pushing out into the countryside on its western edges. These areas are called "new towns" but are, in effect, sprawling suburbs. There is in fact no specific legislation which would allow the building of new towns as has happened in other countries. Thus the city is not really expanding in social and cultural terms but merely in population, new office blocks and suburban estates. In addition, of course, the countryside which was previously so close is now further away and more difficult to get at. The Irish constitution's emphasis on private property rights seems to have discouraged legislators from passing acts which would create a better social and aesthetic basis on which to build new communities.

Despite its many problems, Dublin retains its essential charm and character. The scale of the city centre is still intimate and pleasant for there have as yet been few of the large developments which can so easily disrupt the entire texture of a city. The city does, however, require creative leadership in architecture and urban design. It still lacks a worthwhile pedestrian area. It is still tinkering around with the old motorway and road widening ideas that many other cities have long since discarded. It is still more concerned with the preservation of individual buildings and facades, rather than the conservation of entire areas. The standard of ordinary, day-to-day development is extremely poor. Dublin is now at a crucial stage in its history. No matter what changes in national planning are made, it is destined to expand considerably in the future. But what sort of city will it be? The standards achieved in Dublin will influence the rest of the country. Indeed, it is difficult not to be pessimistic about the future of Dublin. In the past, it was rightly compared with such cities as Edinburgh, Florence, Venice and Prague. Can it be today? Unless more positive and creative policies are adopted, it will surely lose its place on the list of European cities of major and architectural importance.

BELFAST

The second city in Ireland is Belfast — the country's one example of a nineteenth century industrial city. It is also, of course, a regional and

Top– Aerial view of Dun Laoghaire harbour.

Above - A dramatic view of Christ Church Cathedral, Dublin's most historic building, near which archaeologists uncovered Europe's most important Viking site. It is on this site that Dublin City Corporation's new office blocks are being built, despite massive opposition and controversy.

administrative centre and, up to a few years ago, a political one as well. In the past, Belfast was famous for the quality of the ships designed and built in the Queen's Island Shipyard and for the linen and cotton produced in its many mills. It also had a reputation for business and commerce and drew its customers from many parts of Ireland. The establishment of the border seriously affected its business potential, but with the advent of the E.E.C. and the lowering of customs barriers, the commercial influence of Belfast is again being experienced throughout the Island.

Today, unfortunately, the view of Belfast is a city of troubles and unrest — one to be avoided rather than visited. It has long been compared somewhat unfavourably with Dublin. This relationship is not unlike that of Glasgow/Edinburgh, Amsterdam/Rotterdam and indeed many other "sister cities" throughout the world. Dublin is to many people a gay, friendly city, full of easy-going inhabitants. The people of Belfast, on the other hand, are supposed to be dour and dull, their main interest work, and the city itself drab and monotonous. Like many other generalisations, this view does not stand up to close investigation. Belfast is not a dull, monochrome city. It is blessed with fine natural features. Divis Mountain and Cave Hill overlook the city like brooding giants. The city has developed on the flat lands between the mountains and sea. The Lagan Valley is a fine natural landscape close to the city.

Belfast, however, does not have the same close relationship with the sea as Dublin. Nineteenth century industrialisation and the growth of the Queen's Island Shipyard prevented this. The old seaport towns of Carrickfergus and Bangor, however, are becoming more and more a part of Belfast. Belfast also has its medieval core situated round High Street, Ross Street and Castle Lane. Winding streets, small squares such as Arthur Square and Victoria Square, narrow lanes, and a mixture of shops are typical of old cities everywhere. Because of the Troubles, this area has for security reasons been to a large extend pedestrianised. Yet it has none of the nice things associated with pedestrianised areas in other European cities — paving, trees and benches. Its people can hardly be expected to be concerned with such items when their premises may be blown up the next day. It is the intention, however, that when the Troubles are over the old city will remain one in which the pedestrian has preference over the motor car.

In the eighteenth century, Belfast developed south of the old medieval core around Donegall Square, Linenhall Place and May Street. Today, it is just possible to identify its Georgian face amid the later Victorian additions. At the end of the century, Belfast was a small Georgian city of twenty to thirty thousand inhabitants. It was a cultured city in many ways and one that was more influenced by French political thinking of the time than Dublin. There was little indication of the tremendous and dramatic development which awaited the city in the latter half of the nineteenth century. Development continued at a gradual pace in the early part of the century and then the city literally exploded into what was the greatest period of urban expansion that the country has yet seen. The eminent town planner, Sir Patrick Abercrombie, describes this vividly:

> Belfast, for example, suggests a town begun in a leisurely manner, with a designed centre, not indeed very remarkable but having the dignity of a large central square where stands the City Hall: a regular, artificial and urban arrangement. But it has been suddenly over-whelmed by a rush of prosperity: the lava streams of erupting urbanism seem to flow blindly in natural devastating confusion.[1]

The development of Belfast was caused by a series of events. The great famines in the 1840s caused widespread upheaval in rural Ireland and led to massive emigration, principally to America and Britain, but also to Belfast and the Northeast. The internal migration to Belfast came mainly from the other parts of Ulster and the west of Ireland. At about the same time the American Civil War created a tremendous demand for cotton and linen, and together with the business acumen of the Northern people, who had witnessed the beginnings of the Industrial Revolution in Britain and quickly recognised the opportunities made possible by the new technology, spurred on the development of these industries. The people who flocked to Belfast brought with them their intense political and religious outlooks. In most other industrial cities, the political and religious beliefs of new migrants were blurred and indeed changed by new attitudes created by urban conditions. Unfortunately the reverse seems to have happened in Belfast, and the political and religious divisions were sharpened by the effects of urban development. The conflicting cultures of Gael and Planter have yet to come to terms with each other in the small streets of nineteenth century Belfast.

The development of the city followed the typical pattern of industrial cities of the period — row upon row of streets consisting principally of small houses, textile mills and other factories. Belfast did experience the Industrial Revolution later than other cities and so does not have the back-to-back housing associated with the beginnings of the Industrial Revolution. The general standards of building were also higher than in the cities of Northern England. In Belfast, as a general rule, the small housing was developed in a pattern of streets at right angles to the main roads, radiating from the city centre. Along the roads, the major social facilities — shops, pubs and churches — were concentrated and became the focal point of community life. Their names have become part of the folklore of Belfast — The Falls, The Shankill, Newtownards Road.

The building material was brick, used not only for the houses but also for the factories and many churches and public buildings. These areas are not attractive at first sight and the effects of the Troubles, derelict factories, bricked-up houses and "peace barriers" dividing streets make them even more forlorn and uninviting. Despite this, they sustain an active and viable community life. This is particularly true of those parts of the inner city where the physical effects of the Troubles are less evident. Here the houses are usually painted and cared for; the small shops are clean and tidy and obviously prosperous. It is these areas that contain all the vigour and vitality which is very much part of Belfast, reflecting in

High Street, Belfast, at the turn of the century.

their own distinctive way, different cultures and identities. What a tragedy they cannot be fused together. The gridiron lay-out common in industrial cities is by its nature monotonous and particularly so on a flat site. There is a marked absence of small squares or open spaces or even the incidental irregularity to break the monotony. The few spaces that exist stand out by their very isolation. Cromac Square in the Market's Area, for example, is now a rather desolate place but could become an attractive urban space. It is, however, interesting to note that one of the things that united both communities in Belfast in recent years was the tremendous opposition to the proposal for urban motorways within the inner city. They would have practically destroyed many of the older communities — The Sandy Row area and parts of the Falls Road and Shankill Road. The opposition to this proposal crossed all political ideologies and religious beliefs. The proposals have now been dropped, and the city is concentrating on better communications outside the city and more sensitive means of transportation within it.

If Dublin is a Georgian City, then Belfast is a classic example of the

Belfast's City Hall, the high point of Belfast's Victorian architecture.

Victorian one. It has many fine individual buildings and indeed entire areas typified by the Malone Road and the University Area. In 1849 the Queen's College of Belfast, now the University, was founded. Colleges were also established in Cork and Galway in the same period. This gave an impetus to the development of the south of the city, particularly for middle and upper-class families. The University buildings, designed by Sir Charles Lanyon, are a good example of the Gothic Revival style, and together with the later addition of the Library, add atmosphere and character to this part of the city. Unlike Dublin, with its two clearly defined University complexes, the Queen's University is physically integrated with the city — a real meeting of town and gown. The University has expanded rapidly in recent years, and the quality of the new buildings is rather mixed. The area still has all the features of a Victorian suburb at its best — fine terraces of three and four-storey houses, dignified houses in their own grounds and spacious roads with mature planting. Many of the fine buildings and streets are included in the various lists published by the Ulster Architectural Heritage Society.

A feature of Belfast at the end of its period of expansion was great variety in the type of public and commercial buildings, churches, banks, shops and offices that were erected throughout the city in diverse architectural styles and with the high quality craftsmanship characteristic of the standard achieved by the Victorian architects and now more widely appreciated than in the past. Some are in Venetian Gothic style influenced by the writings of Ruskin; others in neo-Classical or early Modern. The crowning achievement of the city's development is perhaps City Hall built circa 1906, and designed by the London architect, Brumwell Thomas, who won an architectural competition for the building. It is a symbol of Belfast's municipal and commercial status: an immense and impressive building, it forms the focal point of Donegall Square and in a sense the entire city. It is a building of borrowed architectural ideas influenced heavily by St. Paul's in London and Wren's City Churches. Another fine example of a typical Victorian building is the Opera House, which is now being totally restored to its former glory. Other buildings of interest from the period that reflect the particular history of the city are those associated with industry and traditions of the city — the mills, factories and workshops of diverse sizes and architectural forms. Many are small, intimate buildings which are appropriate to the scale of the street. Others, such as the large multi-storey mills dominate their surroundings both physically and economically. Nearly all were built in brick. Often a severe style was used reflecting the industrial functionalism of the time, but various architectural details were used to make the buildings look less like factories. The Gas Works is typical of the panache and style of industrial buildings in Belfast. Many of these buildings, particularly the mills and churches, are now being converted for other uses, although not always in the most appropriate way. Others are empty or have already been demolished — the best of them are worth preserving and adapting.

When the Troubles are finally over, there will be a tremendous opportunity for Belfast and indeed all the other Northern cities and towns to renew their bomb-damaged centres not only physically but socially and culturally as well. If this great opportunity is not to be squandered, it will demand vision, leadership and creativity on the part of the architects, planners and all others engaged in the rebuilding. Belfast is fortunate in that its renewal will take place in a changing climate of architectural opinion — the atmosphere, scale and character of a street are now considered more important than individual buildings; the importance of renewal and rehabilitation is more widely recognised. In general there is less of the bulldozer and more of the trowel. It is perhaps too optimistic to expect that the political and cultural differences that divide the city can be removed immediately with its rebuilding. If, however, the city is rebuilt with sensitivity and care for the total quality of life, the seeds of future harmony will be sown.

CORK CITY

The River Lee, just before it enters the estuary, flows through a narrow valley and is contained by small hills on both north and south sides. Here for a thousand years or more the city of Cork has been evolving in a gradual but magical way. There was never a great era of urban expansion comparable to Dublin in the eighteenth century or Belfast in the nineteenth. Cork more than other Irish cities emphasises the importance of "atmosphere" within a city. Except for Patrick Street, there are no really great and dominant streets or squares. The entire atmosphere of the centre is more important than the individual buildings.

It is the second city in the Republic but to many Corkonians it is the first city in the world. It is not without reason that they can be proud of their city. Their pride, however, stems more from a metaphysical feeling of being a Cork person rather than any widespread awareness of the character and beauty of the city — as its generally unkempt appearance would suggest. A seaport, business and administrative centre and University city, Cork has in recent years added another tag to its image. It now contains one of the fastest growing industrial complexes in Ireland with many of the newer chemical industries. Its harbour, a vast, practically landlocked waterway, is a marvellous natural resource with not only tremendous industrial potential that is now being realised but recreational and amenity potential as well.

The natural constraints on development have made Cork a relatively compact city in character and form. The city centre is an island created by the arms of the river as they reach for the sea. It is in an Irish sense an "Ille de la Cité". Unfortunately, the importance of the riverside is still not fully appreciated. Many of the quays and malls are day-long parking lots with rows of cars showing their rear ends to the river. As a seaport, Cork has traditional links with southern Europe and the New World. Like its sister city across the Channel, Bristol, ships can come right into the city centre and so add a romantic dimension to its appearance. Fortunately, Cork has yet been spared the major development disasters which have nearly destroyed the heart of Bristol. In the past, it had strong trading links with Bristol and many of the buildings in the city are built from stone brought back to Cork from the west of England as ballast. It is a small intimate city of hills, islands, waterways and bridges. Streets wind their way up the hillside with elegant Georgian and Victorian terraces side by side with the smaller artisan houses and cottages. The works of man have been influenced by the dictates of topography and nature. It is a city where names are important. Names originating from topographical features are now the basis of cohesive communities: Starch Hill, Spangle Hill, Blackpool, Blackrock, Shandon and Glanmire. The city centre is full of delightful surprises and architectural delights — elegant stone bridges spanning the rivers, pleasant lanes joining the streets together, here and there a glimpse of the spire of one of the city's churches. Their interesting forms and graceful spires, from the elegance of St. Ann's at Shandon to the more dramatic St. Finbar's along the river, are a physical indication of their importance to the social life and architectural heritage of the city. Cork is a city to be explored on foot, not necessarily an easy task particularly on the hills but the explorer will be amply rewarded with

Cork, a city of hills, churches and water – this view looks down Patrick's Hill into Patrick Street.

all the pleasant surprises and exciting views which are part and parcel of a hillside area.

It is a city of commerce with interesting warehouses, fine shops many of which retain their original fronts, elegant and fine homes on Montenotte overlooking the river. It also has its share of good pubs, restaurants and coffee houses. Cork has many fine individual buildings, with good examples of the Classical Revival style from the early nineteenth century. A smaller but highly significant architectural detail is the superb quality of the ironwork which can be seen throughout the city on buildings and bridges, along the quays and on doorways both large and humble. Such great craftsmanship should be cherished.

Through its history, Cork respected the natural constraints of its location. The gradual development of the city was due in part to the difficult building conditions. It is now entering a period of expansion, perhaps the greatest in its history. It is to be hoped that the current generation of builders will in their own way respect the natural form of the river valley, the hill and estuary. It is a sad paradox that despite the benefits of modern technology, the present large-scale urban expansion of cities and towns invariably seeks the easiest land to develop, usually flat land of high agricultural quality. The poorer, more undulating land is left behind. But it is precisely on this type of topography that many of the most dramatic and interesting old areas were built. It will be a boon for urban design when the cost of energy and the importance of agriculture make us look again at the building of cities and towns.

Cork need never import new ideas of planning and architecture. Present-day builders have only to look around the older city and learn from the ways it developed around the hillsides and rivers. Obviously these lessons have not yet been fully learned. Looking westwards from St. Patrick's Bridge one can see a glaring example of how not to build on a hillside. The housing estate sprawls across the hill with little apparent regard for topography or vistas and is dominated by a rather squat and ungraceful church. Any trees which had grown there and might have softened its impact are now gone.

The nature of this compact city of hills and rivers, as one would expect causes major traffic problems. As is too often the case, the usual approach to solve these problems was considered first, namely, the wholesale demolition of buildings, widening of existing streets and construction of a six-lane motorway, elevated in parts and circling the inner city. The classic engineering solution in fact, but one that has never really worked in any city and is absolutely the wrong approach when related to the fragile quality and delicacy of Cork. The opposition which these proposals aroused has resulted in the idea being dropped. Another and more sensible approach is now being considered. It would appear, however, that in the long term the best policy for Cork is less freedom for the private motor car within the city centre and a better public transport system. As modern cities go, there is comparatively little new development within Cork, and the marvellous texture of the city is still relatively intact.

A short distance from Cork and overlooking the harbour is Cobh — formerly called Queen's Town. It is a port of call for the transatlantic liners and, in the past, the last sad parting point for many thousands of immigrants from Ireland to America. It was the major British Naval Base in Ireland. Under the provisions of the Treaty, the Naval Base remained in British hands up to 1936 but is now the headquarters of the Irish Navy. These are historical matters; of more relevance is its quality today. Here the unknowing but perceptive visitor will receive a most pleasant surprise. Cobh is architecturally one of the best "small towns" in these islands. It has delightful terraces and squares, built in the Regency style and nestling into the hillsides overlooking the harbour. At the centre-piece of the town is Pugin's great Gothic Revival cathedral. The architectural splendour of the town is still marvellously intact, except for one glaring disaster in the main square. Casement Square, a marvellous space facing on to the estuary and under the shadow of Pugin's great cathedral, was at a stroke destroyed by the insertion of a single-storey, flat-roofed, precast concrete building.

What of the future? With the possibilities of major oil discoveries off the coastline, Cork could become the focus of vast new industrial and commercial development. Most local people look forward with eagerness and hope to this. A few are more thoughtful and indeed wary. They inhabit a city which is one of the most charming small cities in Europe, whose character has come principally from achieving a balance between man and nature. It will be a pity if in the process of modernisation this sensitive approach to development and town building is not appreciated and practised by this and future generations of Corkonians.

DERRY CITY

Following the defeat of the old Gaelic chieftains, O'Neill and O'Donnell, and their departure for Europe in 1607, a large part of the Northwest of Ireland was granted to the City of London. London then, as many times throughout its history, was facing the problems of over-population. The City Guilds saw a great opportunity for increasing profits and at the same time relieving population pressure. A body known as The Irish Society was set up and entrusted with the task of developing this part of Ireland. It was to establish two new towns: one on the banks of the Foyle, which became known as Londonderry, and the other, known as Coleraine, on the Bann. Both settlements were in a sense the forerunners of what is considered the classic twentieth century planning theory, namely, the creation of new towns to relieve population pressure within a large city. Since then, the city has been known as Londonderry or Derry — you can take your pick. Derry, therefore, is the only city in Ireland which did not evolve gradually from medieval and earlier foundations. Part of the site does include a monastic settlement established by Saint Columcille who is, of course, also associated with the island of Iona in Scotland. Little remains of this, however, and it did not influence future building.

Derry has had its divisions over the years, but despite this its

Above– The finely built stone quay walls and bridges are a feature of the River Lee in Cork.

Left– Cobh, once a major transatlantic sea port, has tiers of terraced houses around Pugin's gothic revival Cathedral.

inhabitants are pleasant and friendly and have a reputation for being a musical people. The layout of the seventeenth century city follows the classical late Renaissance style. The streets are laid out in a formal rectangular fashion converging together in the main central space now called the Diamond. Very quickly, Derry's famous walls were erected reflecting the turbulent background of the city's foundation. These walls, twenty-four feet high and six feet thick were built of local whinstone and are now among the best preserved city walls in Europe. By 1630, they were one of the architectural features of the city and remain so today. The city gates were rebuilt at various times but principally at the turn of the eighteenth century. These are all of distinctive architectural character. The Bishop's Gate is particularly interesting. It was rebuilt in 1889 by Henry Aaron Baker; based on a triumphal arch it has interesting carvings by the sculptor Edward Smyth who also executed the carvings on the Custom House in Dublin.

The old walled city is situated on rising ground overlooking the River Foyle. The view looking west across the river, with the profile of the old city outlined on the hill highlighting the interrelationship of the dark slated roofs and the dominant form of St. Columb's Cathedral, is one of the most exciting urban vistas in the entire country. This view is as much a part of Derry as the more famous walls. It will be obliterated if the rebuilding of the city is not handled with sensitivity and care. The city centre is compact and has a formal but pleasant domestic scale about it. There are many fine terraces and individual buildings of high standard. A feature of Derry is the high quality of the many public buildings in the city, most of which were erected in the nineteenth century during the time of its great commercial importance. These range from the Court-house designed by John Bowden which is one of the best examples of the Greek Revival in Ireland to the City Guild Hall built in 1887 and a symbol of Derry's stature as an important city. The river Foyle divides the city between the old seventeenth century town and its more recent suburbs. Sadly, however, this is also indicative of more serious divisions within the population. The Bogside and the Creggan which are now etched into the folklore of Catholic Derry are on the west side of the river. On the east is the Waterside, the bastion of Loyalist Derry.

Derry has been the capital of the northwest of Ireland for centuries. Donegal has always looked towards Derry as its natural regional capital, and much of Derry's prosperity grew by providing for the needs of Donegal as regards commerce, communications and industry. The partition of Ireland affected both areas. It cut off a large part of the city's natural hinterland and at the same time removed an important focal point for Donegal. It is often said, however, that the real capital of both Donegal and Derry is Glasgow. For many years, the boats, both passenger and trade, travelled daily between the Foyle and the Clyde. Alas, they no longer do so and the port of Derry is gradually closing down but for the occasional coaster.

The city has suffered badly during the past ten years. Many fine

Above— Derry's Guildhall and in the foreground, the city walls.

Left— Bishop's Gate, Derry, built in 1789.

premises have been destroyed and the commercial life of the city greatly disrupted. The centre of the city, in particular the Diamond, has suffered severe damage but fortunately one outstanding building has escaped — Austin's is a fine example of late nineteenth century commercial development with its strong lines and distinctive appearance. While the narrow streets of medieval Belfast still retain an atmosphere of bustle and business despite the security problems, the more spacious atmosphere of Derry can look rather forlorn without lots of people and activity. Like Belfast, there will be an opportunity now to reshape and improve the city. It is hoped that this will also result in an improvement in the relationship between the local communities, for so long divided.

Derry still possesses many advantages. The city walls which have withstood another period of unrest are in good heart and will ensure that the compact nature of the old city is retained. The new bridge over the Foyle, for long a city dream, may at last be built. If so, communication within the city and with its hinterland will be improved. And finally, of course, there is the magnificent Foyle estuary about which it has been said that the entire British and German navies could harbour in it without seeing each other. The city should develop the tremendous potential of the Foyle for industry, recreation and as a pleasant place to live.

LIMERICK

Of all the cities in Ireland, none today evokes the past, and particularly the nineteenth century, more than Limerick with its streets of old houses, warehouses, small shops and general atmosphere of neglect. Proudly situated on the river Shannon, the most majestic river in these Islands, it has a long and interesting history beginning when its charter was first granted by King John in the year 1197. John's Castle, one of the city's more important historical buildings still dominates the Shannon. This fine complex, however, is still awaiting restoration to its full potential.

The city plan illustrates vividly the contrast between the informal atmosphere of the older city whose street patterns were laid down a thousand years or more ago and the more formal streets and squares of the eighteenth century city. More than the other cities, it suffered an economic decline in the nineteenth and early twentieth century. Its very physical fabric is proof of this, large areas in the city centre are ready for renewal and improvement and have been so for many years. The sheer administrative and legal difficulties of rebuilding the city has, however, up to now frustrated the best efforts of the city fathers and as a result the city is expanding rapidly at its edges at the expense of its heart. Limerick is also unique among the larger cities in that it still has the atmosphere of a large country town. This is particularly noticeable on market day when farmers from the surrounding countryside come to market to sell their produce from small vans and carts, an activity which has not changed much for hundreds of years.

The development of the Shannon International Airport, a mere twelve miles away, has given a recent impetus to the growth of Limerick. The airport and industrial estate have brought increased prosperity to the region but not yet to the city centre. The lack of urban renewal may turn out to be a blessing: Limerick must surely learn from the mistakes made in other cities. It has a wonderful natural asset in the Shannon, a river of majestic quality and size comparable to the Loire or any of the great rivers of Europe. The Shannon estuary, west of the city, is one of the finest natural harbours in Europe, as yet relatively undeveloped in terms of either industrial and transportation potential or its recreational and environmental qualities. A beginning is now being made to realise its industrial potential: a large aluminium smelter is in course of construction at one of the deep water sites. The effect that this large, capital-intensive and potentially polluting industry may have on the environment or indeed its long term economic effects on the region have yet to be measured. Ideally, it should act as a catalyst for the other developments in the estuary and eventually for the regeneration of the city centre, which in the final analysis is the heart of the entire area.

Limerick is now after many years of fighting an important centre for third-level education. The Institute of Education is a university in everything but name, and is bound to add diversity to the social structure of the city which for years has been famous for its introspection. Unfortunately the campus is situated on the outskirts where its immediate impact on the city will be diminished.

Limerick has always been a business and administrative centre serving a large part of the West and Southwest. The many fine stone warehouses to be found throughout the city are indicative of its commercial history. Some are of high architectural quality, particularly in the harbour area where they impart a curious Florentine atmosphere. In their own way, they are more like commercial palaces rather than warehouses.

Like other Irish cities, Limerick also has its distinguished churches. Despite the decline in other matters, the late nineteenth century did see a resurgence in the development of churches, particularly Roman Catholic ones. St. Francis' Church and St. John's Cathedral are particularly distinguished but there are many other examples. In fact, there are many fine individual buildings throughout the city, but in Limerick they have to be looked for more assiduously than in the other cities. Limerick in a sense is a city of fine individual areas. It has the Georgian grandeur of Upper O'Connell Street and Perry Square; the spacious quality of St. John's Square with its curiously French atmosphere; the classical feeling in the area overlooking the river which includes the Custom House, St. Mary's Cathedral and the Court House; the robust and military quality of St. John's Castle; the fine stone work in the warehouses; the intimacy and atmosphere of the old medieval city; and, of course, the River Shannon, which is everywhere part of the city. Unfortunately, it would appear as if Limerick people themselves are on the whole unaware of this fine and distinctive architectural heritage. A massive clean-up operation would help to tie all these distinctive areas together and give the city an identity of its own.

Top– Browne Doorway in Eyre Square, Galway City.
Above– King John's Castle, built in the early 13th century, and the River Shannon in Limerick.

On reflection, Limerick is a city whose quality and character is too often dismissed out of hand: it has the River Shannon and King John's Castle, but little else. This is a mistaken impression, however, for which the casual visitor cannot be blamed. He or she cannot be expected to be aware of the other areas of quality and distinction which are worth a visit when even the local community seems unaware of them.

There are other Irish cities, no less historical, no less interesting, and, of course, of supreme importance to their own citizens. Armagh, the ecclesiastical capital of Ireland, with its two cathedrals on twin hilltops, its medieval core, and the Georgian elegance of the eighteenth century, is one example.

Waterford, founded by the Danes and the site of Norman landings, is a busy seaport and a city with a fine architectural heritage of interesting streets and squares and good individual buildings.

Galway, the capital of the West, is a city of Gaelic culture. For centuries it was practically a city state, but because of its relatively isolated location never gave rise to a "Tuscan style" civilization. Architecturally it is the least known of Ireland's cities but this is due primarily to the lack of local awareness. It has a fine central space, not really presented at its best, and a shopping area with narrow streets and bustling crowds which in its own way is one of the more exciting in the country. Its recently completed cathedral is the last of the line of modern Catholic foundations. Its architecture, however, has lost its way. Aspiring to traditions, it lacks the scholarship, detailing and craftsmanship of the earlier churches, both in the building and in the handling of its surroundings.

Kilkenny is the smallest city and, together with Armagh, the only inland one. It is the centre of a region with important historical associations. Its great era was in the seventeenth century when, for a short period, it was the capital of Confederate Ireland. The Confederate Parliament sat in Kilkenny from 1642-1648. Kilkenny is situated on the Nore: the great castle of the Ormonds dominates the centre. The castle has been bequeathed to the people of Kilkenny and is being sensitively restored by the State both for the benefit of the city and the country. Architecturally, Kilkenny is one of the best-known places in the country and refreshingly, the local people seem more aware of their architectural heritage than inhabitants of most other cities.

It can be argued that the appearance and general character of Ireland's cities is an accurate barometer of a country's concern for its architectural heritage. Where the cities lead, other towns and villages will follow. Can we be optimistic about the future of Irish cities? Despite the general lack of concern in the past decade, the fact that they retain many of their distinctive qualities is in itself grounds for encouragement. But much more remains to be done. In a period of growth and change it cannot be expected that the overall quality of the cities will remain untarnished unless there is more awareness by the community at large. The problems must be tackled at all levels — the professionals, the politicians, the entrepreneurs, the general public, but perhaps above all in the schools.

A medieval street in Kilkenny.

Part Two

GROWING UP
IN IRELAND

THE 1890s AND 1900s
IN CLARE

Edward MacLysaght

NE DAY IN JULY 1905, when I was seventeen years of age, I was cycling with my cousin Tom Gubbins along a country road in south County Galway, a few miles from the Clare border. We had come from Lahinch, where Tom was staying with us, and were exploring what was then for us unknown country. As we trundled along the rough road dodging the puddly holes which later would be mended with a scattering of loose stones (our bicycles were made before the free-wheel type was in regular use), we heard an unusual sound behind us and in a few moments a yoke, the like of which we had seldom seen, pulled up beside us.[1] It was a motor car. The day was fine and the hood was down — even with it up the driver would have had no window to open to address us. "Kindly tell me," said he, "am I on the right road for At-Henry?" I was about to say that I had no idea when Tom, quicker than I to realize that we had been accosted by what in those days was a *rara avis,* namely an English tourist in an automobile, replied "I suppose you mean Athenry: we call it Athan-Rye, you know, *Ath an rí* — the ford of the king. Keep right on and you'll get there." "If," he added as the man moved off, "if he doesn't break down on the way." Cars were unreliable then. I remember even some years later when we had a car ourselves and chanced a journey to Dublin in it, we counted at least two punctures en route a probability. My own belated comment was "Why didn't you tell him that after Athenry, if he was going to Dublin, he'd come in due course to a town called Mull-linger as he'd pronounce Mullingar I suppose."

Perhaps it was that At-Henry incident which stimulated in me as a boy an interest in the question of the pronunciation of personal and place names. It used to grate on my ears to hear the good old Clare name O'Dea pronounced by anglified people as O'Dee and, to go further afield, the two syllables of Maher reduced to Mar, almost Mah. When an American calls Minogue Minnogew, we laugh at him. But the laugh is against our-

Edward MacLysaght (on right) at nine years of age with his younger brother Pat.

selves when we fault his MahOney for that is much nearer to the original Irish *Mathúna* than the "correct" way we pronounce it now with stress on the first syllable and the second almost muted. I must not, however, digress further; how aptly my father used to say that my second name should be "Tangent". More to the point would be to tell the reader who those two boys were and how they came to be in the neighbourhood of Athenry that summer day seventy odd years ago.

Tom was a distant cousin and a close friend of mine: his home was a few miles outside Limerick where his people were in the bacon-curing business. At that time I still had no fixed home and spent most of my time, when not at school, living in a shack we had, located near the end of Lahinch golf links on the road to Liscannor, another village on the Atlantic seaboard. During school holidays Tom and I exchanged visits.

Family history can be boring to people not personally concerned with it. I must nevertheless very briefly outline my background in order to show how I came to be growing up in Co. Clare. The MacLysaghts, now more often called Lysaght with the old prefix Mac dropped, are an ancient but unimportant Clare family, an offshoot of the O'Briens, originating at Kilfenora a few miles north of Lahinch. Our particular branch, from circumstance rather than from temperament, was migratory. This began with an ancestor setting up as a goldsmith in Limerick at the end of the sixteenth century, his son marrying the heiress of a landed family in Co. Limerick, only to be dispossessed as an Irish papist by Cromwell and transplanted back to Clare, settling not far from where we now live. Various adventures found them by the end of the eighteenth century as farmers in Co. Cork.[2] So we come to my immediate forebears. My grandfather being a younger son (and so landless) was an architect in Cork. His son, my father, was one of the innumerable emigrants of the nineteenth century but one whose main aim was to do well enough not only to keep in close touch with his homeland but also to resettle his own family in Ireland.

He would personally have preferred Hazelwood, his uncle's farm in the parish of Doneraile where he was reared, as our permanent home, but in 1906 when he was in a position to implement his plans there was no prospect of that so he seized the opportunity to acquire an extensive but largely derelict farm a few miles from the one our people had owned, till they gambled it away before going to Co. Cork. This is Raheen in the parish of Tuamgraney, the present home of my family. The first few years of my life there certainly come within my growing up period, and before I speak of the years leading up to the outbreak of the First World War, which I feel should be the terminal point of this essay, I must not pass over my childhood without some reference to it.

My first memory in life, appropriately enough, is of the packet steamer which brought us on our journeys between Cork and Milford Haven — Rosslare and Fishguard came later — for my early childhood was spent partly in Wales and partly in Co. Cork. My father always felt himself really at home at Doneraile, and I may mention that he was a great friend of Canon P. A. Sheehan, the author of *My New Curate,* who was parish priest of Doneraile. My memories of my childhood in Victorian times are too hazy to be recalled. My clearest recollection is of an afternoon, I think it was in 1899, when we had begun to visit Lahinch frequently; I was with my father and mother and my young brother Pat in a train on the narrow gauge West Clare Railway.[3] What I remember so clearly is the sound of the little engine labouring up the steep gradient near Corofin and the way the train finally stopped, apparently miles from anywhere. That was nothing in itself: what fixed it in my mind was my father telling me afterwards that Percy French was on that same train and the breakdown prompted him to write one of his best known songs: "Are you right there Michael, are you right, do you think we'll be there before the night." It was not till a few years later that I began to regard myself as essentially a denizen of Lahinch. Before we actually had a dwelling there we used to stay at the Golflinks Hotel, but even then we were accepted as belonging to the place through our connection with nearby Kilfenora and the fact that my father was captain of Lahinch golf club.

In one's earliest years the principal influence in life is usually one's parents. In my case this was certainly so. My father was often away for months. His job at that time as foreign salesman for a Welsh steel works

Top– A turn of the century photograph of the Lahinch railway station with the seaside town of Lahinch in the background.

Above– "Kilkee", a steam-powered engine belonging to the West Clare Railway.

took him on long sea voyages to Australia and other distant places. When he was with us I recall him first as an entertaining teller of stories and particularly as a person who instilled in me a lasting love of Irish music: few evenings passed when he did not sit down at the piano and play Irish airs, my special favourite being *Cailín deas crúidte na mbó*. Looking back to the time when I was ten or twelve, I see my father emerging primarily as a friend rather than a parent. On the other hand, beyond the influence for good that a lovable, helpful and essentially honest woman has on a young boy, my mother was responsible for only one of my main interests: she was an expert horticulturist and botanist and it was from her I acquired my interest in everything to do with gardening and forestry. It was only later when the peaceful years before 1916 were over that she was to show her true colours by her worthy part in the resistance to the Black & Tan aggression; in a word she turned out to be what I once described as a "tough saint" during the two years when Raheen was raided no less than twenty-four times by Crown forces. That, however, belongs to a period not covered by this essay: I have written of it elsewhere.[4]

Whatever about the rich on the one hand and the very poor on the other there is little (except perhaps his essentially rural environment) in the life of a boy of middle class like Tom and I which differed in Clare from that of one of the same age anywhere else. First the growing interest of the teenager in sport or books or gardening and, after sixteen I suppose, girls too; so it is not just the personal aspect of the growing-up stage that I should recount but rather the effect of what I might call history in the making on such a youth and for that matter on the whole population.

Before specifically considering this in regard to the years between 1900 and 1910 I think it would help to very briefly look at the far reaching changes which have taken place in the course of this century. I and my contemporaries — there are few of them left now — whose memories go back to before the turn of the century, are actually unique as we are the only generation in history who have witnessed in our lifetime two different worlds. Physically railways, bicycles and telegraphy were the only modern inventions in general use which differentiated the Ireland of my young days from that of the eighteenth century. In a few places electricity had taken the place of oil lamps and candles, and unbeknownst to us there may have been telephones in some of the main post offices, but these things did not come into the life of us in Co. Clare or of the average man and woman anywhere.

A glance at the record since 1900 will show that the change is equally remarkable in the social field both in respect of services and class. Apart from the great change for the better in the lives of the bulk of the people resulting from legislation applicable to the then United Kingdom of Great Britain and Ireland as a whole, which introduced social services such as unemployment assistance and old-age pensions, some belated attempt was made by the government, after nearly a century of neglect, to deal with the special case of Ireland. The establishment of the Irish Department of Agriculture is one example. From within too there were indications that the long period of national stagnation which followed the death of Daniel O'Connell and the failure of the Young Irelanders was at an end: the foundation and growth of three indigenous organizations, the Gaelic League, the Gaelic Athletic Association (GAA) and the Irish Agricultural Organization Society (IAOS), as well as the Irish Literary renaissance, are proof of that.

I know now, but of course I did not realize it at the time when I was only fifteen years old, that the 1903 Land Act more than anything else was to bring about a complete change in the social set-up, not only in rural Ireland but also indirectly in urban life. The "big house" of the landlord with its butler, maidservants, grooms and gardeners ceased to exist, largely for economic reasons. It is no exaggeration to say that it has disappeared as an element in the structure of present-day Ireland, though some have survived at least as the homes of old landed families (as I know from my own experience when working for the Manuscripts Commission and the National Library for forty years after the time now under review). Within ten miles of my present home in Co. Clare there were five "big houses"; now not one of these remains. The last to go, quite recently, was Maryfort (formerly Lismeehane) the home of the O'Callaghans, whose name, despite their disappearance from the area, is perpetuated in

Ennistymon Falls, Ennistymon, Co. Clare at the turn of the century.

the nearby village of O'Callaghan's Mills.

The one "big house" at which I was a regular visitor was Ennistymon House — still there indeed, but now a prosperous hotel. There lived Henry Macnamara, the owner of one of the most extensive estates in Co. Clare. In spite of his historical and religious background — the Macnamaras are one of the three ancient, principal Irish septs of Thomond — he was a typical tough Protestant landlord. It is worth noting that this anomaly was to be found more frequently in Co. Clare than anywhere else: witness for example the Protestant O'Briens of Dromoland, direct descendants of Brian Boru. Though somewhat in awe of him, I rather liked old Henry; I cannot recall his wife at all, I think she was Australian. It was not the company of these older people that induced me so often to cycle the short journey from Lahinch to Ennistymon but the young members of the family — there were seven of them. Val was a normal boy just my own age. Francis, three years older, was already a "character" foreshadowing the dilettante poet so well described in his daughter Nicolette's book *Two Flamboyant Fathers.* Of the four daughters I only remember Eileen, who a couple of years later married the local police inspector. At meals there I very seldom heard a word about politics; the garden, farm, sport and local gossip were the usual topics of conversation when I was there. I remember that I found being addressed as "your honour sir" by the under-gardener rather embarrassing.

Apropos of "big houses" I was about to add Kilteragh, Sir Horace Plunkett's place, but it was not a "big house" in the sense I have been using the term. It was not the old home of the family or the hub of an estate, being in fact a mansion on the outskirts of Dublin. Yet it could hardly be classed as a suburban residence since it had a farm attached which was much used for experimental work connected with Plunkett's cooperative movement (IAOS). In any case it was not till after I had passed the transition stage between the adolescence and maturity (when did I reach maturity?) that I several times spent a weekend at Kilteragh. Incidentally, would it be out of place to say here that the volume on Sir Horace Plunkett in the "Irishmen of To-day" series was written in 1916 by me? There is much about Plunkett and the co-operative movement in it, but it gives more of my own views on the past, present and future of the country as a whole. So much so indeed that one purchaser of the book wrote to the publishers and demanded his money back on the ground that it contained mainly the latter.

Before I come to what I have called the transition stage, which I look back at as perhaps the most enjoyable part of my life, I should say something of the one movement in the national rejuvenation campaign which, prior to 1916 when politics became for most of us a real live issue no longer a dream, enlisted me as a really enthusiastic supporter. The Gaelic League was more than an organization working for the revival of the old Irish language: its ideology advocated other means of combating what we called the "West Briton" mentality. The seed sown in my teenage mind grew rapidly so that in due course I wrote three books in Irish and I am able to say that in the case of my eldest son Fergus we have never yet spoken a word of English together except when the presence of a third person made it necessary. My plans for its use outside my own family — the creation in fact of a *nua-ghaedhealtacht* (newly created Irish-speaking district) in an English-speaking area —were, in spite of my father's approval and the willing cooperation from such good friends as Father John O'Dea, Pádraig Ó Cadhla, Denis MacMahon, and Conor Clune (of Bloody Sunday fame), in due course to fail. I would be remiss, however, if I did not stress this aspect of my teenage environment and outlook in an account of growing up.

As a teenager the G.A.A. did not mean much to me, though as Clare began to emerge as a leading county in the truly national game of hurling I began to take a spectator's interest in it and was duly elated when Clare won the All Ireland championship in 1914.

My own game, apart from playing rugby at school, was golf. I was at school in England. That has little or no bearing on my growing up in Clare, but as it has some bearing on my upbringing I will quote here a few relevant lines from my book *Interesting Times.*

The boys whose rigid conventions I was inclined to flout seem to have regarded me as a "mad Irishman". Going to school in England may have an anglicizing effect on Irish boys with a unionist background, but it certainly tends to strengthen the nationalist outlook of those who, like myself, were brought up to feel emphatically that they are Irish, not "West Britain".

It is not surprising that it was golf, since I used to say, without strict

Lahinch Strand with the Golflinks Hotel in the background.

adherence to the actual truth, that "I was reared on Lahinch golf links". I should have become a more accomplished player — I never got below a handicap of 5 — because I was coached by the local professional, another Macnamara popularly known as Willie Mac. He was a friend of mine too, but of a very different type from the Macnamaras of Ennistymon House.

While Ennistymon, Kilfenora and the other places in northwest Clare were fairly typical of rural Ireland in the West, Lahinch was different inasmuch as it did not suffer in the same way from the misfortune of chronic unemployment. In any area of small farms the work was carried out by the parents and one son: with no local industries to absorb the rest of the family, emigration was the inevitable result. At Lahinch the upkeep of the golf links provided a number of regular jobs as also did the hotels, though this potential was still in its early stages in those days before tourism had become the major industry it now is.

I began this sketch of my early life with a picture of two boys cycling in Co. Galway where there were some larger farms employing farm labourers. As Tom and I pedalled along that country road enjoying our long summer holidays without a care in the world, it did not occur to us to consider the lot of the men working in the fields, saving hay with few mechanical aids. A couple of years later, when I was at the same work myself, my indifference changed to concern. Being in close touch with the situation, I soon began to realize what life was like for the men I was working with. With hindsight one tends to compare the farm labourer working a sixty-hour week for a paltry nine shillings with his grandson today earning £50 or more for a mere forty-four hours, not to mention overtime and annual holidays. The discrepancy is only minimally due to inflation. The plain fact is that the working people of 1905 were grossly underpaid and by modern standards overworked. The conditions of workers in large towns, even though they got three shillings a week more than the rural workers, was worse because they had, especially in Dublin, to live in unbelievably squalid slums which were much more unhealthy than the country cabins and they lacked the plot in which to grow potatoes that many farm workers had. There is no need to labour this point. I am remembering growing up and how the realization of the economic basis of our country, added to my dislike of the social set-up, changed me from a carefree idler (not quite an idler perhaps) into a hard worker.

Before I pass from my teenage period I will look back for a moment to my carefree days at Lahinch. My time was occupied swimming in the river beside the impressive ruin of Duagh Castle or in the Atlantic on the other side of the sandhills, making frequent calls to shops or friends and doing the daily chores, rather than improving my form on the golf links. Occasionally I went out in the curraghs with the Liscannor fishermen in the day; sometimes I ventured to drop in to Reynolds' pub at Lahinch. In both I heard much Irish spoken and thus got my first introduction to it as a living speech. Oddly enough, for he must have been an Irish speaker, another man I got to know very well in that area (which I was fond of calling "the cradle of my race") never used it in my hearing. He seemed to me, a teenager, to be an old man, though in fact he was no more than sixty years of age. His name was Andrew Lysaght, perhaps a distant relative, but we had no evidence of relationships. He it was who first stimulated my interest in family history and that, followed up, meant Irish history, so I owe much to Andrew.

Whether at Lahinch or later at Raheen how did we occupy ourselves during the long winter evenings — long enough even though we usually went to bed about ten o'clock. As a boy I suppose I read books or played games, I simply don't remember. From about seventeen on, as semi-grownups, with no television to watch or even radio to listen to, we were quite happy reading a book or playing cards at home and sometimes "cuarding", or visiting a neighbour's house, where we were sure of interesting conversation and occasionally of music and even dancing — mostly sets, as we called them, hardly ever the waltz or the polka. There were other aspects of the non-working life of the community with which I personally had little to do. I hardly ever, for example, attended a wake, and to go to funerals except one of a close relative was not expected of a teenager, though it was certainly an obligation on older members of a family. Nor did I then take much interest in folklore though at Raheen we lived near the cottage of the famous Biddy Early.[5] That, with me, came later. Once I got to the working stage, I went to bed early because I had to be up soon after 7.00 a.m. for the milking at eight and that, need I add, meant seven days in the week. Even in those pre-bureaucratic days there was paper work to be done at night — milk records, wage sheets, correspondence and the rest. I recall also the toughness of the working day on special fast days like Good Friday when our meals were devoid not only of meat but also of milk and butter — that reminds me of the notable relaxation in the discipline of the Catholic Church which I might well have mentioned when comparing the daily life of the people of today to that of seventy years ago.

And so I come to the final stage in what may be called my growing up process: at last settling down in Raheen, not into some temporary abode as we had been doing over the past years, but into a permanent home — permanent so far as anything is permanent. (Three of my grandsons are approaching working age in it now.) There was the additional satisfaction that it was in a place near where our family was known to have formerly lived. True, it is a few miles from the actual spot but the feeling of traditionally belonging certainly counted with people seventy years ago — and does I think now too. To find nearby a field called "Lysaght's field" was pleasing just as years before when I first began to observe things like street names it was pleasing to notice a "Lysaght's Lane" in Ennis and the same in Lahinch. Absorbing traditional background was undoubtedly one element in the growing up process.

My father, though he spent his early days on his uncle's farm in Co. Cork, never took to farming himself, so when in 1908 we entered into possession — or more accurately at that time, a Land Commission tenancy

Haymaking in the first decade of the century.

— of the large farm at Tuamgraney called Raheen, the onus of running it, young though I was, fell to me, his elder son. Everything to do with a farm interested me from my childhood. My mother told me once that when asked what I intended to be when I grew up, my reply, translated into adult language, was "a literary farmer". By the time I began at Raheen I had spent long enough at Hazelwood to become a fairly competent worker, that is to say I could milk a cow and make a reasonably shapely cock of hay.

Now no longer a spectator but an actor, albeit a minor one, in the national scene I would have a chance to participate in the movements which had begun to attract me as an outsider. As an inexperienced young man not long out of my teens, however, I could have accomplished little more than the day to day running of the farm by myself. Here again my father comes into the picture.

Not long after we went to Raheen he decided that something must be done, with Tuamgraney in mind, to improve the situation of at least one of the depressed and poverty stricken places west of the Shannon. He forthwith established the nursery industry there which has, seventy years later under the management of his grandson William, become one of the largest of its kind in Ireland. Its establishment actually changed the appearance of the countryside for miles around us, for within fifteen years not only had the farmers obtained from the nurseries more than a million young trees to plant as shelter belts and groves but also the Department of Lands, starting at Raheen, carried out an extensive programme of afforestation in east Clare. This has led more recently to the siting of Ireland's largest chipboard factory in the parish as the final stage in this development, the extent of which I am sure my father cannot have envisaged. I also mentioned that his plans were social as well as economic: he built, for example, a fine ball-alley in 1911 (which I can still count as within my growing-up period) and this did much to put Co. Clare in the front rank of the game of handball, now one of the most popular in Ireland and of international interest.

The nursery was the only one of the "Raheen Rural Industries" established by my father soon after we went to Raheen which survived and turned out a success. The others just faded away due, I am inclined to believe, as much to the serious disorganization of normal life in Ireland — which resulted from intermittent warfare from 1916 to 1923 — as to the fact that our plans may have been over-ambitious. The two main concepts in which I was particularly interested came eventually to nothing. The first was the establishment of a co-operative community somewhat on the lines of that setup in the 1830s at Ralahine in another part of Clare — it failed as the result of the bankruptcy of the gambling landlord who promoted it, and the meanness of his successor.[6] The second was our particular contribution towards the creation of a *nua-ghaedhealtacht*. They belong to my earlier days only as a dream. As a reality they date from 1913 when I was, nominally at any rate, grown-up. I have told these stories elsewhere, and it would be out of place to treat them at length in this essay.

By way of a final look back to my growing-up days I do think we can claim that the youth of the first decade of the century were more actuated than those of today by the philosophy enshrined in the words of the late President John F. Kennedy: "Ask not what your country can do for you but what you can do for your country."

Above– George Otto Simms (on left) c.1921 with brothers Gerald and Harry and sister Dorothea.

Top, right– "Combermore", the Simms' family home in Lifford in the winter of 1928.

Centre– The study at Combermore with George Otto's mother at the writing desk and a photograph of grandfather, James Simms, over the bookcase.

Right– Student days in Botany Bay, Trinity College Dublin, 1930.

THE 1920s IN DONEGAL

George Otto Simms

HOME IS WHERE one starts from. In my case, this saying does not quite apply. Although I was born in Dublin, my childhood home still stands on the slope of the Town-Parks in Lifford, Co. Donegal. After being released from Miss Gavin's nursing home in number seven North Frederick Street, within easy reach of the Rotunda hospital where the skill of Doctor Purefoy effected my delivery, I moved to Lifford where there is record of my baptism at the age of four weeks in the Church of Ireland parish church.

I was born with a caul.[1] A subject referred to in the family now and again when David Copperfield was the current book for reading aloud. The yellowing parchment of this membrane that capped my baby head was placed, after labelling, in my mother's bureau and is now in my possession. Sailors take note!

From the last days of July 1910 onward through twenty-five years, the growing years, Lifford was the home-ground for my rooting and maturing. My parents had four children in all, both my brothers and my sister were born in the house named Combermore, built near the hospital, and formerly the medical doctor's residence.

The trees that swayed in the wind round the house on blustery days are early memories. Tall beeches creaking, evergreens whispering and whining, shielded us from the gusts and the rushes of the storm as we lay in bed, snug and secure. This sense of permanence was strongly felt; the continuity and stability of the family's home life coloured the experiences of the early years. To this day, in spite of changes — trees ageing and fallen, fields altered and roads widened — home, now happily occupied by a brother and his family, still has its drawing power. The return of the near-native always includes a memory, some re-enactment of a scene from early life, some fresh appreciation of the place's charm and beauty, unnoticed when unthinkingly accepted. The awe and wonder are felt, deeply and physically, but are rarely mentioned.

Growing up in the valley, with the hills in front of us and behind us too, was a gentle, quiet process. The life of the home was regulated in a routine that kept us healthy and yet never seemed oppressive. We ranged freely enough in what were country surroundings, with the town life of Strabane but a mile away in the bordering county of Tyrone. Two cows were kept for the milk supply; a pony also, and sometimes a donkey grazed in the field beside the wood that sheltered the house; a hay-field, besides, supplied fodder for the loft's winter store; another acre provided vegetables and fruit.

The rivers that glinted in the sunlight on a wintry morning, seen from our windows through the bare branches of the trees, lent distinction to the Lifford-Strabane neighbourhood. Their stately flowing waters shaped the valley. The Mourne and the Finn met before our eyes and formed the broader Foyle, sending it on its way to Derry and the Lough beyond, a stretch of some fifteen miles. Often in flood, rich in fish, majestic in their onward flow, we found these waterways as they dominated the landscape, friendly and companionable. Not with the eye of the tourist or of the visiting stranger, but with familiarity and affection we named and claimed as part of our life these rivers and their tributaries, the heather hills and each peak of their ranges. Purple-headed Knockavoe and the sprawling contours of green-topped Croghan were special and constant companions. The Finn that had its source in the Donegal highlands more than twenty miles away was treated with a due respect; records of frequent drownings provided their own warning for people growing up. The Finn claims a life each year, the saying went.

The county boundary between Tyrone and Donegal was not a political border in those days. My father, who since his marriage had lived in Lifford, crossed on foot each day the old stone bridge, with its twelve arches spanning the Foyle, to his solicitor's office in the Bowling Green. Strabane. An unchanging route brought him in daily touch with those he met on the high foot-path above the river-holms; these daily workers saluted one another in the morning and repeated the greeting on their return journeys at the end of the day. We were quick to recognise these movements and to people our own childhood world of imagination and fantasy with the more notable of these commuting characters.

Before 1921, Lifford seemed to be almost part of Strabane; its population numbered some four hundred, its houses were largely residential with few shops or business premises. In spite of this Lifford was the county town of Donegal, with its courthouse, a fine, dignified building; its administrative offices in the county house; and near my time, though not in my memory, a gaol. Strangely, however, any conversational reference to "town" signified Strabane with its five thousand inhabitants, its shops, its market day each Tuesday and, added to its Thursday fair days at the beginning of each month, two monster hiring fair days on 12 May and 12 November similar to those described by

Above– General view of Strabane and the River Mourne, c.1920.

Right– Fair-day in Strabane with Abercorn Square in the background.

Below– Bowling Green, Strabane. The two-storey building on the left near the crowd houses the offices of solicitors Wilson and Simms, where George Otto's father practised.

Patrick MacGill of Glenties in *The Ratpit* and other books.

The Simms family apparently began life in Ireland in the early seventeenth century. Coming from England with Sir John Kingsmill of Hampshire, they were allocated land near Castlefin, some six miles south-westward from Lifford, up the Finn valley. James Sime and John Sime, his son, are mentioned in the 1659 Census of Ireland; they probably had a small holding in the townland of Magherireagh in the parish of Donoughmore, where of the 20 people, 18 were English and Scottish and 2 were Irish.[2] In the muster-roll of 1630, which records the names of Kingsmill's men and the type of arms they carried, one of the men armed with a sword only was James Symes and one without arms was James Symes the younger.[3]

Subsequently, my forebears moved down-river from Castlefin to Strabane, and in the last century Strabane was their home. References to canal development, the hotel and the lawyer's office illustrate their involvement in the life and business of the town. A burying ground for the family was the churchyard of Donoughmore near Castlefin, a place of ancient parish history where traditions linked the worship of the church dedicated to Saint Patrick with the early days of Irish Christianity. Here the incoming seventeenth century families found themselves sharing an ancient heritage and experiencing a sense of pride in the history of many earlier centuries.

Lifford seemed to us more ancient than Strabane. In fact, however, both places had medieval associations. In Strabane there was a Franciscan foundation, but Clonleigh, the name of the parish in which Lifford was built had traces in and around the ruins of the old church on one of the routes to Derry that recall the days of Colmcille, the St. Columba of Iona fame. Lifford church is dedicated to St. Lugadius, one of twelve in the crew that accompanied Donegal-born Columba on the voyage out to Iona in the year 563. The ancient site lies on high ground above the Deele as it flows to join the Foyle at a further point and can be seen with its encircling fortifications from the Windmill road, on Croghan's slopes, a favourite viewing point on the walks of our childhood.

Our father's interest in history stimulated our reflections upon the past; his books which lined the study in our home included the list of those recommended for his degree course at Trinity College Dublin as well as the legal volumes of required reading for the examinations of the Incorporated Law Society. His own devotion to the life and worship of the Church of Ireland led him to further studies in church history and doctrines and a recognised qualification from the Sunday School Society for teaching the faith to the young.

My father was one of five sons in a family of six: a sister had died in her early twenties. My father was the only one to remain in his native Strabane. His brothers scattered, one to China, another to Canada; the eldest, ordained after graduation at Trinity College Dublin, began his ministry in the Church of England, not an unusual step in the 1890s for members of a crowded divinity school when George Salmon was

Provost and John Gwynn with John Henry Bernard and others were their teachers. My father's twin brother spent a life-time in the service of Sion Mills, acting as agent for that linen firm on the Continent, residing in Courtrai and Brussels. French and German, added to their courses in Latin and Greek, gave the brothers a competence in communication and, incidentally, not a few European contacts. Governesses had supplemented the instruction gained in Strabane Academy, where Aeneas Kerr reigned as headmaster.

My Simms great-grandfather had two sons and six daughters. The daughters all married locally into families that bore names such as Doyle, French, Donnell, McCrum, Montgomery and Hall. Among the numerous cousins of my father, one in particular, Jane French, had an unusually close connection with us. After leaving Miss Brown's school in Strabane's Abercorn Square, she lived abroad in various French and German households as companion and teacher. In 1895 she married my mother's widowed father, Otto Stange, whose background had been in Germany and Australia before he settled with his two daughters in London. This "Oma" who later became my godmother, thus had a double relationship with us — the children of her first cousin and also of her step-daughter.

The considerable coming and going between Germany and Lifford in the early days of my parents' married life ceased abruptly, when I was four years old, with the outbreak and tragedy of the First World War. The strains which this produced for families caught up in the conflict lay in the background of the war years and long after. Too young to perceive the loneliness and embarrassments rarely mentioned in my hearing, I was brought up largely unaware of these inevitable tensions. The sense of security and happy relationships within the family and throughout the neighbourhood was maintained seemingly unruffled and unimpaired. The barriers that war erected to separate and estrange were happily removed twenty years later, as a memorable visit I made to Germany in the thirties clearly proved. My father's twin was held in Ruhleben civilian prison camp in Germany where he had been caught unawares in August 1914 while on a routine business trip.

My "Oma", whose home had been first in Bremen, then in Brussels, spent most of the war years among our family, unable to join her unmarried step-daughter in their Belgian home. As children we thus had the benefit of a lively and colourful personality, who amused us and provoked us in turn. Singing and telling stories, she introduced us to the local community in Strabane whose people she knew so well, summing them up with all the piquant humour for which she had become locally famous. We often fell to imitating, under cover, her down-right utterances spiced with the vigour of Tyrone's phrasing and idiom. Admiration rather than mockery tempted us to offer pale reproductions of scenes and conversations that were in fact inimitable. Visits with her to the houses up the hill that she had frequented as a girl, introduced me to a fascinating list of the elderly and the house-bound, the "characters", both celebrated and obscure. She drew the best from all of them.

Top– The north side of Lifford Church (Church of Ireland), parish of Clonleigh. The church, built in the 1600s, is dedicated to St. Lugadius, one of Colmcille's companions.

Above– Hughie O'Donnell's public house in Lifford.

My first schooling was next door. From the house across the hayfield through the trees at its fringe, it was a simple matter to climb the wall which separated our home from the grounds of the Prior Endowed School. I was five years old on the first day and remained for nearly five years. At the end of my time there, I had the advantage of receiving my first lessons in Latin from the headmaster, the gifted Arthur James Gloster, who had taught my brothers before me. Many years later, after his death in retirement, his widow allowed me to choose what books I might wish to have from his library. Only then, did I appreciate the standards of his learning and the thoroughness of his methods of teaching. Latin, Greek and, perhaps surprisingly, Hebrew were offered by him to pupils who often distinguished themselves in the field of languages and literature after the foundations of grammar and syntax had been soundly laid. Judging by his books, their markings and pencilled *marginalia,* he had a deep feeling for poetry, including the work of contemporary writers. Eleven years after my last lessons in Latin and Greek with him, he renewed his contact with me by postcard when he had observed an examination result of mine at the university. His laconic "well done" which broke the long silence was both a shock and a spur.

I was nine when I left the Prior for a preparatory school in England, following my eldest brother. The school was in the parish on the Surrey-Hampshire border where my father's brother was vicar, and had been highly commended by him. During my time there, I was the only boy from Ireland. I found myself cross-questioned by my contemporaries, since Ireland was much in the news in that year 1920 and the Lord Mayor of Cork was in Brixton. It was challenging and stimulating to look back from across the water and to attempt to give an account of my country. Of course, some of the boys had visited Ireland. One master was full of praise for her scenery and plant life, a keen gardener, he made me feel at home as he sang the praises of Co. Donegal and the *osmunda regalis* that he found to his delight on a stay at Killybegs.

I realised how little of my country and its troubles I knew. The limited experiences in the Finn valley hardly equipped me for a balanced state-ment of the issues that were constantly in the headlines. Yet undoubted-ly my appreciation of my home was strengthened and the three holiday periods in the year made their special impact. Letters from home also made communication with my parents more personal and intimate than might generally be supposed. My brother, who had left before I entered, had clearly told tales of Lifford and some of the town's personalities with stories that were passed on and embroidered in the few years between his departure and my arrival. I was somewhat taken aback to be asked by one, who later became a distinguished English poet, with an abruptness which was designed to tease: "How's Paddy Sullivan?" I remember stammering some answer shyly and hypocritically about the familiar figure that drove a donkey cart and had a cheerful word for every passer-by as he sold his goods. I remember too my efforts at defending and commending the good name of our neighbourhood. After all, could we not see the spire of Derry Cathedral from the hill behind our house and was not its siege an important fact of history, mentioned in every English history book? I was even able to add some items about this from George Walker's Diary, one of the books in my father's study, when the history master turned to me for some local colour. Lundy's cave in the glen above Strabane was duly described, as was "the breaking of the boom" and the more revolting details of the diet of the besieged as the days in the diary moved slowly on. At quite a different level Mrs. Alexander, the writer of some hymns we all knew and sung, became a subject of boasting as she too was part of Strabane — a citizen of no mean town.

The holidays have a special significance for boarders in schools far away from home. The ritual of travel at the beginning and end of term was charged with emotion. Strabane station was in our eyes a junction of high importance. All sorts met on the platform that linked us with the world outside, with the help of no fewer than three railway companies. Of these the Great Northern was by far the most dignified; the stately puffing required to gain momentum on the gradient across the Mourne towards Sion Mills and on to Dublin or Belfast was clearly heard from the bedroom windows of our home. When aboard the train, waving to those who saw us off and less certainly to the small crowd of pedestrians and vehicles held up at the railway gates until our carriage had passed through, our enthusiasm for trains increased. The County Donegal Railway seemed friendlier with its narrow gauge; there was the Letterkenny branch and also the line that stretched westward to Stranorlar, branching to Donegal, Killybegs, and Ballyshannon in one direction and to Glenties in the other. Finally, the Midland Railway, which was in fact the narrow gauge under another name, traced from Strabane the route to Derry on the right bank of the Foyle. Not only children took delight in the trains, many a grown-up converged towards the complex of platforms, broad and narrow gauge lines, signal boxes and all sorts of rolling stock to be in touch with communications, to fetch the papers and, in war-time, to pick up hot news. The busy and bored, the commuters and the tourists would often find waiting for their train a social event — a summer meeting to be welcomed and enjoyed. Today the station and the trains are no more. The story of the railways, however, has been attractively recorded and published in several volumes. When our father's cousin from Lifford married an eminent engineer who was responsible for designing the curve in the line from Strabane to Lifford in order to avoid the swampy terrain that lay between, we indulged in further pride and, quite unjustifiably, took a proprietary interest in this piece of ingenuity. It has subsequently made railway history.

Our interest in trains increased during the summer when holidays by the sea became part of the year's programme. August was reserved for visits to such places as Port-na-Blagh and Marble Hill in Co. Donegal and also Portnoo. Affection for the hills and headlands, the yellow strands and the lonely roads that wound past lakes and through rocks and heather was shared by us all. One brother climbed almost all the

Top– A typical Donegal coastal scene. This one at Tranarossan Bay.

Above, left– A railway bridge, spanning the River Foyle, under construction at Lifford halt on the Strabane and Letterkenny line, c.1906-7. George Otto's father was solicitor to the line.

Above, right– Engine No.6, the "Columbkille", crossing Lifford Bridge, viewed from Lifford halt.

significant hills and mountains in that very large county; another brother embarked on marathon walks. I found myself developing their tastes in a lesser, lazier fashion. Yet such easily provided recreation in the open air, in surroundings full of the spectacular and the unexpected, is still associated with great happiness and the kind of relaxation that is enjoyed after coming back home with aching, tired limbs and soaking clothes, clinging clammily to the skin.

Most of this pleasure of holidays continued a tradition which was well established before I was born. But the conventional pattern pleased me, and I was content to join in this annual enjoyment of all that the county we loved had to offer. Not until I had grown up was there a break in the rhythm of these memorable summers. My father with his brothers had similar memories long before. In their day, the eighties of last century, they did not have the full advantage of railway travel when they visited their mother's sister and her husband in Rosbeg to spend the summer weeks on the Hamilton farm near Dawros Bay. My father seemed in later years to become a different person when, on his way to those parts, he passed a certain point on the road. Crossing the Reelan river or making off "over the mountains", as he expressed it, seemed to serve as some kind of elixir. We, his children, found such an experience contagious. The environment left its mark on the family's life; its members were more communicative and more closely knit and, in a strange way, more self-contained in these temporary surroundings.

Yet there was more than scenery and surf-bathing in the experience. Going over the mountains signified entering another kind of atmosphere — a special neighbourhood — with friendly people to meet each year. The seaside was strongly associated in our minds with the inhabitants who belonged to the district and welcomed us to their houses. The fishing, farming, hay-making, turf-cutting and house-keeping, all carried out in the local style, gave us the feel of the place. I remember the freedom of access granted to me through all sorts of doors. The more often our visits were repeated, the greater appeared to be the attraction of the familiar scenes and the same old roads we never tired of walking. Others would ask me if I did not become weary of the same scene. Had not the possibilities of Portnoo been exhausted? Surely there were other places in Ireland to be explored, not to mention countries further off. But wider travel was to come later. In my early years these Donegal holidays involved more than sight-seeing. My father's interest in working at the Irish language revived each year on these August visits. We used to join in the learning of words and phrases with the help of Eugene O'Growney's grammar, but there was little opportunity to hear conversations and obtain the feel of the idiom or turn of phrase. Some of the houses which we visited in my father's company, however, were Irish speaking, and we picked up snatches of songs and sayings. I can still recall the sounds and inflections heard first round the turf fires of Kilclooney and Kiltoorish in Boylagh country. This memory became alive when in later years I spent a longer time at the language with a scholarly friend in

Glencolumbkille and tried to build on the first steps learned with my father. Unfortunately, I did not persevere sufficiently to gain any kind of fluency, although my father would often speak of a famous occasion in court when he used his Irish to extract from a witness who knew little English the desired reaction to convince the judge that her evidence was sound. Apparently the reliability of the woman's eye-witness account was being questioned during cross-examination. Did she or did she not see the incident referred to? The magistrate was becoming impatient and no headway was being made. The woman had interpreted "Did you see" as "D'ye see", that is, "Do you understand" and nothing more. My father perceiving that the two-fold meaning of the English word "see" was causing the confusion, interposed in Irish "Did you see him with your own eyes?" *(An bhfaca tú le do shúile féin é?)* whereupon the witness's own eyes brightened with obvious intelligence. She answered convincingly in the affirmative through Irish, and the judge was assured of her credibility.

The events in Ireland which followed the First World War altered in a dramatic way the atmosphere of Lifford and Strabane. Their geographical position and strategical importance in the days of danger and uncertainty leading up to the Treaty caused my parents no little anxiety. Yet the civil war which ensued was a time of excitement rather than fear, since my life was sheltered and protected from the risks that many ran in those troubled days. Light-hearted, faint disappointment was felt when raids and alarms took place in my absence during the school-term and not in the holidays, which were uncannily free from such violent happenings. I was eleven years old when the political boundary separated Lifford from Strabane. In practice, communications between the two continued unbroken. There were external signs of the new situation which could not go unnoticed: the appearance of customs houses manned by uniformed officials, strict and watchful. The barrier was set up but a few yards from the entrance to our family home. The scars of the Troubles were still to be seen on some of Lifford's water-front houses, their walls pock-marked with bullet holes. Windowless, burnt out buildings had a gaunt and forlorn look in the lingering interval before the new Lifford emerged. Shops sprang up and a brisk air of business transformed the streets as branch-houses of leading Strabane firms, with their well-known names, established a presence in what had become another country. Green pillar-boxes, green military uniforms and bilingual public notices in Irish and English were only samples of further outward and visible signs of a new order. Smuggling stories by the score, hugely and humorously embroidered in the telling, helped to lighten the darkness of those uncertain days. Countless anomalies in local life and loyalties during the period of settling down and accepting the situation mollified much ill-feeling. There were frustrations and resentments for everyone to share, but, if business was unusual, life went on with surprising resilience in the face of events which have now become part of history. What some people called rather grandly "the battle of Lifford", however, does not receive a mention in the records.

In retrospect, it was remarkable that all the necessary adjustments, with their accompanying irritants and controversial stresses, were endured without much apparent damage to human relationships in the district. If there were radical alterations in government and in the administration of the state, the parish, at any rate, continued with its life unaltered and the diocese of Derry, in which the parish was situated, held its boundaries as before.

Although the Church of Ireland parish church in Lifford was the only place of worship in the town, the parishioners were few in number. Many of them had a strong sense of community and took an active part in social concerns, sharing their talents with the whole population. Inter-denominational life did not express itself in any organised or deliberate way. The proverbial difficulties of making contacts across the religious divisions were probably recognised and left undisturbed. In childhood days, I learned about Christian traditions other than my own through visits to houses in the neighbourhood and by observing the pictures and symbols of the faith so obviously in a style and tradition unfamiliar and different from my own. On one occasion I overstepped proprieties by following a funeral, in casual overalls, out of sheer curiosity. Usually, there was respect for these differences; nearly always, there was reticence on the subject of religion. There was certainly no dialogue at that period. For myself, I found people fascinating for their variety and their company. The opportunity of working with and among them drew my thoughts towards serving in the Church's ministry even in those early days before my confirmation.

These inklings of adult life, when the growing up drew to a close, have remained with me over the years. The place called home and the people surrounding it gave me more than I knew at the time. Here were roots. In later days, I often met in far-off, distant places others whose life had begun in the self-same valley and immediately the county's name and the physical features of the countryside supplied a touch of kinship. Those who were mere names at home were hailed as friends when among strangers. The Donegal Association is made up of those who share this heritage and most mixed tradition. We all have walked the roads and stopped to drink in the view and catch the tang of heather and turf smoke in the air. In Lifford we still remember the strong aroma of the old flax dams, the grass of the green brae where the salmon nets were spread, the winter when the river was frozen over, the day the church tower was struck by lightning that ripped the ivy from the clean stone. Others, known and unknown to me, also had these experiences to remember. All of us found ourselves belonging mysteriously, even mystically, to the community before that term became over-worked and ran the risk of losing its colour and spontaneity.

The last years of growing up were in my student days. Lifford's Carnegie library in the old court-house served the county. Here the biographies, history and literature were on the open shelves for browsing. The story of the county and of Ireland was not confined to books, for the friendship of Andrew McIntyre helped me to appreciate the culture and traditions he so clearly loved. There was magnetism in his story-telling. The soft voice from the north of the county spoke of books and writers with an intimacy and affection that held the listener fascinated and admiring. I often thought of the manner in which he related all that the county had produced in song and saga and had given to the world of literature. His critical appreciation, lively with humour, sparkled as he showed me the range of his studies. With but little persuasion I might have become a librarian. I had grown up.

THE 1930s ON ARAN

Breandán Ó hEithir

M Y MOTHER'S PEOPLE, on her father's side, have been in Aran for hundreds of years; probably since Queen Elizabeth I granted the islands to the O'Flaherty clan with whom she was anxious to make peace. Older people in Inishmore would have known my mother as Delia Mhaidhc and her father was Maidhc Mhicil Phádraic Bhartlaiméid Bhrian Bhartlaiméid Bhrian Bhartlaiméid.[1] The family was settled in the village of Gortnagopple for that length of time. Her mother's people came to Inishmore around the middle of the nineteenth century. My great-grandfather, Thomas Ganly, was of Ulster Protestant stock and came to Aran to build a lighthouse and a pier. A tolerant father had allowed Thomas Ganly to follow his mother's Catholic faith. He liked Inishmore and married a widow with a good holding. She died within a year and he then married the young daughter of a neighbouring blacksmith and smuggler called Mícheál Riabhach Nee.

My father came from Clare to teach in Kilronan school in 1927. His family got on the wrong side of the Bishop of Killaloe during the Civil War and all his applications for teaching posts in the diocese had been ignored. The inevitable "friendly" priest, a neighbour's child, came with sound advice: "Pat, the Bishop is an old man. He can't live forever. Get a school in some remote place and come back to Clare when he's gone." My father was twenty-four when he came to teach in Aran, and I was a year older when the good God finally called Bishop Fogarty. The point is worth noting by anyone who might have ideas about playing that kind of hide-and-seek with an Irish bishop. In this case it didn't matter too much since my father married my mother, who was principal of Kilronan Girl's School, and became an Aranman by desire.

According to the findings of the numerous scientists who came to measure our heads, examine our teeth and perform tests on our blood, I am a fairly typical Aranman. According to the scientists the typical islander comes of very mixed stock and in many physical characteristics is closer to the East Anglians and the Cockneys than to most of the mainland Irish. This can be taken seriously or with pinches of salt of varying size. Anthropological jokes aside, I am probably of more mixed stock than the typical islander in this generation but whether that is a good or bad thing is for others to judge.

Temperamentally the O'Flahertys were stern and austere; the Ganlys gay and feckless; the Hehirs introverted and generous; and the Murrihys garrulous and rather Jansenistic. Politics were the only common bond. Both my grandfathers were imprisoned in Limerick during the Land War for doing physical damage to bailiffs, and Thomas Ganly's son, Thomas, had to flee to America after shooting a member of the same profession.

My father and mother both disapproved of non-constitutional political action and the more violent of our ancestors were never held up to us as examples to be imitated. My mother believed in a rather aggressive brand of pacifism which demanded an iron will and spartan self-discipline. Nevertheless, when a first cousin of mine arrived suddenly from Co. Tyrone, having shot a policeman there in 1941, he stayed with us for weeks before the Special Branch came from Galway and took him to the Curragh, where he was interned. In our house family always came first and such things as politics and religion some lengths behind.

My first clear memory of life in Aran concerns the general election of 1933 (when I was three years old) when my father and a crowd of de Valera supporters lit a bonfire on top of a craggy hill near our house to celebrate the victory. In doing so they dragged a clump of withered briars across a field belonging to our nearest neighbour who was an ex-member of His Majesty's Royal Navy, a strong Cosgrave supporter and the owner of a double-barrelled shotgun. Although no shots were fired on that occasion the scene was sufficiently dramatic to remain vividly in my memory.

When I tell the story I notice that some people express surprise that party politics were so firmly rooted in such a remote place. This merely betrays an ignorance of the political and social history of the islands and particularly Inishmore. We know almost nothing about the shadowy tribe who built the great stone forts; apart from the fact that they must have been fleeing from some mortal enemy and had the ability to move huge blocks of stone to very inaccessible places. The legion of holy men who left a more permanent mark on the islands must have had some form of local government and certainly had strong links with the Continent. Descendants of Brian Boru ruled the islands for over three hundred years until Queen Elizabeth made her deal with the Connemara O'Flahertys. From 1582 until the Treaty of 1922 the British Government maintained a continuous military presence on Inishmore. It is very important to remember that the English language had taken firm root and was the official language of Church and State from the middle of the nineteenth century. After his first visit to Inishmore in 1896, W.B. Yeats noted the purity of

Right— "This picture was taken in 1940 when I was ten. I was as proud as I look of my new soutane and surplice with its beautiful smell of starch and bleaching. The angelic look was also fairly authentic."

Below— Tiny stone walled fields on Inisheer. There are no gateways and a farmer will knock down and rebuild sections of a wall to allow his cows to enter and leave a pasture.

133

the English spoken by some of the islanders he met. It is worth noting that the Irish language is stronger in Inishmore today than at any time for a hundred years.

It is no wonder then, that a bitter dispute about language involving my own family clouds my earliest memories. My father, as well as being a member of the Fianna Fáil party since its inception, was also a convinced supporter of the Irish revival. The language had just ebbed from his native townland in Clare, as it was later to ebb from the rest of the county, but he worked hard to master Aran Irish. I cannot remember which language I first spoke (presumably it was Irish for I was looked after by a succession of maids) but I cannot remember a time when I couldn't understand and speak English. I suspect that my mother, who was sceptical of all causes once they seemed too popular, was partly responsible for this situation. My annual visits to my grandparents in Clare also played a part. English had become the language of the home among a growing number of families in the village of Kilronan although it was spoken by others with great accuracy and a rich vocabulary. Matters came to a head when the Fianna Fáil government introduced an annual grant for Gaeltacht children whose home language was Irish. My father issued an ultimatum: he wasn't going to sign the necessary forms for anyone who didn't decide to use Irish as the language of the home during the coming year.

At this point the Catholic Church, in the person of the parish priest, took a hand in the affair. A man with an almost pathological horror of the Irish language, he seemed to take pleasure in forcing English on the most monolingual of his flock. He was also directly opposed to my father's brand of politics and as school manager he had more than a little control over his activities. As if all that was not enough, there was an even more sinister element involved. My uncle, Liam O'Flaherty, had written novels in which the Catholic clergy — and particularly some thinly-disguised former parish priests of the Aran Islands — had appeared to no great advantage.[2] So "evil" indeed were some of his works that the Irish Government in its wisdom had banned them. When my father refused to sign forms for a number of families, the parish priest took their part, and I got my first glimpse of a collision between Church and State in de Valera's Ireland.

My memories of the actual conflict, although fragmentary and hazy in part, are very real and owe nothing to knowledge gained later. It was as good a way as any to learn the realities of Irish life at first hand and in an almost claustrophobic community; to see the pitfalls that yawn before the unwary crusader, the loneliness of the individual in such an isolated place who is attacked by one authority and only grudgingly backed by another and, most important of all in the end, the quiet courage of simple and vulnerable people who cannot find it in their hearts to side with Might against what they believe is Right. The language battle was short and what bitterness it generated was soon forgotten. The parish priest failed to show the courage of his particular convictions and made the mistake of insulting a high-ranking inspector in the Department of Education. This was the deciding factor and the parish priest was moved sideways to a more placid part of the diocese.

His replacement was as enthusiastic about the revival of Irish as my father was and although he kept away from politics, seemed partial to Eamon de Valera. But unfortunately for my family, he was even more obsessed than his predecessor with bad books and their authors and the necessity for suppressing them. Unlike his predecessor, he read books and had certain simple ideas about what they ought to contain. The result of all this was that the campaign against my uncle Liam (in the person of my mother) grew in intensity. The central figure was beyond the parish priest's range but my mother was a fixed target.

My mother kept her brother's books locked in a press for safe keeping but one resourceful maid found the key and read some of them. She came to the conclusion that all she had heard about them was indeed true and hared off to confession. Part of her penance was to seek out and destroy this cache of filth. Luckily, the girl had a problem when it came to destroying her employer's property and my mother found her at the range, book in hand, still struggling with one part of her conscience. On another occasion the parish priest turned up at the school, took my mother's two classes away to the sacristy and got them to "confess" that my mother had boasted about her brother's writings. Two little girls refused to obey, even when slapped, and that particular plot failed. Eventually, she was prevailed upon to let the matter go to a higher authority which it did. There was no formal reaction for in those times the Church could not be seen to react to complaints from mere laity. But positive persecution ceased and life became much easier.

Through all these years the thing that made the greatest impression on me was my mother's deep and sometimes oppressive relationship with the Almighty. Even now I find it difficult to comprehend how she could divorce Him so completely from the activities of some of His servants on earth. All through her struggles with local and visiting clergy she remained a regular daily communicant. When someone said to her that she must find it difficult to confess to a man who was doing his best to deprive her of a job in her native place, she shrugged it off in her usual laconic manner: "No tramp from the County Mayo has the power to shake the grip I have got on the hand of God." In those days we were plagued by a succession of parish priests from that county.

My own relationship with the parish priest was almost cordial and the fact that I became a dedicated altar-boy at an early age helped me to develop a love of ceremony and ritual that I never fully lost, even when my simple childhood faith flickered and failed. Missions, given by a platoon of terrifying Redemptorists, were the high-point of my association with Church affairs. I rang the "Sinner's Bell" with a fierce dedication as the congregation knelt and prayed for "the sinners of the parish who had turned their backs on the Grace of God". I knew them all, of course, and as I tolled the bell I wondered where they were at that moment and what they were thinking as the sound of the bell rang out over the island.

Pat Mullin was probably reading a book or perhaps writing one.[3] The doctor was undoubtedly reading a book if he wasn't actually doctoring in one of the three islands and deciding that he would probably go to the last few days of the mission, if only to hear the priests fulminating against the excesses of *an corp lofa seo* (this rotten body of ours) and to chuckle at the memory of the parish priest's efforts to monopolise his own services completely during the last epidemic of flu. Old Pádraic in Kileaney could be doing any one of ten different things. When one missioner approached him and asked him why he didn't go to church, he replied that he didn't consider himself to be suitably dressed. The missioner decided to give him the soft treatment and said, "My good man, Jesus Christ didn't have grand clothes to wear." Pádraic considered this proposition which hadn't occurred to him before and replied, "That may be so but neither did he have to walk into Kilronan Chapel."

But all experience in Aran was heightened by the closeness of the community, the long folk-memory that connected present-day happenings with the past and, above all, the physical surroundings. The changing of the seasons was far more dramatic and powerful than it could ever be on a larger mass of land. In winter the Atlantic pounded the high cliffs to the south with great earth-quivering thuds which vibrated through the soles of the feet on the flat rocks overhead. Great gobbets of spume were whisked inland from the breakers and made salt the water in the barrels under the eave-shutes. Old men and women leant against the wind as they toiled up-hill and stooped to seek the shelter of the stone walls. Such was the force of the elements that even inanimate things were given character and a kind of life. The old S.S. *Dún Aengus,* our only link with the mainland, was constantly sought by hundreds of eyes and the people shouted to each other over the howling wind, *"Meastú an dtiocfidh sí inniu?"* (I wonder will she come today?). I remember standing behind a huddle of women, enjoying the shelter given by their thick flannel skirts and heavy paisley shawls, as they watched the *Dún Aengus* wallow and plunge towards Kilronan pier lamenting the severity of the weather. One old woman, who had walked from the far end of the island that morning, said, "Indeed it's a terrible day and let's not forget the poor *Dún Aengus* herself and the battering she's getting!"

In spring the light got stronger and although seas still ran high, the shores were now full of men with pitchforks gathering seaweed. It was spread to dry on the foreshore then stacked in great wine-red cocks to be burned as kelp in autumn. Broad ribbons of red weed and tufts of tasselated black weed were spread on the greening fields to fertilise them and later men with spades turned the earth over it and planted potatoes. It was the lambing season and little boys got up at the crack of dawn to be first at the scene of a birth and then run to the owner with the good news. On Easter Sunday the bearer of good news was rewarded with a gift of fresh eggs. The evenings were spent searching for birds nests and the school playground was full of arguments about the number of nests each boy had found. You only shared your nests with your closest friends and with the birds themselves who gradually got to know you from your

136

Above— Inishmore men prepare to take their cattle to the Kilronan pier for shipment to the mainland.

Left— The leisurely loading of a bullock onto the MV "Naomh Eanna" at Kilronan, Inishmore reflects the comfort of life there compared to the other two islands. The long white building in the centre background was the old "Atlantic Hotel" where John Millington Synge spent his first night on the Aran Islands.

137

regular evening visits. It was always sad to come and find the parents and fledgelings gone; but not terribly sad because it also meant that summer had come.

Summer brought the tourists or strangers as we called them, not as numerous then as they have now become but always interesting to watch as they trooped down the gangway to run a gauntlet of persistent jarveys. One of these found his own place in island annals by telling a startled American lady of middle-age that he was prepared "To ride her around the island for ten shillings." Remarks of a witty or ridiculous nature never seemed to want for an audience in Aran, no matter how privately or indeed intimately, they were uttered. I always found it curious and rather frightening.

Autumn was my own favourite season on Aran. It was kelp-burning time and for weeks on end the northern shore of the island would be enveloped in clouds of creamy-white smoke from the blazing kilns. From early morning until well after dark laden carts and empty carts clunked and clattered back and forth through the island and Kilronan pier piled high with hundreds and hundreds of sacks. There was great rivalry between families as to who would have the record tonnage and the top price, for kelp was tested for quality. It was also potato-digging time and it was wonderful to see the lines of freshly-dug potatoes looking so rich and almost exotic in the stark, grey surroundings of stone walls and bare crags. The September fair in Galway was the last great outing of the year to the mainland and after the special holiday for potato-picking we went back to school and the island settled down to prepare for Christmas and the advent of winter.

Judged by the standards of the times, in any part of Ireland, our family circumstances could only be described as comfortable; by island standards, we were well off with two state salaries to sustain us. Times were not good anywhere in the mid-thirties and while I have no memories of real poverty around us, I have vivid memories of real deprivation. Small wonder then that the introduction of the dole (unemployment assistance) was hailed in places like Aran as a definite social revolution. It certainly helped to turn the Congested Districts (and all the Gaeltacht areas) into Fianna Fáil strongholds.[4] This was brought home to me shortly after the first National Coalition came into office in 1948. An old man from the most westerly village in the island came in to see my father in a very agitated condition. He had just heard that de Valera was gone and wanted to know if the dole was also going to be taken away and "the bad days we knew returning".

I associate the coming of the dole with the first paper in the Irish language that I ever read, *An tEireannach* (The Irishman), edited by Seán Beaumont and widely read in the Gaeltacht. Our local poet wrote a song in praise of de Valera for having introduced the dole and it was published in this weekly paper. It was followed by another song in praise of the "Free Beef" scheme which was introduced as a means of disposing of the "beef mountain" created by the economic war with Britain. Under this scheme people who were entitled to the dole were given an allowance of free beef according to the number of dependants they had. This struggle, during which blood was spilt and which turned the ranchers of Ireland into raging revolutionaries, was taken as another sign of social progress in Aran. When de Valera's son Brian was killed in a riding accident in the Phoenix Park almost everyone on the island signed a message of sympathy to the family. When he visited the island in 1946 the whole population turned out to see him, including a ninety-eight year old man, and we were told that when he landed in Inishmaan the people knelt down.

And I also remember the long line of men, many of them well past middle-age, sitting on bags of straw under the swirling winter rain, breaking stones for the county council roadworks. When the roadworks reached our house they ate their lunch of bread and tea in our store, and the cans of tea were heated on the range in the kitchen. The hours were long and the work was hard but work was scarce and men were glad to get it. Whenever I come upon the shortest poem written by Yeats, I remember those days and those men.

"Parnell came down the road, he said to a cheering man 'Ireland shall get her freedom and you still break stones'."

Just before the outbreak of war in 1939 we built a house of our own on the brink of a cliff about a mile west of the village of Kilronan. Previously we had lived in the teacher's residence in the village, as draughty and as damp as most of these monstrosities seemed to be in all parts of Ireland. At this time there were four of us — my sister Máirín, who was four years younger than me, my brother Éanna and my sister Mairéad. The new house, coupled with the move out of Kilronan and the outbreak of war, marked a turning point in my life. I became more interested in the political and social history of the island, spent more time in the company of older people and read all the books I could lay my hands on in English and in Irish. The war made us all more conscious of the importance of radio and it brought Europe into our kitchen in a real way.

My father, who was very pro-German, got the *Daily Mail* war-map of Europe, complete with Axis and Allied flags. When the Maginot Line was broken, when Norway was invaded and when Rommel rampaged through North Africa, the little flags on our kitchen wall kept up with the action and we became familiar with places like Tobruk, Narvik, Bengazi, and Valetta. Lord Haw Haw came to us nightly and another German broadcaster spoke to us in Irish every week. Getting batteries for the radio was the only problem but a resourceful man from Kileaney started a system of barter with some English trawler skippers: they brought us high tension batteries, tea and bicycle tyres and they got butter, whiskey and meat. In this way we were able to follow the war from our remote and neutral rock in the Atlantic. To ensure our immunity from attack from the air, army engineers came and built a large whitewashed EIRE on the highest spot on the island. It remained for years after the surrender of Japan, and even the Korean war, but when last I went to visit it I found it had been cleared away.

Our new house made me more aware of the physical beauty of the

Left— An old lady of Inishmore pictured at the Seven Churches in the early part of the century. She would probably have remembered the Great Famine which was mercifully mild on the islands.

Below— Dún Aengus will always be Inishmore's greatest tourist attraction and the tourists in turn will be surprised to find that most of the jarveys who drive them from Kilronan to see it have never visited it themselves. Even a small island can afford to have its own mysterious places.

island and the varying moods of the sea around us. On a clear day in early spring or autumn one could see an unbelievable sweep of land and sea from our front door: Mount Brandon and the mouth of the Shannon along the Clare Coast to Black Head; the sand dunes near Salthill; and along the Connemara shore to the Twelve Pins and Slyne Head. With the aid of binoculars one could see Croagh Patrick and pick out individual houses in Carraroe and Garumna. It was a pleasure to start the day, at any time of year, by contemplating this segment of coastline and sea with Inishmaan and Inisheer lying to the east of us. We were probably the first to spot the boat from Galway, on days when her arrival was doubtful, as the tiny black dot came over the horizon. At night the lighthouses winked at us from Loop Head on the Shannon away to the south, from Inisheer, from Black Head to the northeast, and from Slyne Head near Clifden to the northwest. My mother, who had the enviable capacity to observe the elements for hours on end, developed an almost infallible method of forecasting the weather from studying the beams of the lighthouse on Straw Island which was opposite the house.

The house stood near a hill, the third steep one on the road west from Kilronan. It was a lonely road at the time and as we never seemed to go to bed before midnight, we became a halfway-house for people who felt like a rest or needed to have a rest before completing their journey west. Sometimes they came in parties and after a cup of tea in the warm kitchen and a drop out of the bottle, flagging spirits were revived and three o'clock in the morning would find my teetotal father yawning and thinking of school at nine while Mac Phatch Sheáin sang *Brídín Bhéasaigh* or Pat Bhairtlín made his way through *The Thirty-Two Counties*.

My father's main interest in life, outside of school and the family, was people. A true-born democrat, he was in no way concerned with a person's wealth or standing in society; unless they were erudite, odd, expert in the Irish language and in local history, or engaged in intrigue and politics they held no interest for him. After a short time on the island he knew more about local history and family trees than my mother did. Like most Clare people he had a deep interest in "tracing" relationships to remote degrees and was always consulted by my mother when her own family tree needed pruning. She affected to know even less than she actually did and as she usually worked through the medium of parables, I took it as a ruse to discourage us from taking too deep an interest in what she considered to be other people's business.

Her passion for gardening brought these matters to a head on more than one occasion. My father, although he was the eldest son of a small farmer, had no interest at all in gardening and my mother's fear that his two sons would follow in his footsteps were only too clearly realised. Ever since the introduction of the dole and social insurance and Gaeltacht grants for housing my father had a new method of indulging his interest in people and in the social history of Aran. He rarely came home from school to have his dinner with the rest of us as there usually was a battery of official forms waiting for him in the school porch. Other people preferred to come to the house to discuss their business but nobody would be so rude as to come directly to the point of their visit which gave my father the opportunity to broaden and deepen his knowledge of various island matters. As a result of all this he has an unequalled knowledge of Aran history and it was from him rather than from my mother that I got my sometimes painful love of the Irish language.

In 1944 I passed the Preparatory Colleges examination and was called to Coláiste Einde which was located in Drumcondra Training College in Dublin. Its Galway base had been taken over as a military hospital. The war was coming to an end and Lord Haw Haw's voice sounded strident and hysterical, and as soon as the war ended emigration began to drain young people off the islands at a startling rate. Some went to America; the others to England. Only one other boy and myself and a lone girl, out of the class I went through Kilronan school with, remained in Ireland and only the girl stayed in Aran.

Emigration was nothing new to us. My mother never saw her eldest sister, Mary, who kissed her as she slept in her cradle before setting off to Boston. When Mary died people called to our house to sympathise and it was one of the most unreal occasions I ever witnessed and far more distressing for my mother than if she had known her. Some of the mourners had gone to school with Mary and were able to describe her and tell stories about her. She shouldn't have gone away at all for she was being appointed a monitoress in the local school. But when she heard that another girl said she had used influence to get the post, Mary got up and said, "If she wants it that badly she can have it" and went to America. I think that story upset my mother more than anything else when Mary died: she would have done the very same thing herself.

After four years in boarding school, three of them in Galway, I got a scholarship to University College Galway where I spent three idyllic years doing just as I pleased until fate, in the shape of a degree examination, caught up with me. From 1944 on, Aran was becoming the place where I spent my holidays and the grip of the mainland got stronger and stronger as the years passed. Like a lot of island people I settled easily into city life; first in Galway and afterwards in Dublin. Still Aran was and is the place I call home automatically, although my immediate family have left it now and the house is sold. My last link with the island community died with my brother, Eanna, who taught in Inisheer and was one of the pioneers of the co-operative movement on the islands. He died young and left a wife and children to mourn him. He was also the only one of our family to make a practical commitment to the island community and for that reason he will be remembered there in a way that the rest of us will not. In my own case, although the wish was there, the attraction of the city was always too strong and the older I got the more the necessary inquisitiveness of life in a small community oppressed me and made me scuttle for the relative indifference of the city of Dublin.

The fact that I grew up in Aran must have affected my outlook and attitudes in many ways that I am not fully aware of myself. All I can say about it now is that if I could re-live my life and choose a place to grow up in, I would choose Aran without any hesitation. I might be tempted to eliminate the more irritating and unpredictable traits of some of my ancestors but would probably resist it without too great an effort. Life in Aran changed dramatically during my lifetime; changes being more apparent and more striking in an island community than anywhere else. Most of the changes please me but my Aran now exists only in my memory.

Breandán walking along the cliffs of Inishmore.

THE 1950s AND 1960s IN DERRY

Nell McCafferty

I T WAS NOT ALWAYS like this, with armed British troops patrolling the streets and families riven by internment, imprisonment or death by bullet. There were not always armoured tanks and bombed buildings; the gates in the old walled city of Derry, high above the Bogside, were not always closed against us at dusk. I was born in 1944. When I was growing up animals roamed freely through the wide open spaces of Bogside and children chased butterflies. Sheep and cattle were driven on the hoof to Rossville Street Market, horses drew milk carts, hens were kept in backyards, Susie Kildea had a goat in the field she called a farm and greyhounds abounded because they could be trained to race in the fresh air and win a few shillings.

Unemployment being what it was — some things never change — people turned their hands to anything to earn a bob. Even our garbage was minted by Billy and Thomas, two little brothers from our street, who wheeled a foul-smelling open cart up and down the terraced hills collecting brock — the local name for waste food. They delivered the vegetable peelings and potato skins and bread crusts to Mister McIntyre who kept pigs in a shed three streets away. The pigs supplemented their diet in the field that is now a little housing estate. We followed in the wake of the pigs, collecting worms which we used for bait to fish in the pond at the top of our street.

Sergeant Duffy's Bogside barracks were famed for their vegetable gardens, the produce of which graced his family table. The irony was not lost on his daughter when she later urged her own children, including me, to repulse his successors, the Royal Ulster Constabulary, in the Battle of Bogside, 1969. Our vantage point in that battle was the roof of the High Flats, a multi-storied block which replaced the old Rossville Market. Our war cry was "one family, one house", because Bogside had by then bulged to the boiling point, the overcrowding spilling onto the streets in riotous rage. When I was a child the pace had been rather more leisurely.

I was born in my own home, number eight Beechwood Street, delivered by Nurse McBrearty who lived in number two. My godmother, Sadie Gallagher, shirt factory worker, lived in number eleven. Annie McDaid, retired shirt factory worker who lived in number six, was always addressed by us as "Aunt Annie". Granny Doran, who lived in number ten, baby-sat us when my parents escaped their six children and hurried off to the pictures.

In that matriarchal street, there was little need of male figures. The men in any case frequently departed out of our lives, away over to England in search of work. My own father spent the statutory period of exile there, as later, did four of his six children. So the women were much used to their own company, taking, indeed, great delight in it. Our summer play was supervised by a group of them, gathered together around Ettie Deeney's door. Every day at two o'clock, after she had fed us, my mother sent me to see if Ettie was out standing at her door. She always was, and my mother would take off her apron, pick up her cushion and meander up to Ettie's where she sat herself on the ground amid the circle of females and indulged in the exchange of hot news. Occasionally she picked out one of her nearby brood and instructed us to go into the house and bring her up a single cigarette. One woman, one cigarette, in those post-war ration days.

The ritual was repeated at seven in the evening after tea, there being no television to compete with conversational talent. There was no sliced pan or tiled fireplace then either. Our kitchen was dominated by a large black range, the bane and pride of my mother's life, throwing out great heat and producing lovely baked bread. Her scones were famous, especially on Saturday nights when we tried to coax them newly warm from her and slap melting butter on before the midnight hour was struck and the fast began for Sunday morning communion.

Each woman had her own recipe, a little of this, just enough of that, and "How much baking soda did you say again, Mary?" They exchanged their produce in civil competition, though victory was conceded to my Aunt Vera's buns. Aunt Vera lived on Foyle Road, beside the river, a fair walk from our house. The distance was nothing to her when making a visit. Through the streets she proudly walked, bearing her gift of fluffy buns topped with icing, slit with cream and borne in outstretched arms on a tray covered with a teacloth. One of us playing round the corner usually spotted her coming. As she strode into sight, modest withal but sure, shouts of greeting would assail her from the family gathered round the front door to pay her hungry homage.

Both women in turn conceded victory to Aunt Mena's confections, as classy as her pretensions and twice as substantial. Her cakes were always glacé, her biscuits macarooned, her sandwiches contained watercress grown in her own garden on the rarefied heights of Glen Road.

My Aunt Nellie, who lived within the walled city, went in desperation to a Protestant neighbour and learned how to make toffee, bribing us by the paper bagful.

None of them had a patch on Mrs. McDaid, whose gravy rings were such that people bought them from her. Every Sunday after dinner we were dispatched to Tyrconnell Street to buy a dozen of the golden sugared circles of light dough. Nor was she alone in home enterprise. Mrs. Deery stuck thin sticks into apples, immersed the fruit in a boiling pan of syrup and sold the cooled concoction as toffee apples right out of her front window.

My Aunt Mary, however, took the biscuit. She lived just outside the Walls, beyond Bishop's Gate, in Bishop Street. Every 12 August she used open her front room as a cafe in which she fed hungry Orangemen who had travelled from all over the North to celebrate the siege of 1689, when Protestants had successfully defended the walled city against the Catholic army of King James of England. They were quite happy to eat bacon, eggs and sausage in that Catholic household after a rousing chorus in the streets of "God bless King Billy and to hell with the Pope". The Pope had backed the Protestant Dutchman against James, but what the hell. Anyway the hearty fry Aunt Mary sold them far surpassed the dogs and rats their ancestors had eaten during that famous siege. Let bygones be bygones. Sure didn't Nixon engage in trade with China?

Chronic unemployment rendered even children to ways of making money. My pal Joe and I personally dismantled the air raid shelter at the foot of our street, selling the thin iron rods that threaded the stone blocks together to the rag and bone merchants. Every penny counted, a fact of which we were acutely aware at the age of six, when we were dressed up to receive the First Holy Communion.

The Catholic Church held that such a day constituted a calendar occasion in one's life; a red letter day, so to speak, which it was because it plunged our parents into debt in an effort to fit us with the customary and expensive white dresses and veils, dark suits and shoes. After the religious ceremony came the equally fervent round of relatives and neighbours, in the unexpressed and prayerful hope that their money gifts would equal the cost of the outfit.

The Church was the repository of all our hopes in the fifties, not surprisingly, because prayer held out the only hope in a politely gerry-mandered city where the majority Catholic population never achieved official control. The docks were running down, the railways were closing, no factories were being built and housing was at a standstill. The family rosaries which we said every night were shorter by far than the litanies that we tacked onto the five decades. "God send John a job; God send Jackie and Rosaleen a house; Holy Mother of God look down on Peggy in America, on Leo in England; Jesus and his Blessed Mother protect Mary that's going out with a sailor..."

Derry was then a rollicking port of call for foreign fleets — the Dutch, Portuguese, Italians, English and Americans. The free-spending sailors sailed in and out, dancing and dating between times, taking many women away as brides, leaving quite a few unclaimed babies. Scarcely a street remains in Bogside that does not contain an unmarried mother or a

Right– Nell at first communion in Derry, 1950.

Below– Relaxing outside of Ettie Deeney's door on Beechwood Street in 1949.

daughter married into the forces. I was old enough to notice girls being beaten through the streets by angry fathers who had gone down to the ships to retrieve them and young enough to welcome the sailors because they played the juke box non-stop and gave away their loose change before departure.

Bogside was open to sea and land then. The river was not blocked by Army nets nor the roads straddled by army encampments, hemming us into Ulster. Bogside gave onto open countryside, and we roamed at will among the fields and streams and orchards often crossing the border which separated North from South only three miles distant from the city. We availed freely of the many lanes and by-ways giving access to the Republic; they are now called "unapproved roads", spiked by the British Army and often as not mined by the IRA in hope of blowing up a foot patrol.

We did not call it the Republic, of course, because national politics had not tangibly intruded upon us. I always thought it was called the "Free State" because cigarettes and butter were cheaper there. Crossing the border had all the romance of entering a foreign country. At our back-door we had Donegal, with sea and sandy coast, mountains to climb and a strange language called Gaelic if you penetrated far enough. There were also two monuments, magical to any child. Grianan Fort, atop a wind-swept height, came complete with underground tunnels and ramparts along which we could swagger and fight. The round fortress, with walls three feet thick, was built centuries ago without benefit of cement, thus providing cracks and crevices for a handy scaling of its walls.

Nearer home, more suitable for a family picnic, was the Stone Man — a conical heap of stones on the crest of the hill that sloped gently up out of Derry. On the way to it we stopped at a spring well for pure water, good for our health, and on the way back we gathered blackberries for home-made jam. A farmhouse provided eggs and buttermilk for practically nothing, and then it was downhill, singing all the way home.

Buncrana, a sandy resort on the wild Atlantic shore fourteen miles away, called for more resourcefulness and planning. Cars were in short supply and everyone relied on the Lough Swilly Bus Line. The trip always began with a swift despatch of notes around the clan, from my mother to Aunt Maureen, Aunt Nellie and Aunt Mary. Aunt Mary was the pivotal pin since she knew the times when her husband John, the bus conductor, would be on duty. The notes would go thus:

Dear Maureen,

What do you think? The wanes and the heat are getting on my nerves. Do you think you could raise the fare to Budgen? John will be on the two o'clock bus, but Mary says he won't be leaving Budgen again till after nine tonight. And what about the men's dinners?

Yours sincerely,
Lily

Back through the dusty streets we raced with the unvarying reply.

Dear Lily,

God knows I am suffocated. I have only five shillings. Could you lend me a couple of bob till Friday? I'll bring egg and onion sandwiches. What about the tea? You bring a flask and we'll send the wanes to a house for hot water. Never mind the men's dinners, they can heat them in the oven when they get home. It's us will be stuck with starving wanes all night waiting for John's bus.

                                    Yours sincerely,
                                    Maureen

Off we'd go to wait round the corner from the regular queue. The bus would come to a halt, with half the top seats empty, and fourteen children's fares became three halfs and two adults. Should an inspector board to check tickets, we were instructed to disperse through the double decker naming everyone Mammy.

Sometimes, on Sundays, our fathers would follow, paying full and dignified fare, to join us on the beach where they borrowed navy-blue knickers from the girls to use as swimming trunks. Unless of course they were offered overtime which no working man could afford to refuse. All his working life my father supplemented his job as a storehouse clerk with the British Admiralty with Saturday and evening work as bookie's clerk at the dog-track. That of course was long before the greyhounds were destroyed with tear gas and had nervous breakdowns every time shooting broke out.

When I took my parents to Buncrana in my car in 1977, I had to pass through a British army checkpoint, British and Irish customs posts and an Irish police checkpoint before arriving in that resort's main street where I was charged with double parking and later fined in court.

My Uncle John was not the only relative with an important job. My Aunt Nellie was secretary in the Rialto, and my Uncle Jimmy was doorman in the Strand Cinema. They were married to each other, and between them supplied us with numerous free passes to the pictures. Derry was much engaged with picture shows then, and we were more than proud of our showbiz connections. It was only natural that we graduated from screen to stage: I followed my sisters Muireanna and Nuala onto the boards for the annual pantomime — a vast entertainment organised by the Catholic Church every winter with profits going to the Church building fund. Local talent was exclusively used for such productions as *Oklahoma,* supplying everything from costumes to scenery to musicians and resulting in massive interference with the script in order to accommodate our native wit. St. Columb's Hall is now used for Bingo sessions run by the clergy. It was during one such pantomime, at the age of eight, that I fell in love with the Principal Boy who was a woman, making my young passion acceptable.

I had had sexual experiences as a child, of course, though I did not know that that was the name for them. Around the age of seven our gang had discovered that extremely pleasant physical sensations could be

150

Above – Bogside mothers at a neighbourhood shrine.
Right – Apprentice Boys Parade, 1970.

induced by "spieling" up a lamp-post and pretending to be stuck half-way up, wrapping our arms around the pole and clasping it between our frantically screwing legs. I have a vivid memory of our mothers emerging simultaneously from their front doors, each equipped with a duster with which they whipped us about the shins. "Get down outta that," they whispered fiercely, beating children off the lamp posts which we were happily screwing up and down the street. They never said why, but their guilt transmitted itself to us. Children always sense these things. To clinch the matter, our fathers said nothing about it, if indeed they were ever told, rendering the action utterly unspeakable.

The streets were rich with amusements. We played handball against gable walls, tied rope swings around telegraph poles, chalked hop scotch on the pavement squares, wheeled hoops, dug holes for marble games in the dirt, roasted potatoes in the back lanes over little fires, gathered chest-nuts for conkers, shot pieces of paper from elastic bands and organised gang warfare, a not unusual occupation given the notables after whom Bogside streets were named — Wellington Street, Nelson Street, Blucher Street, Waterloo Street. Our heritage and intimate knowledge of ambush spots served us well in 1969, when the Battle of Bogside began in earnest.

Football and rounders, a derivative of baseball, were the major team sports. Girls took part in rounders with no taboo on sexual identity; my brother Hugh made sure I always got a place on the football team. An attempt was made once to introduce us to that most Republican sport, hurling, but the sight of waving sticks of wood slashing at shins and forehead deterred the bravest among us. The first and only practice session took place in the Celtic Park, a field purchased and reserved exclusively for use by the Gaelic Athletic Association. It was hardly ever used since the GAA forbade its members to play English football. Today it lies totally silent but still green, and the Southern Tricolour flies above it to remind the Bogside and the British army of our real goal in life.

Sister Agatha, who was in charge of my education at the time, had a different, more practical goal. She and Sister Oliver ran the Wee Nuns, so called because it was the smallest school in the town, comprising only five classrooms and supervised by the two religious and three lay teachers. She might not thank me for it now, but I never associated Sister Agatha with religion. She instructed us in the basics of faith, but her eyes really came alight when it was time for reading, writing and arithmetic. She followed her pupils' careers long after they had left infant school, making sure they got jobs by badgering the town's employers with her personal guarantee that all her children were skilled in numeracy and literacy. She visited our homes discussing our futures with both parents: a rare woman indeed in that town of little hope.

She was in many ways a forerunner of the comprehensive idea, handling many levels at once within the same classroom and developing each child according to their particular ability. When I fumbled at art or knitting, she would snort with contempt and settle me down before a hardbacked copy of *Robinson Crusoe* or *Lorna Doone*. I was reading prose texts while other children pursued cartoons with subtitles or engaged in painting and craftwork. Her war cry was legendary, "If you can't do that, you'll never get a job."

It was a shock to leave her and go to St. Eugene's, where the enrolment reached the hundreds. I was quickly and anonymously absorbed into a class of forty, all of us preparing frantically for the Eleven-Plus examination which determined our future lifestyles. Success meant a scholarship to grammar school and middle-class aspirations. Failure meant the shirt factory, where women were eternally girls, financially supporting men on the dole.

I was beginning to change anyway, spending less time with Joe on the streets and more time with Monica and Philomena whispering romantic fantasies under the trees in Lone Moor Road. Joe had been my lifelong companion, climbing into my pram, I am told, when I was a baby. We had often opted out of the gang, preferring our own silent company on solitary excursions to forbidden places — the docks, where we fed grain to pigeons; the railway line on Letterkenny Road, where we stayed on the tracks until the engine was almost on top of us; the bakery, where we dodged between parked savoury vans, hoping to steal a sugared bun.

Our favourite occupation was to climb up on someone's back wall as dusk fell and gaze at the family scenes in bright warm kitchens. We used sit like cats, silently looking at them eat and talk and fight and move about. Once; from a Cable Street wall, we saw a man strike a woman several times and we heard her scream and watched her raise her arms for protection. Her children clung about her, hissing and crying with fear at their father. We had to get down off the wall when the father stepped outside to the toilet in the yard. We visited that house often, because the police were sometimes called to referee and it was very dramatic.

Joe was illegitimate and an only child, though I was unaware of it at the time. I knew that he was dealt with more tolerantly than others in the street. Hardly a word was said when he climbed aboard a stationary tractor, started it and drove it into the gable wall at the foot of Beechwood Street. I was sent early to bed though I had only watched. When his mother died, he was sent round the corner, literally, to other relatives, and I began to transfer my affections. I had passed the Eleven-Plus in any case and was set apart by my school uniform. The only thing left in common with childhood friends was the onset of puberty.

It came gently enough, bringing with it menstruation as a gift from the Blessed Virgin and a second-hand bra as a hand-me-down from my sister Muireanna. Nevertheless none of Monica's afternoon theatre in her father's tool shed had prepared me for it. Monica, large and laughing, was the doyenne of our romantic scene. Daily she improvised plays in which she took all the parts, ad-libbing on the general theme of going to her first prom which we had learned about from Archie comics. Her audience, seated on the floor, was mixed in gender, united in response. We lapped it up, as she described for us her off-the-shoulder satin gown suspended from an orchid presented to her by Rock, who had called for her in a

Children playing on lower Linenhall Street on top of the walls of Derry.

white sports coat, pink carnation and his father's borrowed car. He had made the price of the tickets by operating a newspaper delivery route which puzzled us somewhat because paper selling in Derry was a man's occupation, jealously defended against encroaching children. Rock and Monica ate hamburgers and double chocolate malteds in between waltzes; more than once Monica had to scratch out the rich girl's eyes, sending her home in silk shreds; at the end of the prom Rock presented her with a fraternity pin and they kissed. Oh God, it was wonderful and we couldn't wait to get started ourselves.

Daidser McDaid and I won the competition for the longest kiss on Hallowe'en night, pressing our closed mouths firmly together for a count of eight hundred. I only broke off our back-lane marathon because I could hear my mother calling us from the front street to come in for the family rosary. Later I grew to prefer the embraces of Fits McLaughlin who always ate chocolate before kissing. With his looks and personality, he needed something extra going for him.

All the Derry boys were wiped out in the summer of fifty-six when a real live American teenager came to spend his vacation among us. His name was Billy Brown. He wore blue jeans and white teeshirts and tartan shirts and canvas sneakers, a technicolour movie among his Bogside contemporaries, so thin and pale in dark sweaters, grey flannels and dusty, black laced-up brogues. Billy was tall and tanned and muscular. His eyes passionately dark in a sea of runny blue. His teeth gleamed; he didn't even have pimples. Boys vied to walk along with him, girls struggled to stand beside him.

Myra Collins got him. She relayed all his conversation to us, supplying Monica with dialogue that kept her theatre open seven afternoons a week for that whole season. Billy was a god come down among us, giving us a vision of the promised land — fifty flavours of ice cream, gangsters, hot dogs with mustard, a bedroom of his own, his Dad's car, eternal sunshine, unmelting snow. In September, before he left, he shook hands with all the boys and kissed all the girls. His lips, we agreed afterwards, were warm and dry. Derry boys were always coming down with cold sores and snotty noses.

American relatives were a dime-a-dozen at the time but they were older versions, without the remotest trace of a Yankee accent, and they worked at three jobs per week and were always crying to leave that lovely land. They nevertheless, on their trips home, brought tales to tantalise and taunt us. My Aunt Peggy, for example, had been courted by Captain Van Hooten who made his fortune in coconuts and spread diamonds at her feet. Like any true Derry woman, she had spurned him to marry her Joe, who had also emigrated from Derry, and they worked together on the railroads. She shovelling coal into furnaces; he collecting tickets on the Long Island line.

When she came home, once every few years, there were Big Nights to which all relatives, neighbours and friends were summoned. Plates of sandwiches and cups of tea and bottles of stout and glasses of sherry were laid out in sumptuous array. The children were instructed to do their party pieces before being sent to bed. Muireanna and Nuala played the piano; Hugh and Paddy and cousin Desmond sang *The Halls of Montezuma,* I drew tears with my *Green Glens of Antrim,* and Carmel, being youngest, made a fortune in loose change. We did not go to bed but huddled on the landing, peering through the banisters as the adults told stories in the kitchen, harmonised in the sitting room and decamped out into the street in the wee small hours to dance in large circles, bang pots and pans with spoons and yell and cry in turn about the return of the emigrant. It was a bad party if one frying pan at least wasn't dented beyond redemption. America is only a package deal away now, and we fly out to see them. The Big Nights are no more.

I'm glad to record that Monica made it to the States, marrying an officer from the American Naval Base in Derry. Her pal, Bridget, did less well. She was left behind holding a baby, rearing it in consort with her married sister in the Derry tradition. Others have trickled home bearing bad tidings of divorces or bigamy or houses with no swimming pools. I was effectively debarred from courting such risks and pleasures by attendance at Thornhill College-cum-convent, secluded among manicured green lawns three miles by bus outside the city. It was a single sex college, run by nuns and unmarried lay females, untainted by hint of anything male. We were forbidden even to speak to the workmen who occasionally laboured there.

Our horizons were narrowly confined. We could become nuns; failing that, teachers; failing that, it was understood though not mentioned, we might consider marriage. The educational emphasis was on English, French and Irish. Some oddballs studied maths and rudimentary science. Of course we must have some pleasure and céilí dancing on a Saturday night met with approval. While Monica and company rocked and rolled in the Crit ballroom, I was doing the martial march of the *Walls of Limerick,* stepping it out to a tune that glorified the martyrdom of the Irish at the hands of the English in a town south of the Border — the location of which I did not then know. Our wild Gaelic whirls in the parish hall were supervised by a priest.

It was not love of things Republican that sent me to spend all my summers in the Gaelic-speaking area of Rannafast in the wilds of Donegal. I won scholarships at school, presented by the Irish Government, that provided me with paid bed-and-board holidays in that lovely spot. I became proficient in a foreign language good for University entrance examinations, sneaked out of my first bedroom window for a moonlit walk, learned to smoke and noted that Irish-speaking people were very poor.

Monica too was learning about the joys of the Republic, courtesy of the Protestant ethic that closed Derry's cinemas, dancehalls and pubs on the Sabbath. On Sunday nights, teenagers raced across the border to dance and drink, fleeing dour Ulster for the merry South. I, of course, spent Sunday nights poring over homework, reassured by all and sundry that I

Top, left– Two Bogside residents pause at "Free Derry corner", so-called after the famous "Battle of the Bogside". *Top, right–* Bogside boys and soldier confront one another on Rossville Street on 14 August 1969 – the day British troops entered Derry. *Above–* Much of the traditional working-class housing of The Bogside has been demolished to make way for modern houses and flats. Pictured is the rubble of Nelson Street in 1969.

was meant for better things. Contact with the outside world and Elvis Presley was maintained by listening to "Top of the Pops" from eleven to Sunday midnight via Radio Luxembourg. While Monica and her pals returned on Monday morning to the hard reality of bench and counter, I was dreaming among books, snug in a schoolgirl desk.

I was turning into a right little snob and suffering because of it. I knew that I would never become head-girl, a position reserved for the daughters of doctors, teachers and businessmen. I began to wish for a bathroom, blushing at the thought of Friday night locked into the scullery with a tin bath and pots of steaming water. I felt shame when friends called and I had to show them to the lavatory out in the yard. I never told them about the bucket on the landing into which as children we used relieve ourselves in the middle of the night. I resented being squeezed in the double-bed between Muireanna and Nuala, with Carmel in a cot in the corner.

Thornhill College was meant to make us feel those things, and parents connived innocently at it. We were sent there, after all, to better ourselves, and the only place to go after Bogside was upwards and outwards.

The prospect, if a little complacent, was enlivened occasionally. Mairead Fleming staggered the teacher by enquiring if Hamlet had an Oedipus complex. Rita McLaughlin refused to join the Children of Mary, pronouncing herself an atheist. We worried about having crushes on each other after someone smuggled in the *Well of Loneliness.* We were relieved to find from the forbidden *Lady Chatterley's Lover* that sexual intercourse consisted of threading violets through a man's pubic hair.

There were two occasions when we were instructed directly on politics. A young firebrand teacher decided to dispense with Church Apologetics and have us read *Animal Farm* instead. She may very well have wished to warn us merely of the evils of totalitarianism, but the head nun, when she heard of it, arrived in freezing fury to instruct us and her that Communism was to be dealt with in prayer, not reason.

The second occasion struck rather nearer home. We were taken to a free educational film in a city cinema. The Protestant schoolgirls sat in one block of seats and we sat across the aisle in another. The boys were to come next day, sexual integration being considered the marginally greater danger. The cinema darkened, a drum roll began, the curtains parted and onto the screen flashed a picture of Queen Elizabeth the Second, Monarch of England, Scotland, Wales and Northern Ireland. The Protestants stood smartly on their feet. Our escort, Miss McDevitt, an elderly aristocratic lady in tweeds, remained firmly seated. We took our cue from her and sat stolidly through the national anthem.

Miss McDevitt never afterwards alluded to the incident, and we knew better than to ask her why she did it. They followed the Queen; we followed the Pope. The division was as simple as that, neither British nor Irish prime ministers having heard of us at the time. In such a small society the lines had occasionally been crossed, of course, but always discreetly. The matter was too painful and confusing to be dwelt on at length. My father's brother Joe, for example, had fought in the British

Army in the First World War and his name was inscribed on the War Memorial within the walled city. But we never attended the annual commemoration ceremony, an occasion for underlining British citizenship.

My maternal grandmother was a Protestant who converted to the Catholic faith in order to marry. My mother retained contact with her relatives by post and the rare exchange of visits between Derry and Belfast, but we knew not to discuss religion or such dangerous topics. They were decent people but... different. Very nice, good people but... different. My grandfather may have been a policeman but he was a Catholic, and you could trust him. In any case he had joined the force before Ireland was divided and was originally a member of the Royal Irish Constabulary. It was not his fault that the force converted to the title Royal Ulster. We kept his helmet for years, with the Irish emblem on it, to prove his good faith.

With these dim memories and equipped with English, Irish, and French, I left Derry at seventeen and went to Belfast, thence France and London. I returned to Derry in 1968, aged twenty-four, and joined the dole. We had all grown bigger and there was little room at the Inn. Two brothers and a sister were already crossing back and forth to England in search of jobs and houses. Bogside was both bulging and static. Something had to give and it seemed illogical to blame the Pope who was stuck over in Italy. Blame was traced to the Queen and all who supported her.

But that's another story.

Part Three

THE PEOPLE AND THEIR TRADITIONS

FAIRS
AND PILGRIMAGES

Sharon Bohn Gmelch

FOR HUNDREDS OF YEARS Ireland presented a picture of small villages and isolated homesteads scattered thinly across the landscape. A large proportion of the population still lives in rural areas, their lives geared to mesh with the demanding daily and yearly rounds of agricultural work. Before the era of modern transport, people had little opportunity for regular social contacts and as a result looked forward to periodic gatherings at fairs and religious celebrations. The saying "He missed the mass but hit the gathering" meant a person late for church still had something worthwhile for his trouble. The lure of traditional gatherings such as fairs and pilgrimages remains strong in Ireland today, despite the dramatic changes which have taken place in recent years.

FAIRS

About six miles from Aughrim I began to fall in with droves of bullocks and sheep, in charge of two or three dogs and a herd, or with whole families of mountain people driving nothing but a single donkey or kid. These people seemed to feel already the animation of the fair, and were talking eagerly and gaily among themselves. I did not hurry, and it was about nine o'clock when I made my way into the village, which was now thronged with cattle and sheep. On every side the usual half-humorous bargaining could be heard above the noise of the pigs and donkeys and lambs. One man would say: 'Are you going to not divide a shilling with me? Are you going to not do it? You're the biggest schemer ever walked down into Aughrim.'

A little further on a man said to a seller: 'You're asking too much for them lambs.' The seller answered: 'If I didn't ask it how would I ever

Opposite – Bishop greets pilgrims at the base of Croagh Patrick.

get it? The lambs is good lambs, and if you buy them now you'll get home nice and easy in time to have your dinner in comfort, and if you don't buy them you'll be here the whole day sweating in the heat and dust, and maybe not please yourself in the end of all.'

Then they began looking at the lambs again, talking of the cleanness of their skin and the quality of the wool, and making many extravagant remarks in their praise or against them. As I turned away I heard the loud clap of one hand into another, which always marks the conclusion of a bargain...

When I reached the green above the village I found the curious throng one always meets in these fairs, made up of wild mountain squatters, gentlemen farmers, jobbers and herds. At one corner of the green there was the usual camp of tinkers, where a swarm of children had been left to play among the carts while the men and women wandered through the fair selling cans or donkeys.[1]

That scene described by John Millington Synge at the turn of the century is familiar enough even today. Traditional country fairs where farm animals are bought and sold are still held in approximately seventy locations in Ireland. As recently as 1965, however, there were over five hundred towns and villages holding livestock fairs. The dramatic change reflects many things including the growing importance of cooperative livestock marts and weekly auctions in the Republic which compete with fairs and of government marketing schemes and purchasing boards in the North. Road transport has also facilitated the movement of livestock to these auctions and allowed dealers to buy stock directly from farms. Fairs were once widely distributed through the countryside. Today they are found primarily in the rural West — thirty-one in Galway and Mayo alone — where small farms abound and modern marts have made fewest inroads. Even where livestock marts exist, many farmers in these areas still frequent the fair to sell their sheep.

In past centuries, fairs fell at the turning points of the pastoral year: spring horse fairs in February and March; Lammas fairs for sheep and wool in July and August; and cattle fairs in October and November. Most places held from one to six fairs annually. With the spread of cattle rearing in the nineteenth century, however, monthly fairs became common.

Formerly country fairs were organized into a recognised sequence beginning with the trading of goods and animals and ending with games and sporting events. Larger fairs such as Puck Fair in Killorglin, Co. Kerry and October Fair in Ballinasloe, Co. Galway still follow this pattern. Puck Fair lasts three days beginning on 10 August. The first day, known as "Assembly" or "Gathering Day", is the scene of its famous horse fair when hundreds of horses of all descriptions as well as large numbers of travelling people (tinkers) gather. On the second day, "Fair Day", herds of small black Kerry cattle, dual-purpose Friesans, Blackface Mountain sheep as well as a sprinkling of donkeys and goats crowd the streets as farmers in wellington boots and rumpled suits wander about examining each others' stock in minute detail. On the final day, "Scattering Day", a general carnival and series of sporting events and competitions, from angling to donkey racing, are held. The week-long Ballinasloe Fair begins with a horse fair, followed by three days of sheep trading, stock judging and awards, then a cattle fair and a final day of general fair-going when exhibits of the latest farm machinery stand side by side with a carnival on the fair green.

Fairs have a long history in Ireland. In modern Irish the word for fair is *aonach*, similar to *oenach*, the term for the regional festive assemblies of early Celtic Ireland. Many writers have suggested that modern fairs are continuations of these ancient gatherings. While some no doubt are, the two cannot be directly equated. As folklorist Maire MacNeill has pointed out, trade and tribute-raising (then made in the form of cattle) was alien to the festive and sporting spirit of the ancient *oenach* which was essentially a religious, political and social assembly whose underlying purpose was to unite the people of a region or tribal district. The modern *aonach* or fair, on the other hand, is primarily a commercial event albeit with an important social and entertainment role. Modern fairs such as Puck Fair which do appear to be direct survivals of early Celtic gatherings occurred fortuitously.

Commercial fairs really began in the twelfth and thirteenth centuries with the arrival of the Normans. At that time the expanding commerce of feudal Europe was largely stimulated by the trading conducted at great fairs. Fairs were of such importance that the legal right to hold one could only be granted by royal charter. Norman settlers arrived in Ireland eager to obtain land grants and set up feudal fiefs. They realised the value of fairs and wished to control and encourage them by granting concessions to traders who came to the fairs held within their domains. In some places they may have claimed lordship over the old native *oenachs* held in the territories they seized, but more frequently they established new fairs near their manors and in the towns near their mills. Puck Fair's transition into a livestock and produce fair no doubt began during this period when the Norman Fitzgeralds built a castle and manor at "Kyllorgelan".

It is from this period also that an interesting present-day custom dates. The central event of Puck Fair is the crowning of a large male goat (*poc* in Irish) "king" of the fair. Captured in the nearby mountains each year, the goat is bedecked in ribbons, bells and restraining ropes and paraded through Killorglin on the back of an open lorry in the early evening of Gathering Day. To the roll of drums and cheers, he is crowned and hoisted atop a wooden tower in the town square. From there he presides over the fair and the hordes of people and animals below, while munching cabbages which are periodically raised to him. Until the mid-1800s, he stood garlanded in leaves and flowers on the battlements of the old castle. Despite the pagan overtones of paying homage to a male goat – symbol of fertility and licentiousness – the custom has a tamer origin.

During the Norman era it was common for a symbol of the fair to be paraded through the town and then raised above the roofline so that people outside the village could see it. In some places such as New Ross and Limerick a huge glove representing a hand and thus denoting protection was attached to the end of a pole. In other places an animal was used. There was once a Puck Fair at Mullinavat, Co. Kilkenny and a ram known as "King of the Bens" was once enthroned at Greencastle, Co. Down. White was the usual colour for such symbols, perhaps in allegorical reference to justice and fair play, since fairs were recognised periods of abeyance and a time of special privilege. Trading concessions applied and peasants were exempt from arrest for debt. As MacNeill points out, it was undoubtedly the idea of interregnum which gave rise to the expression "king of the fair" as applied to the fair's symbol. The length of time the symbol was on display marked the duration of the fair. Puck Fair is one of the very few places, if not the only one, in Western Europe which has retained the practice.

Fairs began to take on their modern form after the seventeenth century upheaval in land ownership and the change to money rents. Irish tenant farmers then had not only to produce goods but also to convert them into cash by bargaining at fairs. Fairs thus became even more important to the peasantry. Their numbers continued to increase into the nineteenth century with the spread of cattle rearing as the main activity of Irish farms. Patents to hold fairs continued to be granted by the English Crown until late in the century.

Country fairs were once capable of meeting all the normal trade needs of rural households. They provided an outlet for the surplus items such as chickens and butter which country people produced as well as a place where specialised goods such as tobacco and matches could be obtained. The only other source for such goods were itinerant tradesmen and tinkers who travelled through the countryside. But they might never visit the more isolated farms, and families had to rely on the tradesmen who congregated at fairs. Weavers were there with frieze, linen and drugget; spinners with woollen yarn and flax; the cooper with churns and noggins; as well as tinsmiths, shoemakers, basket and creel makers, carpenters, livestock castrators and vendors of poteen — Ireland's homemade brew. The relative anonymity of the fair with its bustle and crowds also meant that certain types of goods such as second-hand clothing, shoes and boots could be purchased without embarrassment. Today stalls of inexpensive clothing made from synthetic fibres as well as imports from India and Korea have replaced the second-hand booths. Expanded bus service and increased ownership of private automobiles has also made towns and the shops located there readily accessible to country people and hence there is less economic need today to attend monthly fairs.

Most important, fairs provided a place where farmers could buy and sell farm animals. Irish farming has long been a mixed economy in which most farmers have a small amount of arable acreage but considerable grazing land. Their livelihood depends on some form of livestock production with occasional cash crops. Cattle are raised on almost all Irish farms,

Above– The crowded town square of Killorglin as "King Puck" is about to be hoisted atop his tower-throne. In the middle of the square a vendor's lorry displays religious pictures, fancy teapots and kitchen supplies.

Right– "King Puck" at the beginning of his three-day reign.

especially in the West and South and on small farms everywhere. Despite modern livestock marts, monthly fairs still provide a major outlet for stock sales for farmers in more isolated areas. Much of the cash income of small farmers on the Iveragh Peninsula in Kerry, for example, comes from the sale of young cattle, sheep and other animals to local consumers and dealers and outside buyers from Tralee, Limerick and Cork who attend the monthly fairs at Killorglin, Cahirciveen, Sneem, Waterville and Kenmare.

The ritual of buying and selling at fairs has a lingering appeal for many farmers and some prefer it to auctions or accepting a guaranteed price from a dealer. Proving one's ability at dealing was once considered a "rite of passage" for males in rural Ireland, and the simpleton who exchanges his cow at a fair for some worthless trifle is a stock object of derision in folktales and stories. The amount a farmer receives does depend largely on his dealing abilities and on the persistence of both buyer and seller. Intermediaries are widely relied upon to help forge agreement over the hesitancy of the seller and the obstinacy of the buyer. They may be a friend of either party known for their wit and experience, an interested bystander or a traveller who specialises in "tangling" or "blocking".

"I'll give you thirty-eight for the two," offers the buyer. "I'll not take down forty. I could have been gettin' it coming in the road. Clear to pocket at that... Aye, I was offered forty-two all up," challenges the seller, while walking off a few paces. "You'll get it again," comments an onlooker. "You have the nicest wee stuff in the fair. Aye, a grand pair of colourly calves." "Come on now, boys. Divide, that last two pounds, both of you, and make it a dale," cajoles the tangler. The buyer swishes his ash plant in the air, "I'll give you thirty-nine and not a penny more." "Down forty, they'll not be sold the day," retorts the seller. "Go on now and make a dale," says the tangler as he tries to grasp their hands and force them together.[2] Once agreement has been reached, buyer and seller spit and slap hands. The flanks of the animals are crossed with a red marker and the numbers of their ear tags checked. The appropriate certificates of health are found and buyer and seller retire to the pub or bank to conclude the transaction. The tangler receives a few pounds for his trouble.

Besides the risk and vagaries of dealing, selling at fairs has always posed other disadvantages. In the past, farmers from more distant areas had to drive their cattle along the roads for as many as ten miles. By the time the cattle arrived they had already lost some of their value, and the cost of the return trip made selling imperative. At one time local landlords, the owner of the fair green as well as city corporations levied tolls on the animals sold: a shilling on a horse, a half-shilling for a cow or bull, one penny for a sheep or goat, thus adding to the farmers' costs. In many parts of the country, tolls were excessive or levied illegally. The Report of the Commissioners on the State of Fairs in Ireland of 1853 cites the case of a toll collector in Roscrea, Co. Tipperary who demanded 4d. in toll on a goat, which was sold for only 2s. 6d., even though goats were not listed

Top– A group of countrymen discuss the merits and weaknesses of the blinkered piebald mare to their left at Puck Fair. *Left*– Horses being coaxed onto the back of a dealer's lorry. *Above*– Tying a knot in a horse's tail was once believed to ensure that "the luck of the beast" remained with the new owner.

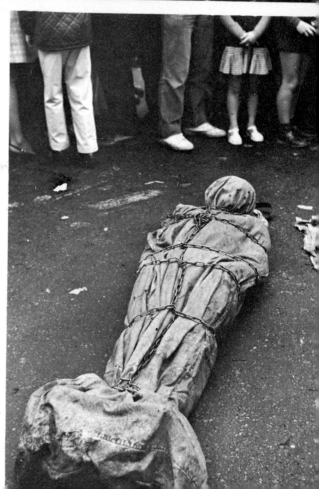

Top– The fair green at Moy, Co. Tyrone is crowded with people, cattle and horses in this photograph taken at the turn of the century.

Above– Animated faces at Puck Fair.

Right– A street entertainer at Puck Fair performs one of his feats of skill and strength by squirming out of a chained bag.

on the toll-board. He claimed they fell into the category of "horned cattle" and were taxable as such. In some places "through" tolls were collected at the entrance to town on everything that passed whether it was sold or not. Toll abuses were of such proportions that they became a matter of parliamentary inquiry in the Irish House of Commons as early as 1635. By 1853, they had been abandoned in the eastern half of the country although they persisted in places like Galway City and Cork in the West and South.

Given the unpredictability and uncertainty of fair-going, it is not surprising that many magical folk beliefs and superstitions once surrounded it. For good luck, country people used to carry a borrowed article made of metal; others tied a knot in the end of the tail of any horse they wished to sell. A handful of earth on the back of any animal they purchased ensured that "the luck of the beast" remained with it. Sellers still routinely hand back a pound or two in "luck money" to the purchaser of animals at the fair.

Besides their strictly commercial functions, fairs also bind people together through a network of economic and social relationships. Contracts with tradesmen and specialists to perform services in a farmer's household have to be fulfilled. In the past, many young men and women from the western counties were hired at fairs to work in households in the more prosperous parts of the country from May until November. Many went as servants, others as ploughmen, dairymen, turfcutters, potato diggers and harvesters. Country people relied on the shopkeeper's credit, as the shopkeeper relied on their business. Fairs also provided people with an opportunity of meeting people from beyond their immediate neighbourhood. It was a recognized practice for bachelors to be on the lookout for a mate. Marriages were often initiated and arranged at fairs. While "matches" are rare among country people today, travelling people continue the practice.

Country fairs thus provided one of the basic rhythms in the lives of rural people. Dates of important events in the community and household were often measured by the date and cycle of local fairs rather than the calendar. According to Synge,

> The greatest event in West Kerry is the horse fair, known as Puck Fair, which is held in August. If one asks anyone many miles east or west of Killorglin, when he reaped his oats or sold his pigs or heifers, he will tell you it was four or five weeks, or whatever it may be, before or after Puck.[3]

Fairs also provide entertainment. In the era before radio, television, cinema, and improved transport, this was especially important. Cock-fighting and bull-baiting as well as jugglers and itinerant theatre groups were once common. Faction fights which flared up between rival kin groups were also a major attraction. Until the 1900s, countrymen carried "knuckledusters" and wore heavy felt hats partially as a defence against the blackthorn shillelagh. One fair achieved such notoriety that its name became a synonym for a riotous meeting. Donnybook Fair, held on the outskirts of Dublin for six hundred and fifty one unbroken years before it was abolished in 1855 as a "public nuisance", was for centuries one of the most important livestock and produce fairs in Ireland.

Horse-racing, fortune-telling, games of chance, ballad singing and dancing are old entertainment forms which continue to be enjoyed by modern fair-goers. Canvas-covered stalls still line the streets offering an assortment of cheap glass and dishware, plastic trinkets and toys, souvenirs, fruit and sticky sweets. Dulse and yellowman stalls are a feature of Ballycastle Fair, Co. Antrim. Dulse is a seaweed gathered and dried locally; yellowman is a locally-made hard toffee. At the larger annual fairs, carnival rides and rifle ranges compete for attention with sideshow performers lifting weights and wriggling out of chains. Many towns which have lost their livestock fairs, retain the carnival and festivities associated with them.

To a large extent, fairs provide a sanctioned "time-out" from conventional behaviour. The normally quiet atmosphere of rural villages and towns is shattered by music blaring from loudspeakers and throngs of people and animals milling about. Bright flags and Christmas lights colour the normally grey scene. Cattle, sheep and horses are allowed to take over the town, fouling its narrow streets. Pedlars and street merchants fill the town, competing with established shopkeepers. Travelling women and children beg and offer to tell fortunes openly. Normal shop and pub hours are extended for the duration. Instead of closing at 11.30 p.m., the pubs at Puck Fair remain open until 3 a.m. and reopen a few hours later. Many find the convivial temptations great. To accord with the pubs' booming business, police tolerate a higher level of drunk and disorderly behaviour than normal, even though extra men are often called up to deal with the crowds. At some of the larger fairs, people can be seen sleeping in public places — on the footpaths and in parked cars and vans. It is this combination of commercial activities and fun which continues to draw people to fairs despite modern marketing facilities and newer entertainment forms.

PILGRIMAGES

There has always been a close link between the secular and the religious in Ireland, between fairs and religious celebrations. Irish fairs were traditionally held on or immediately following religious holidays — saints' days or the moveable feasts of Easter and Whit Sunday. Parish religious celebrations, known as "patterns", held on the feastday of the local patron saint included secular festivities. Such patterns, however, were not the only form of popular religious devotion. Pilgrimages to sacred sites have been a part of Irish life for centuries. In the modern world the large-scale devotion to religious sites is perhaps nowhere more apparent than in Ireland with its elaborate network of holy wells, monastic ruins and major national shrines at which close to a million people gather each year. Over half of the 2,499 people surveyed in one study of religious beliefs and practices had been on a pilgrimage at least once in their life.[4]

Top— A travelling woman pauses with her child in front of a stall selling an assortment of trinkets and souvenirs at Puck Fair.

Above— Nuns kneel at Our Lady of Knock Shrine. On the evening of 21 August 1879 fifteen people from the tiny village of Knock, Co. Mayo were witnesses to an apparition of the Virgin Mary, St. Joseph and St. John the Evangelist. Knock is now a major Marian shrine.

173

The earliest Irish pilgrims were sixth and seventh century monks and clergymen who renounced the world and wandered aimlessly over land and sea throughout Ireland and Europe in perpetual exile. The word pilgrim comes from the Latin word *peregrinus* meaning foreigner — a stranger passing through to a much desired destination. This form of perpetual pilgrimage, however, was very different from the idea of penitential pilgrimage which was also introduced by Irish missionaries at this time and which evolved into the pilgrimage seen today.

In the early days of the Church, pilgrimages of varying duration were imposed for serious transgressions such as murder, incest, forgery and sacrilege especially when committed by monks and the higher clergy. The seventh century *Penitential of Cummean* notes that a monk who commits murder "shall die unto the world with perpetual pilgrimage". According to one tenth century Anglo-Saxon writer, the early Irish penitential pilgrim threw away his weapons and wandered "far and wide across the land, barefoot and never staying more than a night in one place... He fasts and wakes and prays by day and night. He cares not for his body and lets his hair and nails grow freely." Voluntary pilgrimages were also under-taken for venial or lesser sins. Both types were still aimless wanderings, although for a specified period of time, and took the place of exile or banishment as a punishment for sin and anti-social behaviour.

The idea that a pilgrim had only to go to a particular shrine to obtain grace and have his sins remitted did not develop until the ninth century and did not command universal acceptance until the eleventh. By then growing numbers of the humble as well as the mighty were going on pilgrimage in Ireland and throughout medieval Europe. A number of famous Irish monasteries and universities established between the fifth and tenth centuries were visited by pilgrims at this time, including Clonmacnoise, Co. Offaly; Glendalough, Co. Wicklow; Monasterboice, Co. Louth; the Aran Islands; and Inis Cealtra in the middle of the Shannon River — a major roadway for early pilgrims.

Devotions at holy or "blessed" wells, many of them pre-Christian in origin, were also common. The present-day pattern at St. Brigid's Well, Liscannor, Co. Clare is just one example. It is held on *Domhnach Chrom Dubh* (Black Crom's Sunday), the last Sunday of July, and is the remnant of an ancient Lughnasa festival. Lughnasa was one of the quarterly feasts of the old Celtic year when the Irish assembled at traditional sites to celebrate the coming harvest with festivities dedicated to the god Lugh. The contemporary pilgrimage to Croagh Patrick in Co. Mayo has a similar origin. Many pagan customs and rites were absorbed into Christianity.

With the decay of the Celtic monasteries, Continental religious orders took their place. Abbeys such as Mellifont, Co. Louth and Jerpoint Abbey, Co. Kilkenny were founded and with them new pilgrimages established. It was at this time that St. Patrick's Purgatory in Lough Derg, Co. Donegal achieved notoriety as the place where a pilgrim could physically enter hell. Henry of Saltrey's *Tractatus de Purgatorio Sancti Patricii,* first published in 1140, recounted the pilgrimage of the mythical

Knight Owen and his descent into the island's famous cave. It became a medieval best-seller and provided one of the inspirations for Dante's *Divina Commedia*. On medieval maps, St. Patrick's Purgatory is one of the most dominant landmarks featured. Its reputation was such that the famous and wealthy of Europe travelled hundreds of miles to reach its shores. Only later did Lough Derg become an important place of pilgrimage for the Irish.

The island continues to attract pilgrims. During its brief pilgrimage season from June 1 to August 15, an estimated 20,000 people arrive to take part in what is described as the most rigorous Christian pilgrimage in the modern world. The setting is austere. The lake is surrounded by low heather-clad mountains untouched by signs of life. Arriving at the shore, pilgrims climb into deep-hulled, power-driven open boats to begin the one mile journey to Station Island or the Island of St. Patrick's Purgatory. The appearance of the island itself is other-worldly. Its buildings, which appear to float on the surface of the water, contrast starkly with its desolate surroundings. Docking at the small pier, one's first impressions are immediately reinforced by the silent, staring faces of people huddled against cold grey stone walls, coats draped over their knees and feet. The initial imagery is that of an early sanatorium or little-known leprosarium. In a line, newly arrived pilgrims file past the buildings nearest the pier. Entering the small grassy courtyard they are confronted with a scene from an earlier period of Irish history. It is the penal era when Irish Catholics furtively practised their faith on isolated islands and at mass rocks hidden deep in the countryside. In gradations of grey, men and women kneel to kiss St. Patrick's Cross, clamber over sharp rocks in their bare feet and stand in ankle-deep water engrossed in prayer.

Croagh Patrick was a more popular place of pilgrimage for the native Irish during the Middle Ages than Lough Derg. It drew peasants from much of the western seaboard as well as the upper classes from all over the country. In one of the earliest references to this popular pilgrimage, the *Annals of Loch Cé* report that in 1113 a thunderbolt fell on the mountain on St. Patrick's Eve killing thirty fasting people. While natural events could not be controlled, man-made interference could. The mountain and pilgrimage route were protected by both the ruling families of Connaught and the Church. In 1224, the *Annals* praised the reign of order established by the O'Connor family noting that the only crime committed in Connaught had been the robbery of a pilgrim on his way to the Reek. The thief's hands and feet were cut off. In 1543, an Irishman found guilty of strangling his son was sent on a penitential pilgrimage to fifteen widely separated shrines including Croagh Patrick. On his return with certificates from each, he was granted absolution. Parish priests in counties Mayo and Galway as late as the nineteenth century sent parishioners to Croagh Patrick for penance; and *Turas na Cruaiche* or the journey to the Reek and its imposition as a hard penance became a common theme in songs and folktales in the province of Connaught. It is still a popular pilgrimage site, drawing up to 80,000 people each year.

Although pilgrimages to holy places can be made at any time of year, most shrines and wells have one or more special feast days associated with them. On that day people come from many miles away to pray and perform "rounds" of the well or shrine and its associated ruins. The basic action of Irish pilgrimage is the "round", that is, the practice of walking in right-handed circles a set number of times (usually three, seven or fifteen) around a series of "stations" while reciting short prayers — typically Aves, Paters and Credos. Rounds may originally have had a practical purpose, keeping people moving in the same direction in an orderly fashion. The set number of short prayers may have prevented them from going around too quickly and perhaps from darting off to the fun fair which often accompanied religious gatherings. Stations may involve one or a series of Celtic crosses, chapels, wells or drystone "altars". Many are mounds of stone and earth known as *leaba* meaning bed. Some are possibly the remains of ancient burials; others the ruins of early beehive cells and other structures. The right-handed round is very old and in Celtic times may have been linked with sun worship and stone circles. The right-handed turn, known as *deiseal* in Irish, from *dheas* meaning south, was in pre-Christian Ireland equated with summer and hence good luck. It tied in with the Celtic idea that the seasons moved from north (winter), to east (spring), to south (summer), and to west (autumn).

Gatherings at holy wells and other pilgrimage sites were first disrupted in the ninth and tenth centuries when Vikings, primarily Norwegians, began plundering Ireland's rich monastic centres. Many were destroyed and their abbots and monks killed or forced to flee to the Continent. Others such as Kells in Co. Meath survived and were rebuilt. A second serious disruption occurred following the twelfth century Norman invasion.

In the sixteenth century the Reformation brought fanatical attempts to stop pilgrimages and "popish superstition" in general. Irish priests were forbidden to teach the faith, and the peasantry was forced to retreat further into popular devotions, themselves outlawed. In 1536 Thomas Cromwell's "New Injunctions to the Clergy" ordered the taking down of all images associated with pilgrimages and religious gatherings stating that "wanderings to pilgrimages, offering of money, candles or tapers to feigned relics or images, or kissing or licking the same, saying over a number of beads not understood or minded on, or such like superstition" was conducive to image worship. In 1552, Clonmacnoise, after surviving Viking and Norman raids, was finally destroyed by the English garrison of Athlone who carried off bells, books, images, treasures and every scrap of glass in the windows. Lough Derg which had become a symbol and rallying point for Catholics was demolished in 1632 and again in 1680, its cave and wooden statues destroyed, stone crosses thrown into the lake and pilgrims prevented from landing.

English persecution of pilgrimages and the Catholic faith increased with the arrival of Oliver Cromwell and the ensuing penal era. The "Act

Top, left– A penal cross dated 1702 is one of the earliest yet discovered. These simple wooden crosses were sold to Lough Derg pilgrims as souvenirs until the mid-1800s.

Top, right– St. Patrick's Purgatory on Station Island in Lough Derg, Co. Donegal seen from the air.

Above– Pilgrims perform one of the nine stations to be made at St. Patrick's Purgatory during their three-day stay.

to Prevent the Further Growth of Popery" in 1704 forbade "the riotous and unlawful assembling together of many thousands of papists to the said wells and other places". A fine of ten shillings was placed on every pilgrim and twenty shillings on "all and every person and persons who at such assemblies build booths, sells ale, victuals or other commodities". Public flogging in default of payment was decreed, and magistrates were directed to demolish "all crosses, pictures, and inscriptions that are anywhere publicly set up, and are the occasion of any popish superstitions". Despite all this, gatherings and pilgrimages continued. St. Patrick's Purgatory was rebuilt, and according to contemporary sources country people flocked to holy sites. It is during this period that "penal crosses" were manufactured and sold at Lough Derg as pilgrim souvenirs and from there were spread throughout the countryside.

Not all religious gatherings and pilgrimage sites waned as a result of persecution. A natural evolution in the popularity of shrines and wells has also taken place. Over the years holy wells have dried up or been desecrated and thus lost their following. Shrines have waned with the growing popularity of competing sites which resulted from reports of miracles, the acquisition or display of relics or the canonization of a local man. Popular piety has created new pilgrimage sites with disconcerting spontaneity. Ballyvourney, Co. Cork founded by St. Gobnait in the sixth century grew in popularity as a pilgrimage site during the seventeenth century after the death of Father O'Herlihy, a popular local priest. Modern pilgrims still kneel in front of Father O'Herlihy's tomb located at the side of the ruined church, lift the weathered leg bone left lying on top of the tomb and with it make the sign of the cross.

Why is pilgrimage so popular in Ireland? What draws people to sacred sites? There are many reasons: ritual persists despite different interpretations of its meaning. Some, particularly the young, claim to go merely for the "crack" — the sheer adventure and challenge. For many, penitential pilgrimages like Croagh Patrick and Lough Derg are exciting rites of passage into Irish Catholic culture, a necessary experience at least once in one's life. But for most people, pilgrimage is primarily a religious experience. Those who visit the shrine of St. Oliver Plunkett in Drogheda, Co. Louth do so to honour the martyred saint whose sacred relic is venerated there. At penitential pilgrimages such as Croagh Patrick, Lough Derg and Lady's Island, Co. Wexford, Catholics participate in the redemptive suffering of Christ and the saints. All the historical and legendary accounts of St. Patrick on the Reek, for example, stress his suffering. Consequently, many believe that physical hardship and sacrifice are an essential part of following in the footsteps of Christ and the saints and of pilgrimage generally.

Most pilgrimages do involve some form of hardship. To begin with, many pilgrims travel long distances to get to the major national shrines. During the medieval era travel was especially difficult; pilgrims were faced with dense forest, poor roads, bandits and natural catastrophes. Today, in an age of organised tours and modern transport, some pilgrims choose to walk or cycle rather than travel comfortably by car, bus or train. Walking has long been regarded as the most virtuous method of going on pilgrimage.

Pilgrimages are usually physically demanding in other ways. The real hardship of Croagh Patrick is the climb itself which is especially difficult once the mid-point has been reached and the ascent of the steep, scree-covered cone begins. The mountain is high by Irish standards, rising 2,510 feet above the surrounding plain. The path to the top is roughly two and a half miles long. In the past pilgrimages were always made in bare feet; such mortification of the flesh being a sign of piety. A Protestant minister who climbed the Reek in 1836 reports that he and his two companions were immediately noticed and heckled as "Sammies" (Protestants) by the other pilgrims because they were wearing shoes. Although it is no longer prescribed, many people continue to make the climb in their bare feet as extra penance. Pilgrims at Lough Derg spend the entire three-day period in their bare feet.

The performance of traditional stations at holy wells and shrines is also penitential — kneeling on hard rocks, walking over sharp stones, making numerous rounds and repeating a seemingly endless number of prayers. At Croagh Patrick conscientious pilgrims make a total of fifty seven rounds and recite a minimum of one hundred and thirty six prayers. At Lough Derg the devotions are even more impressive and exhausting: pilgrims make nine lengthy stations while on the island. Each station involves making forty rounds, kneeling at fifteen different places, reciting two hundred and fourteen short prayers as well as seven decades of the Rosary, and renouncing the World, the Flesh and the Devil three times. This yields a total of approximately three hundred and sixty rounds, two thousand prayers, and sixty three decades of the Rosary. During an earlier period the pilgrimage was a month long. The pilgrimage to the Skelligs once involved an eight and a half mile sea journey, a nerve-racking climb to the top of Skellig Michael to follow the stations and kissing a stone carving overhanging the sea.

Early nineteenth century accounts of pilgrimages note the pilgrims often performed rounds on their knees. One such circuit was felt to be the equivalent of the required seven or fifteen on their feet. At Lough Derg, pilgrims still maintain the old devotional customs of fasting and vigil. For three full days they refrain from all food and drink except for the dry toast and black tea served twice on the island. Two days and a night are spent without sleep and given to almost continuous prayer before they are allowed a few hours rest. Pilgrimages in general, Lough Derg in particular, retain all the basic ingredients of Celtic spirituality: solitude, repetitive prayer, vigil, fasting, and physical endurance.

The prospect of starting one's spiritual life anew has always been part of pilgrimage; baptismal imagery is common at shrines. In the Middle Ages when millenarian fears were rampant in Europe and people believed in the imminence of the Second Coming of Christ and of divine judgment, pilgrimage fulfilled a real spiritual need. By inflicting severe physical

echoed by others, including a hospital administrator from Belfast who explained, "In ordinary life you get soft. This experience brings you back to basics." An Irish priest from Tampa, Florida has come to Lough Derg on eighteen of his last twenty annual return visits to Ireland. To him Ireland itself is a "retreat" and "time for reflection" after living in the States. Lough Derg is thus a retreat within a retreat.

Because pilgrimage is viewed by the Catholic Church as a meritorious act, individuals who undertake it may gain indulgences or a remission of the temporal punishment due to sin. The concept of indulgence is based on the belief that God and the saints together have a limitless amount of merit which the Church as the "minister of Christ's Redemption" can transfer to the faithful. Proximity to a holy place and the performance of the prescribed religious devotions provides believers with the means of acquiring some of this limitless merit and thereby expiating their sins. An indulgence of two years and two quarantines (forty-day periods) was granted by Pope Eugene IV as early as 1432 to pilgrims who climbed the Reek on the Sunday before the feast of St. Peter's Chains (1 August). Over the years, various pontiffs have reaffirmed the holiness of Croagh Patrick through the granting of both partial and plenary indulgences for devotions associated with the mountain. Pope Pius III first granted indulgences to pilgrims at Lough Derg in 1503, in 1870 a plenary indulgence was granted in perpetuum by Pius IX. Indulgences for the pilgrimage at Lady's Island were granted in 1607 by Pope Paul V.

For the individual, pilgrimages and gatherings at holy places can also, and usually do, have more immediate and mundane purposes. Cures and the solution to daily problems have always been one of the main goals of pilgrimage. A twenty-nine year old shop assistant making her third pilgrimage to Croagh Patrick had come to be cured of "infertility". (In the early 1800s it is reported that only those pilgrims who were barren and wanted children, performed the rounds and prayers at St. Patrick's Bed on the Reek). A travelling woman had come to ask for relief from asthma for her children. Her father-in-law, who has been climbing the mountain for thirty years, had come for his arthritis. It is a common superstition among both men and women that climbing Croagh Patrick or attending Lough Derg for three years in a row will bring luck in finding a spouse. Some young people had come to ask for good results on their exams. A large proportion of the pilgrims to Knock shrine in Co. Mayo come for physical cures: the *Knock Annual* is filled with letters signed "a friend of Mary" and "a client of Mary" telling of miraculous cures and of petitions granted.

Persons whose requests have been granted, return the following year in "thanksgiving". Frequently vows are made to undertake pilgrimage a specified number of times in exchange for requests. One sixty-year old woman came to Lough Derg the first time when her nine-year old child had been taken seriously ill and there appeared to be no hope. "I stormed heaven with prayers and then I came to Lough Derg." She promised to return the following year if the child recovered and has been coming back ever since. A fisherman who was saved from drowning promised to go to Lough Derg every year for the rest of his life. A man whose wife recovered from cancer has been performing the pilgrimage at Lough Derg each weekend of the season for several years.

Resorting to saints for healing reminds one of past centuries when diet was poor, the incidence of disease high and medical knowledge rudimentary. Physical illness was often believed to have a spiritual cause and hence penance at the shrine or well of a saint helped not only sin but also illness. John Clyn, once Franciscan Friar of Kilkenny, notes in his annuals that in 1348 great numbers of people flocked to St. Moling's Shrine in Graiguenamanagh, Co. Carlow to wade in the water, "many thousands might be seen there together for many days: some came on the score of devotion, but the greatest part of the fear of the pestilence which raged at that time with great violence."[7] He was referring to the Black Death which soon after took his own life. Pilgrims to Ballyvourney in the early eighteenth century concluded their devotions with a *rann* or special prayer to St. Gobnait: "O Gobnait, keep us safe from all kinds and sorts of sickness, especially from the Small Pox."

Female fertility in particular was felt to be a gift from God and therefore barrenness was a sign of God's displeasure. Feast days of saints drew especially large crowds of the sick. Dust, stones, scraps of cloth which had been in contact with the saint or his shrines were applied to the body. The same things eaten or drunk were believed to have more effectiveness; relics dipped in water or wine were common methods of healing practised in the pilgrimage churches of the eleventh and twelfth centuries. Similar practices have persisted into recent times in Ireland. At St. Olan's Well in Aghabullogue parish, Co. Cork a small, oval quartzite stone kept on top of a large standing stone known as St. Olan's Cap was used by pilgrims — until the mid-1800s when it was removed by the parish priest — to cure disease and aid childbirth. If worn on the head while making three circuits of the church it would also cure a headache. A new stone is now at the well but it reputedly lacks the same magical powers.

Because water cleanses not only surface dirt but also symbolically cleanses deep-seated disease, holy wells were believed to have special curing properties. By drinking some of the water or applying it to the body, relief is still sought for many ailments — skin diseases, muscular aches and pains, sore eyes and fading sight, toothaches, and sterility. Some holy wells are believed to give relief to any illness; others are associated with specific complaints, such as *Tobairín na nUalacán* in the parish of Killeagh, Co. Cork which once provided a remedy specifically for vomiting. Drinking water from the well used to be a part of the ritual: cups and glasses are still found at wells where devotions go on. Some wells such as Wether's Well, Co. Kerry and those at Struell, Co. Down also have bathing or dressing houses where the body can be immersed and bathed privately. In some cases moss and other growths near the well were taken and also applied to the body. Healing is believed to be accomplished by virtue of the water itself or as a blessing granted to pilgrims

Above— The holy well at St. Gobnait's Shrine in Bally-vourney, Co. Cork. Two sons assist their mother in collecting water to be taken home with them. Note the cups on top of the well which remain there for other pilgrims to use.

Left— The stone is covered with tokens and votive offerings left by visiting pilgrims, including a crutch, cane, crucifixes, ball-point pens, coins, rosary beads, broken plaster religious statues, and even a tooth brush. This rock marks one of the stations at St. Gobnait's, Ballyvourney.

who performed the prescribed rituals with good intentions. A common Irish tradition, however, is that wells are also inhabited by magical fish — a trout, eel or "golden fish" which only appears to a person about to be cured.

Pilgrimage sites for believers are manifestations of divine or supernatural power. Climbing Croagh Patrick, for example, provides pilgrims with the means of tapping the potency of sacred objects as well as the holy site itself. Pilgrims once handled *An Clogh Dubh* (The Black Bell of St. Patrick) believed to be the bell used by Patrick to banish demon-birds from the summit in 441 A.D. Until 1836, it was kept by the hereditary custodians of the church lands of Aghagower (an important abbey on the original pilgrimage route). It was taken out each pilgrimage day and carried to the summit where for a small fee pilgrims kissed the cross engraved on it and then passed it clockwise around their bodies three times. This was believed to cure rheumatism. Before the modern chapel was opened in 1905, pilgrims entered the small hut that housed the altar, paid a penny to the clerk and were allowed to kiss what were said to be further relics of St. Patrick including a small wooden crucifix. Women took pebbles from St. Patrick's Bed home with them to cure barrenness. Modern pilgrims continue to chip pieces of rock from St. Patrick's Bed for luck. The plaster from the gable wall of the church at Knock was stripped bare within months of the apparition of the Virgin Mary that occurred there in 1879. Pilgrims still take home clay from the ground and poke their fingers into a hole in the side of the church where the original gable wall can be touched.

In thanksgiving and remembrance, pilgrims have typically left small tokens or votive offerings at the shrines they visited. At the major curing wells crutches and canes are still to be found, as are coins, flowers, buttons, nails and religious objects such as rosary beads, crosses, pictures and delph figurines of saints. A common practice still found at holy wells is that of tying a bit of rag or cloth, often part of the pilgrim's garment, to the hawthorn tree or bush which inevitably seem to be growing nearby or securing it between the rocks of the well. The leaving of souvenirs no doubt symbolises the leaving of disease, worry and trouble at the well. At one time there may also have been the belief that a person could actually transfer his or her disease to the cloth or rag they left behind.

Traditionally pilgrimages have always been happy occasions — like that described in Chaucer's *Canterbury Tales.* As at other social gatherings, people took great pleasure and enjoyment in the fellowship of others. This festive atmosphere is evident today on the pilgrim buses and trains to Knock shrine: talking, laughing, food sharing and tea drinking are as much a part of the atmosphere as reciting the Rosary. In the past, the great patterns or festivals held at holy wells were especially festive. They were public holidays when no work was done and secular pastimes were added to the devotional exercises. Tents and stalls lined the roadway as they still do at some of the large pilgrimage sites today. Drinking, dancing, singing, games and sideshows, and sporting events (particularly wrestling and boxing) were popular as they continue to be at many fairs. Aran islanders from Inisheer still travel by curragh to the Clare shore and from there walk to St. Brigid's Well where they make the rounds and then spend the night in vigil, singing much of the time.

Perhaps inevitably things get carried away when people gather and drinking takes place: free-for-alls and faction fighting became common-place at many pilgrimages and patterns in the eighteenth and nineteenth centuries. Writing in 1873, Sir William Wilde described the pattern of Glendalough in the following way:

> The scene was remarkable, and I and my friends often spent a large portion of the night walking among the ruins, where an immense crowd usually had bivouaced, or were putting up tents and booths, or cooking their evening meal, gipsy-wise, throughout the space of the sacred enclosure. As soon as daylight dawned, the tumbling torrent over the rocks and stones of the Glendasan river to the north of 'The Churches' became crowded with penitents wading, walking and kneel-ing up St. Kevin's Keeve, many of them holding little children in their arms... Dancing, drinking, thimble-rigging, prick-o'-the-loop and other amusements, even while the bareheaded venerable pilgrims, and bare-kneed voteens were going their prescribed rounds, continued. Towards evening the fun became 'fast and furious'; the pilgrimages ceased, the dancing was arrested, the pipers and fiddlers escaped to places of security. The keepers of tents and booths looked to their gear. The crowd thickened, the brandishing of sticks, the 'hoshings' and 'wheelings', and 'nieings' for their respective parties showed that the faction fight was about to commence among the tombstones and monuments, and that all religious observances, and even refreshments were at an end. Police and Magistrates were often required.[8]

Many pilgrimages were stopped or discouraged by the Catholic Clergy in the late 1800s and early 1900s; others were placed under Church control. As early as 1160, the Synod of Tuam had admonished the "revelling, junketing, or boisterous behaviour" found at religious assemblies to "sacred fountains". Nevertheless, merry-making continued. As recently as 1974, the clergy was forced to change the pilgrimage of Croagh Patrick from a night-time climb and vigil to a daytime pilgrimage due to the drinking and "blackguarding" that had been taking place.

Despite the change in hours, a festive atmosphere remains at Croagh Patrick. The crowds at the base of the mountain might be attending a sporting event. The roadway is lined with venders selling soda pop, sweets, sandwiches and tea as well as walking staffs made from branches and broom handles. Turning the corner at Campbell's Public House onto the footpath leading to the mountain, one is confronted with a row of wooden stalls where still more vendors sell an assortment of souvenirs and religious paraphernalia from rosary beads and plastic St. Patrick statues made in Hong Kong and Italy to stuffed toy animals. A short distance up the mountain, a last enterprising vendor, seated behind a folding table and large umbrella, hawks devotional pamphlets through a megaphone:

You just can't go wrong with the pilgrim guide. You don't have to ask unnecessary questions. It tells you what prayers to say and when to say them. Just take a look: see for yourself. Get your pilgrim's guide-book now. Unavailable anywhere else. Once you get the guidebook, you're home dry. Don't go up without the pilgrim's guide.

Finally you are free. A wide stoney path filled with climbing pilgrims leads upward; the atmosphere becomes progressively more reverent as the first devotional site is reached. Nevertheless, the pilgrimage to the Reek continues to present an odd, if not startling mixture of sacred and profane images and activities: rosary beads and Bulmer's cider bottles, aged bare feet and platform shoes, devotional rounds and cigarette breaks. After the devotions of the pilgrimage, the pubs in Murrisk and nearby Westport are packed. People are thirsty and enjoy a sense of accomplishment. Even the most ascetic pilgrim — a young man in black who climbed the mountain in his bare feet, alone and intent — now leans against the stone wall across from Campbell's, staff at his side and pint of stout between his feet. The drinking before and after the climb has long been a feature of the pilgrimage, and Croagh Patrick is referred to derisively by some as only a "pub pilgrimage".

Pilgrimages appear to increase in popularity during times of rapid social change and stress. In the sixteenth and seventeenth centuries when Ireland underwent a period of dramatic social upheaval brought on by the destruction of the monasteries, the proscription of the Catholic faith and the relocation and suppression of the native Irish, popular devotions and gatherings were in fact strengthened. In recent years, the appeal of all the major pilgrimage sites in Ireland has grown steadily coinciding with the quickening pace of modernization and change. Pilgrimage may also represent one of the last defences of folk Catholicism against the rationalizing changes now going on in the Catholic Church. For although the Catholic Church in Ireland is notably conservative, changes such as the introduction of the English mass and in the format of communion and confession are taking place. Much of the mystery and aura surrounding the Church and its rituals is disappearing. In this light, pilgrimages and gatherings at holy sites can be seen as continuing to provide an important element of the religious life in Ireland.

For rambling, for roving, for football or sporting
For drinking black porter as fast as you'd fill
In all your days roving you'll find none so jovial
As the Muskerry sportsman, the Bould Thady Quill.

The traditional sport of Road Bowling in Co. Cork.

THE
SPORTING TRADITION

Garry Redmond

OR ITS LILT and liveliness and the infectious rhythm and gaiety of its tune, the Cork Ballad opposite is accepted as virtually the national anthem of Irish sportsmen; some might say it is the "bottle hymn" of the Republic. No celebration of victory or carousel of defeat is complete until it has been sung, no matter what the sport may be. To purists, of song or sport, who enquire about its provenance — is it true?, is it praise?, it is exaggeration, satire, mockery? — the answer simply is: it's traditional.

Indigenous and unmistakably Irish sports are few enough. The purely native games — native in the sense that they are unique to Ireland — Gaelic Football (codified from older forms in the 1880s) is played between two teams of fifteen who handle the ball, kick it, pass it by hand and score both goals and points. Hurling, the prince of field games and of great antiquity, is also played fifteen to a side on a pitch up to 160 yards long by 84 to 100 yards wide. A small leather, ridged ball is struck with hip-high sticks of ash which are curved to form a broad striking face at the base. They are called *camáns,* from the Gaelic *cam* meaning crooked. Camogie is an abridged version of hurling played by women; after a slow start it is now enjoying a tremendous boom. Currach-racing is still practised by traditional fishermen along the western seaboard in their lath-and-canvas currachs or canoes. Road-bowling is played in parts of Cork where it's called bowls (to rhyme with bowels) and Co. Armagh where it's also known as "bullets": two players throw a steel ball under-arm along several miles of road to see who can do the "score" in fewer shots.

Horse-racing, hunting, show-jumping, coursing and greyhound-racing are not monopolies of the Irish (although greyhound racing or "the Dogs" with the mechanical hare was developed in Ireland in the 1920s), but each has a distinctive Irish tradition and flavour. The horse is so identified with

Ireland that it was used on the first coins of the new state in the late 1920s and some foreigners still seem to think an Irishman is a horse with red hair.

International sports in which Ireland participates, whether in team competitions or individually, are rugby, soccer, golf (amateur and professional), amateur boxing, lawn-tennis, athletics, cycling, hockey, swimming, sailing, rowing, show-jumping and eventing, motor rallying and racing, and, of course, horse racing. There are also devoted if not so numerous, followings for table-tennis, squash, badminton, lacrosse, basketball, volleyball, croquet, fencing, clay-pigeon shooting, bowling, billiards, snooker, wrestling, handball. A major national pastime is betting, principally on horse-racing, but also on greyhound racing and coursing.

A visitor once asked why we had so many "turf accountants", was it because we had no coal? He did not realise that they were off-course bookmakers' shops with their ritual "debt in the afternoon". In proportion to its population, Ireland must be one of the most sport-addicted nations on earth. Every sport has its devotees but some are followed by large and surprisingly knowledgeable factions. Major events embrace the entire public — men, women and children. Irish newspapers regularly carry three, four and five pages of sporting intelligence, and hardly a week passes without news of some event of Irish sporting significance at home or abroad on everybody's lips — in shops, buses, taxis, pubs, right across the land. In past years it might have been Pat O'Callaghan's winning the shot and Bob Tisdall's 400-metre hurdles win at the Los Angeles Olympics; or Jimmy Bruen's winning of the British Amateur Open golf title; or Workman winning the Derby or Reynoldstown the Grand National; or in rugby Jack Daly's Triple Crown winning try at Belfast or Tony O'Reilly's try in the first Test at Port Elizabeth in 1955; or Tull Considine's eight goals for Clare — when was it?, 1932 or 1933? And remember Cottage Rake, and Arkle, and Sir Ivor and Santa Claus and golfers Fred Daly, Harry Bradshaw and Christy O'Connor? These sporting figures, who keep appearing in numbers and quality disproportionate to our population, are household names even among people who have never competed or who have long since passed their active stage. Thus conversation is enlivened and coloured in every season of the year by some aspect of sport, establishing the first notable aspect of the Irish sporting tradition and that is participation.

A player's lease may be limited, but once he's played, he's a follower for life. For instance at the Ireland vs. France rugby international at Lansdowne Road in 1979, I sat near Colonel Jack Burke Gaffney, now well into his eighties, but still sharp of eye and shrewd in judgement. This was possibly the 150th Irish match he'd seen at Lansdowne Road despite there being only two internationals in Dublin each season (three if there is a touring side here) and the fact that he'd been abroad about twenty years. In fact when he first played for Lansdowne (1908 or 1909), the famous pitch ran the other way!

Likewise, at any Munster hurling final at Thurles or Limerick or at any

Placing a bet is as important as watching the race. Here the bookies are busy at Galway Races.

All Ireland at Croke Park, there will be men present who haven't missed a final in forty or fifty years and who can precisely recall other generations of great players and clinically compare the best today with those of long ago. Every big race meeting, golf tournament or coursing meet is an unconscious celebration of all that has gone before. Mind you, memory sometimes goes adrift, but, as Yeats said, "Why should not old men be mad?" After one rugby game I heard an argument between two old stagers. One recalled a match in Limerick in the 1920s, when, he said, Eugene Davy (a famous Irish outhalf) dropped a goal from about 60 yards out on the left — a huge kick. The other disagreed — it was on the right. Eugene himself happened by and was buttonholed. "Remember that match against Garryowen, when you dropped the goal from halfway...?" Eugene thought a minute. "Yes... 1928. Or was it 29?... Yes, just in front of the posts, about the 25. Isn't it good of you to remember that!" "But Eugene, it wasn't the 25, it was half-way, out near the touchline — you've got it wrong. I was *there*."

Where did this vigorous sporting tradition begin? An early manuscript describes a hurling contest which took place before the first Battle of Moytura near Cong, Co. Mayo in 1,272 B.C. The ruling Fir Bolg were challenged by the invading Tuatha De Danann for half of Ireland. Fighting talk, but as a preliminary, "three times nine" of the Fir Bolg engaged an equal number of the De Danann in a hurling match, beat them and then slew them.[1] The De Danann won the second battle of Moytura in which Eochaidh Mac Erc, a Fir Bolg king, was killed. When the king's widow Tailte died, her foster-son, by then a De Danann leader, ordered that ceremonial games be held each year forever in her memory. These were staged at the famous *Aonach Tailteann,* the fair or law-giving assembly held at Teltown, Co. Meath until as late as the tenth century. The games were revived at Croke Park in 1924 and held for some years.

Hurling is described in some detail in the *Táin Bó Cuailgne* (The Cattle Raid of Cooley), the epic of Cuchulain contained in the Ulster Cycle. The boy Setanta first makes his mark by his skill with camán and ball, outplaying more than a hundred youths single-handed and later killing the king of Ulster's watch-dog by driving a ball with deadly accuracy and force into its jaws and down its throat. Thus he became Cuchulain — the hound of Ulster. It is heroic stuff, but implicit in its telling is an appreciation of the skill and grace of hurling, an appropriate training for warriors.

In the *Fiannuidheacht* or Fenian Cycle — the epic tales describing the life and times of Fionn Mac Cumhail and his *Fianna,* the legendary standing army which defended Ireland — we have most likely the first record of an international foot race in Ireland. In this *Bodach an Chóta Lachtna* (meaning The Clown in the Grey Coat), an improbable athlete, gross, raw-boned, ugly, but full of craft and sinew, defeats *Caol an Iarainn* (Slender Man of Iron), son of the king of Thessaly, who demands *árdcheannas agus árdchíos na h-Éireann de bheith aige"* ("to have the overall authority and tribute of Ireland"). If, however, he says, "one warrior among you can beat me in running, single-combat or wrestling,

Old rivals Cork and Kilkenny clash during the All Ireland Minor Hurling Final, Croke Park, Dublin.

I'll do you no more damage than return without delay to my own lands."
Fionn, going to Tara for his best runner, Caoilte Mac Ronáin, meets the
Bodach, who hearing the news says, that with all respect, if Caoilte is
Fionn's main hope, "you're a man without a kingdom". He therefore
takes up the challenge — first stage a 120-mile race from *Luacra na
Mumhan* (near Castleisland, in Co. Kerry) back to Howth. It's a genuinely
funny story, yet full of suspense before the Bodach outstrips Caol, gives
him his come-uppance by knocking his head off with a snowball of
blackberries and flour. He then magically sticks Caol's head back on his
shoulders, but wrong way round, and having made him promise the rent
of Thessaly to Fionn in perpetuity launches him out to sea with a mighty
push that drives the boat seven leagues! The Fenian stories are filled with
running, wrestling and hunting on foot with hounds, described with great
feeling for the countryside and outdoor life: clearly the men who wrote
them were steeped in the pursuits they described.

Important too is the Fenian Cycle, the Fianna's code of *Cothrom na
Féinne* (the equality of the Fianna), under which their warriors could
never take unfair advantage of an opponent's accidental slips or falls or
dropping of a weapon.

Cothrom na Féinne, whether it is still maintained is at least recognised
as an element in the sporting confrontation — not to be overdone, though.
There was a famous Dublin rugby character, now dead, Des Merry, who
hooked for Palmerston for years up to the 1950s. Once, as a guest player
for Bective Rangers on a short English tour, he was in positively Fenian
form against one of the best packs of forwards in England-Northampton.
At half-time, gathering his wind near the touchline he overheard two very
pukka types. "I say, George, the Irish are traditionally vigorous, but isn't
this a bit much? One used to think this was a game for gentlemen."
Whereupon Des Merry, good Dublin Protestant and former sergeant in
the Irish Army, notched up his sleeves, spat on his hands while glowering
at the pair and ambled back to kick-off with the parting shot: "Well, be
Jasus, when I came out on this pitch today I was labouring under no such
f——ing misapprehension." It all depends...

How sporting pastimes fared during the Gaelic Order before its passing
at the end of the sixteenth century we do not know, but hurling must
have been a widespread custom for the Brehon Laws, which regulated
Gaelic society for over a thousand years, prescribed penalties for various
sorts of injuries inflicted or suffered by players of the game. The word
for hurling is *iomáint* or *iománaidheacht* meaning hurling or driving a
ball from a point halfway between *bailtí* or villages. This form of the game
continued into the nineteenth century. It and another version in which
the ball was played without sticks, by foot or hand, were the residual
root onto which the great growth of the Gaelic Athletic Association
(GAA) was later grafted. In Dinneen's Irish dictionary the word *iomáinim*
captures the essence of the game: "I toss, whirl, fling, hurl, drive, urge,
press."

Hurling's significance in Irish society is further attested by two particular Norman ordinances. In 1366 the Statutes of Kilkenny "ordained and established that the commons of the said land of Ireland, who are in divers Marches of War, use not henceforth the games which men call Hurlings, with great Clubs and Ball upon the ground... but that They apply and accustom themselves to use and throw lances and other gentle games which appertain to arms..." (Why didn't we stick to the hurling, lads? If the FitzStephens and the De Burgos had got a few proper belts of the hurdl' we wouldn't 'a had half the trouble we did wi' them Normans!) In 1527 a Statute of Galway proscribed "the Horlings of the littil Balle with. hockie [presumably meaning 'hooky' or curved]Stickes and staves". Ireland did not take readily to the Norman idea of towns, and the conquerors clearly realised the threat native games and pastimes offered to the sort of cultural innovation they were attempting to impose.

If all this seems remote from modern Ireland remember that oral versions of the ancient tales and legends as well as of more recent wrongs "in ballad and story, rann and song" have been recorded in living memory among storytellers in those parts of Ireland where the Gaelic language survived. The tradition has lasted over two thousand years.

By contrast the moulds within which Ireland's games are now played are relatively modern. The first moves towards organisation — apart from racing where the Turf Club had already been an institution for nearly a century — came from Trinity College in 1854 with the founding of Ireland's oldest rugby club (second oldest in the world). This led within twenty years to the formation of the Irish Rugby Football Union and the first international rugby matches. Ironically, in view of its ascendancy character, so offensive to many nationalistic minds, Trinity also had a hand in the revival of hurling. In 1879 it produced an Irish Hurley Union "to foster the noble and manly game in this its native country". Hockey, cricket, tennis, soccer, golf, all received impetus from Trinity men as students or graduates. No wonder, since only the privileged upper classes had the resources and opportunities for sporting leisure. It was the "big house" and the officer class which patronised racing, hunting, shooting, fishing — a world and a style so well portrayed in the writings of Somerville and Ross. The ordinary young Irishman was effectively disenfranchised. His only outlet was the odd race meeting, prize fight or local inter-village hurling or football match (more like a faction fight than a regular game) or poaching his landlord's game.

In 1884 a revolution began. Trinity men, in trying to get hurling going since 1879 had sought advice from the leading authority on the old tradition — Michael Cusack, a Co. Clare schoolmaster who had an academy in Dublin and was organising matches for his students. He was a burly, impressive figure, with a heavy beard — a man of strong nationalistic views. (He was, incidentally, the model for The Citizen in Joyce's *Ulysses*.) Cusack gathered six like-minded men, interested in games and athletics, at Hayes's Hotel, Thurles, Co. Tipperary, on 1 November 1884. There they formed the Gaelic Athletic Association. No need to follow its history through early arguments, disagreements, recriminations and misunderstandings about aims and objects, ways and means. The movement caught on like wildfire. The basic aims were to establish a club for hurling and football in every parish, a standard set of rules for both games which then existed in varying forms around the country and a regular framework of national championships. By 1887 the first such championships were staged: a tide began which has swept on, unbroken by the upsets of revolution, civil war and two world wars.

The GAA is now the biggest amateur sporting body in the country. It claims to be the biggest in the world. It is certainly an impressive movement, especially if one reckons what it would now cost to provide capital for all the fine championship grounds it has developed all over the country. Croke Park, Dublin, headquarters and arena for the big matches, has seen crowds of over 90,000 — an enormous number in proportion to the populations of both country and capital. Recent extensions to provide more seating have oddly enough reduced its total capacity to around 70,000, but now the important games are televised and far greater numbers can watch the best players compete than Cusack and his founding colleagues could ever have dreamed of. Old-timers argue whether the games and their basic skills are as good as in past years. "Now, when we were playing..." — but the force of hindsight is as uncertain in sport as in life. "Oxford," said Oscar Wilde while re-visiting after a twenty-year absence, "is not what it was. But then, it never was." They have a point, though, for although football has grown to vast proportion, hurling has declined if not in the standard of the best county teams, certainly in the numbers playing. In Leinster, despite all the great effort put into schools and young people's competition, only four senior county teams entered the 1979 provincial championships. In Munster, Cork were on top in 1979 as All Ireland champions, but the rest, apart from Clare, who won the National League for the previous two years running, seem to be in decline — though even to suggest it will bring defiant growls from Tipperary, Waterford and Limerick men for daring to put them down. The fact is, however, that more and more people are moving from the land to towns and cities. The old pastime of knocking a ball about "at the crossroads" of an evening in little villages has gone. Yet, paradoxically, Cork hurling, for thirty or forty years acknowledged to be among the best for style and substance has been essentially a city game: the "Bread and Tay Boys", they were often called, lads who came from Shandon Street and Barrack Street.

The Gaelic games, long rooted in the countryside, have naturally reflected the patterns of change going on in the country even though the championship system has not varied since the All-Irelands began. And, of course, while the Gaelic games reach out to all sections of the public, they have come to represent a self-preoccupying attitude, for they have no natural international outlet. The American tours, to Boston, New York and San Francisco by All-Ireland winning teams or "All Star" selections are really for exhibition games; a much-prized "reward" for successful teams, but lacking the elements of genuine, organic competitiveness.

In Gaelic football Ireland's great national amateur game, the ball can be kicked, punched or caught.

Similarly, the visits to Australia and Australian teams' return visits to Ireland in which Gaelic footballers play "Australian Rules" seem rather a forced international growth. Ireland is a conservative country so the All-Ireland system has splendidly served many generations, but in the insistence on the nationalistic basis of Gaelic and hurling, particularly after the Rising and the foundation of the State, there developed the now happily abolished "Ban", which has had profound influence on the whole sporting scene. This was the rule which forbade GAA members to play or attend certain games. Thus there was an implication that those who played rugby, soccer, hockey, cricket and tennis were somehow less Irish than those who played Gaelic football or hurling. One irony escaped the proponents of the "Ban". Many of the Dublinmen who fought in the Rising were by choice soccer men — were they less Irish?

Politics and sport should not mix, but each is bound to affect the other: no game can be played in isolation from the society in which it is played. Thus when the State was founded, the North-South division inevitably had an effect. The GAA had no problem continuing its function as a thirty-two county all-Ireland body but it accidentally did provide a point of polarisation in the Six Counties. Some thirty-two county sports organisations continued to operate as all-Ireland bodies.

The outstanding example of how sport has transcended the complexity of Irish politics is rugby. The natural appeal of the game to our temperament has been noted by no less an authority than Eamon de Valera, who played rugby for a while at Blackrock College. Speaking in the 1950s at an annual dinner of the past pupils' rugby club he reflected on the tremendous quality of the game and how ideally suited it was to the Irishman's natural sporting temperament. What is very clear, and has been for many years is, that when fifteen fellows turn out together in green jerseys no one of them or of the 50,000 people at Lansdowne Road has any doubt but that they represent Ireland. It was not always so, of course. There's a story from the 1920s which Dr. Bethel Solomons, a distinguished and well-liked gynaecologist from a Dublin Jewish family, told. On Saturday evening after an international match he and a group of Irish team-mates took a cab back to the Shelbourne Hotel. Solomons, a very large man, sat outside on the "box" with the jarvey. "Well," says he, "what did you think of that? Didn't Ireland do well today?" The jarvey was unimpressed. "Jasus, are ye coddin' me? D'ye call that Ireland — fourteen Protestants and an effin' Jew!" In the 1940s though, when a Belfast medical student and Methodist lay preacher helped Ireland to win two Triple Crowns, it was widely acknowledged that "they'd die for Jack Kyle in Limerick", pious city of the famous Redemptorist arch-confraternity affectionately called "the Holy Family". And there has never been any difficulty about Ulster Protestants' joining in the balladry of afterwards in which rugby, with uniquely pre-ecumenical tolerance has long combined the tribal songs of divided tradition with equal voice and harmony. You hear *The Boys of Kilmichael, Dolly's Brae, The Holy Ground* and *The Sash* at any Irish rugby "afterwards" and "pass no remarks". It was Wolfe Tone who aspired to an Ireland in which men would be distinguished not as Catholics or Protestants or Dissenters, but by the common name of Irishmen. Sport in some ways has helped to unify the various social, religious and political traditions within the country to the point that Irish teams can represent a United Ireland.

Rugby also shows how the social revolution has worked in Ireland over the past hundred years. Initially rugby was undoubtedly a game of privilege and upper-class, it is now played by all sorts, shapes and sizes. Willie John McBride of Ballymena, Co. Antrim, a small farmer's son, is now one of the most widely-known Irishmen: in New Zealand and South Africa in 1974 he captained a British and Irish touring team. Ireland has provided seven overseas touring team captains in this century. Names like Gibson, Kiernan, O'Reilly, Mullen, Clifford, McKay, McCarthy, Mulligan, Dawson, Slattery, are household words wherever international rugby is played. In France, England, Scotland, Wales, Australia, South Africa and New Zealand, Ireland is known and respected as a country, though small in numbers, with teams which are hard to beat. And in New Zealand there is now call for them to "remember Limerick!" For Munster achieved a historic first win over a touring side in November 1978 and were the only side to defeat the Eighth All-Blacks on its tour of Britain and Ireland. Rugby is based in Dublin, Belfast, Cork, Limerick and Galway. Its seed-beds are now some thirty schools and colleges around the country which in turn nourish forty to fifty senior clubs in all four provinces. It has been argued that some schools' concentration almost entirely on rugby has produced, however accidentally, a kind of counterpart to the GAA's "Ban" which, incidentally, was repealed at the annual congress in Belfast in 1971. I remember in the 1950s taking Andy Mulligan — a Cambridge graduate who played at scrum-half for Ireland to watch Cork and Kilkenny hurling at Croke Park. He was immediately excited by the grace, skill and speed of the game — "that's a game I want to play," he said. "Yes, to be sure," I said, "it is a marvellous game, the perfect summer counterpoint to rugby, but you haven't heard about the Ban."

It isn't possible to say how much wastage of talent may have occurred before the Ban was removed in 1971. Certainly the top class player in any game has a difficulty and there must come a point where he has to choose which game will get his main effort; but it is a pity that so many amateurs have until now been denied, in the formative stages at any rate, more freedom of choice. The games themselves are surely benefiting in the more open post-Ban situation. What is happening now is that players of different sports are meeting and mingling, comparing skills and problems, even sometimes training together. The GAA in particular, in its rank and file, is beginning to emulate rugby which has for many years had a strong tradition of social life based on comfortable pavilions and club-houses which cater for more than the mere playing of the game. There is a danger, however, that affluence and an over-emphasis on sociability may cause the game to suffer; but young fellows today are no longer willing to commit themselves for the "honour of the club" unless they can do so

Top – Rugby. Ireland and Australia show their grit.

Above - Rugby ; Ireland vs France.

in the context of hot and cold running water, all the modern conveniences and a comfortable bar in which to meet and mingle and to which they may bring the steady or the wife.

Professional soccer represents another distinct Irish tradition — sadly, in fact, two Irelands. Since partition the South has had the Football Association of Ireland (FAI) and the League of Ireland (the old Free State League) which play internationally as the Republic of Ireland. In the North the Irish Football Association (IFA) and Irish Football League play internationally as Northern Ireland. Each Ireland, ironically, resembles the other in the fact that for many years its best players have played in the English League — from Elisha Scott, through Jackie Vernon to the Blanchflowers, George Best, Harry Gregg, Pat Jennings, Derek Doogan from the North; from Johnny Carey (great Manchester United centre-half who captained the Rest of Europe against England to celebrate soccer's kick-off after World War II, through Kevin O'Flanagan, Liam Whelan, Noel Cantwell, Seamus Dunne, Johnny Giles and now Liam Brady, Steve Heighway, Don Givens. Ireland miraculously keeps on producing the most talented ball players, yet cannot deploy them in a united team. A few years back there was a marvellous expression of solidarity among all Irish players when Derek Doogan and Johnny Giles contrived to bring Brazil's World Cup team to Ireland to play an unofficial united-Irish team at Lansdowne Road. Exhibition stuff, perhaps, but the three-all draw was pregnant with possibilities. If only...

Soccer in Ireland is predominantly a working class game; its appeal to the working man is surely due to the simplicity with which it can be improvised in any street or open space with a rag or paper ball roughly twined together (the plastic ball is producing already a new generation of Peles, Bests and Stanley Matthews's) — it has never at home achieved the full potential of its support in towns and cities, but its professionalism makes it a separate case in the generally amateur Irish situation. Soccer also represents a uniquely Irish oddity, the degree to which its vast army of followers feeds for its staple diet, upon the richer pabulum of English and Scottish soccer. The interest has been there for as long as Irish players, North and South, have been playing for top cross-channel sides — I remember when I was very young seeing Paddy Moore, back from Aberdeen, playing for Shamrock Rovers. Paddy, a great man for the pint, was going down by bus to the Scottish boat one night and as the bus bumped and slithered over the old Spencer Dock Bridge, Paddy hanging on like grim death, shouted out, "Be careful there, driver! Don't ya know ye'v twenty thousand pounds worth o' footballin' genius aboard?"

In the last fifteen years or so, the overspill of British television has brought top English and Scottish League matches into almost every pub and home on the east coast of Ireland. By popular demand the Irish National Television service relays on Saturday nights during the season the BBC's big soccer feature, "Match of The Day". The televising of European competitions and of the World Cup has given soccer an enormous boost, and the FAI's developing schools and youth coaching courses and competitions are channelling a vast new reservoir of talent. It's estimated that there are now 25,000 soccer players in the Republic. Oddly enough, despite the large numbers playing, soccer in Ireland at the amateur level has never achieved as high a standard as, say, rugby or even hockey. The professional game struggles on against continuing economic difficulties, a paradoxical situation when you consider its large and discerning public. The fact is that the best Irish players continue to be drawn away by the richer magnet of the cross-channel game.

I mentioned hockey which in the last century got an impetus from the revival of interest in hurling at Trinity College. The Irish Hockey Union was founded in 1893 and the game has been played both North and South in clubs and some schools ever since. Perhaps our weather, the greater popularity of other field games and the necessarily limited duration of the school's season have tended to keep Irish hockey as a distinctly minority game. It has, nevertheless, given some great players to British Olympic sides — Harry Cahill, a superb goalkeeper, springs to mind — but in recent years Irish players themselves, by dipping into their own pockets and organising trips to foreign tournaments have brought about a spectacular advance in the standard of the game. Ireland, having played in the last World Hockey Cup in Argentina, now stands among the top ten in world hockey gradings. An isolated, but marvellous expression of Irish sporting will and determination to overcome both practical and political difficulties.

Cricket is another minority game, stronger now perhaps in the North than in the Republic. But did you know that Ireland beat the West Indies in the 1960s — yes — Sobers, Kanhai, Wes Hall and all. Parnell played cricket at Avondale, and there was a time when local teams organised by patrons from the old "big house" played regularly against scratch sides from the best Dublin clubs — at places like Grange, Conn in Co. Wicklow, Scarawalsh in Co. Wexford and Halverstown and Sallins in Co. Kildare.

Athletics is another great Irish tradition which stretches competitively from the O'Connors and Leahys at the turn of the century right up to world cross-country champions John Treacy and to Coghlan, with 22 wins in 23 starts in the 1978-79 season, who has almost literally burned up the boards on the American indoor mile and 1,500 metre circuit. His 3 minute 52.6 second indoor mile record in February 1979 was an astonishing performance, enough to make him famous forever if he never ran another yard. Coghlan, incidentally, is one of a number of outstanding young Irish athletes, male and female, who have emerged in the past half-dozen years or so having first made their impressions in the Irish Community Games, which began as a local idea about fifteen years ago and have now developed a hugely successful momentum. Natural aptitude in the countryside was a solid basis on which organised athletics began to grow in the 1890s, but here again the fact of partition and of the setting up of a thirty-two counties sports body brought about a "split" in the 1930s over the matter of international representation. No need to trace its course. Enough to say that it has been an inhibition on the organised

Eamonn Coghlan, one of Ireland's leading middle distance runners, who broke the world indoor mile record in 1979.

development of whatever athletic potential natural selection may have ordained for a traditionally vigorous rural people. Athletics, of course, is a singularly subjective form of exercise; only athletes know the mysterious inner processes which can sustain the private torment of training against themselves, the clock and the limits of height or weight. Standards are set by competition; the highest by international competition. An athlete may prepare himself or herself in the remote private world of his or her own effort in some lonely field or on the remote byroads of a rural town or village, but if there is not a decent stadium to attract top-class competition, the thing remains no more than aspiration. What gives an extra cachet to the Olympic gold medals for Ireland of Dr. Pat O'Callaghan and Bob Tisdall in the 1920s and 1930s and to the 1,500 metres win of Ronnie Delany in Melbourne in 1956 is the fact that each of them made such a particular assertion of will and determination in the setting which provided virtually no public, national support. To be sure, the Mayo County Council was one of the first public bodies to associate itself, by telegram with Delany's marvellous win; but the David Ben Gurion of Irish athletics, Billy Morton, spent a large part of his life trying to persuade Dublin that Delany and those athletes who would certainly follow deserved the facility of a world-class running track. It is history that Herb Elliott and Ronnie Delany and three others all ran the mile under four minutes in Dublin in August 1958, but the political "split" and the lack of public investment still mean that the Irish athlete who looks to the highest international standard, must look abroad. The athletics scholarships awarded in American universities may be part of the gross materialisation of American athletics, but they have served Ireland well.

So we see that there are as many Irish sporting traditions as there are sports. The beagle runner of some of the fashionable Co. Dublin packs and the beagle racer of Kerry and Cork — celebrated in the sporting ballad of *The Boys of Fairhill,* are blood-brothers to the bowler who throws or the crowds who follow a "score" on a Sunday from Blackpool on the Dublin Hill course to the Blackman and the Horse and Hound, or those who remember when Mick Barry lofted the eight-ounce steel ball over the viaduct on the Kinsale Road; or the forty-year old who has turned out at top of the right for Skeoghavasteen Slashers, or any one of a hundred lads on Pitch Thirteen on a windy Sunday in the Phoenix Park.

There's something in the blood and heart in Ireland that responds to the sporting rhythm. There's the playing of sport; encouraged and moulded by school or family association and now by the publicly available sight of the best of international performances on television. This, indirectly is an element which has in a few years made golf so successful a growth sport that it's almost impossible for newcomers to play. Natural linksland — Portrush, Portmarnock, Baltray, Lahinch, Royal Dublin, Ballybunion, Rosses Point — and some majestic inland courses like Killarney, Carlow, Mullingar, Hermitage and Grange were the training grounds which produced the famous amateurs, John Burke, Jimmy Bruen, Billy O'Sullivan, the inimitable Joe Carr, and pros like Fred Daly, Harry

Top– Horse racing on the strand at Laytown, Co. Meath.

Above, left– Show-jumping at the Dublin Horse Show.

Above, right– Horse racing at Punchestown, Co. Kildare.

Bradshaw and Christy O'Connor. They have put Irish golf on the world map, set a standard by which any aspiring handicapper can play, but since television has brought Jack Nicklaus and Arnold Palmer, Johnny Miller, Hubert Green and Sergiano Ballesteros to thousands more than saw Sam Snead play at Portmarnock the game has burgeoned. As the price of land for new courses has also grown, we find that club membership is very expensive and difficult to achieve; so the traditional supply of young players may be checked by economic forces.

I've left to the end racing which in terms of time alone is the oldest organised sporting tradition in Ireland. The Irishman's and Irishwoman's love and appreciation of a good horse is as old as our history. The "sport of kings", once the privilege of a few, has long been the joy of many. The Curragh, in Co. Kildare, by its very name proclaims the antiquity of racing in Ireland. *Cuirreach* in Irish, means a moor or racecourse, and there are many "Curraghs" in placenames around the land. The organised sport traces to some downy birds of the Anglo class in the late seventeenth and early eighteenth centuries. The Irish Turf Club emerged from the coming together of interested and disinterested men of substance motivated by a love of good horses and the desire to race them and by the further desire to see that those who watched and backed them should get a fair run for their money.

In all the dark days of the nineteenth century when Earl and Sir were the principal patrons and organisers of racing and hunting, the plain people had small say. In fact, under one Penal Law no Irishman who had a horse however valuable could refuse an offer for it of £5 flat.

The names are legion: among jumpers, Golden Miller, Reynoldstown, Brown Jack, Prince Regent, Early Mist, Quare Times, Caughoo, Cottage Rake and on the flat, Workman, Arctic Prince, Sir Ivor, Santa Claus, Larkspur and many more which have won the biggest prizes in English racing. And where do you leave Arkle (and his rider, Pat Taaffe)? That almost humanly intelligent horse was a national institution — and seemed to know it. How many half-dollars he carried on his noble back from the ordinary people who could never go racing, except on the box, or to run around to "Joe Byrne Bets Here, Estd., 1917".

Irish racing is a tradition which has now become an industry; one of the happiest conjunctions of new Ireland and old. In 1945 a state-sponsored organisation, the Racing Board, was established to develop in the changing post-war economic scene certain aspects of racing which up to then had been governed solely by the Irish Turf Club — the traditional ruling body representing owners, breeders and patrons of racing. The Turf Club still controls the taking of entries, the conditions of races, jockey and trainer licences and the stewarding of meetings — all stewards, to their eternal credit, contribute their time and judgement free of charge. The Racing Board, representing all the turf's interests, superintends the general scene, administers the Tote betting system at the track and ploughs money into increased stakes, better amenities, subsidies to transport horses and maintenance of the Irish National Stud, which makes top-class sires available to owners who might otherwise be unable to patronise them.

That's the bare framework; but go to The Curragh on Irish Sweeps Derby Day, or to Fairyhouse on Easter Monday, Punchestown end of April or Galway races in July — and if you can manage it to Cheltenham in March — and you'll savour a timeless Irish racing tradition. Here is a sport, centuries old, once the preserve of privilege and still, in a way, the province only of those who can afford to breed or buy or run a beast; but no one grudges them their economic fat, for the vast community of Irish racing's ordinary patrons is rooted immutably in a simple love of the horse. It is argued that racing, since it encourages so many people who cannot properly afford the funds to keep on investing in their daily fancies is a socially deleterious thing. That's for the moralists who've never savoured the thrill and tang of the course.

At race meetings, at "the dogs", at coursing meets, at Glin or Clounanna or Clonmel or on a frosty day when they beat the open paddocks at Newbridge or Donabate you get near the sporting heart of Ireland — or one of them. Our sporting tradition is long, old and complex. Is it an exact microcosm of Ireland, past and present? Who knows? It is alive and well.

The state-run National Stud, Co. Kildare, plays a major role in Ireland's bloodstock industry.

Clones, Co. Monaghan.

WORDS
WRITTEN, SPOKEN AND SUNG

Seán MacRéamoinn

IF YOU EVER hear the word "brilliant" used about an Irishman, you may take it that nine times out of ten it has to do with his use of words — usually spoken, less frequently written. And even if he's a professional writer the chances are that the accolade has been given not to his work but to his conversation. "A great talker!" This, of course, is the commonplace of the tourist brochure: "Come to an Irish pub and listen to the great flow of talk, as sweet and as heady as the drink itself." And I'm afraid we are too often ready to believe our own propaganda, and give the tourist what he's looking for. For those who don't like pubs, we're willing to put the talk between hard or soft covers or on to the stage.

Clichés however are usually rooted in fact, and the truth of the matter is that Irish culture is overwhelmingly verbal, and almost uniquely so for our time. This will be quickly apparent to the visitor of more sophisticated taste who seeks something more than the "sweet talk". Dublin, he will soon find, has no opera house. Nor does this capital city of a traditionally Roman Catholic country boast a Roman Catholic Cathedral. The excellent National Gallery is well worth visiting but not mainly for the Irish works on view. Most of our good architecture dates from the colonial period, and what remain of its once splendid interiors were decorated by Continental artists for Anglo-Irish patrons. There is a little good statuary, but only a little.

Against this it will be argued that public display or the lack of it doesn't prove anything, that there are good Irish painters and sculptors, architects and musicians (and indeed this is true), and that, anyway, Dublin isn't Ireland. But in the end I think it will be generally agreed that the visual arts are not our strongest suit. That we're not great builders, that a long gap in the development of religious art is only now being repaired, and that music is a very special case, which we will consider later. At the very least, no one will deny that we have never produced a painter or composer to match the achievement of W. B. Yeats or James Joyce — or, for that matter, of Shaw, Wilde, O'Casey or Beckett.

I may be accused of sleight-of-pen here, since some of the great names I have just mentioned can be regarded as "colonial" or Anglo-Irish as our Georgian buildings. The question is too complex to argue now, but I cannot honestly agree. In any case it does not affect the main thrust of my argument. I am suggesting that a verbal emphasis pervades Irish life at all levels — not merely that of "high" culture; that this is mainly, though perhaps not entirely, the result of the fortunes of history; and that this centrality of the word in our culture has had certain very remarkable side-effects in the way we think and behave. I would further argue that the Irish musical tradition, again as conditioned by our history, has close links with the dominant verbal culture which it at once sustains and relieves.

Calling on the past to explain the present — or to excuse it — is a familiar national pastime. "Seven hundred years of oppression" can too often be made to cover a multitude of sins, usually of omission. But there is no gainsaying that a stormy and often ruthless history did stunt growth, did frustrate creative energy and did inhibit the investment and organisation of resources, human as well as material, which carried most of medieval Christendom into the modern age. Indeed that very Christendom, set alight in the dark centuries by Irish faith and scholarship, bears now in its surviving monuments few physical traces of this illumination. Few of our sermons were in stone. The noble ruins of past glories which mark the Irish landscape can hardly begin to compete with the rich architectural heritage of almost any corner of France or England.

Domestic building of more recent centuries, in town and country alike, is, as I have said earlier, almost all colonial: I mean as far as the "big house" is concerned. More modest building of some interest does exist, but, in general, the tenant-farmers and landless or near-landless peasantry lived in cottages and cabins which were mean, comfortless and often plain squalid. More recent times have brought greater comfort and so-called modern conveniences, but the new dwellings are often even less beautiful than their humble predecessors. Again there is little of a decent vernacular tradition in furnishing or decorating, either in private or public buildings. Until very recently the interiors of Irish Catholic churches were as appallingly vulgar as the newest Irish pubs now are.

And yet enough of beauty, occasionally of splendour, remains to remind us of what once was — a Book of Kells, a Tara brooch, a Holy Cross Abbey — and what might have been. There are even hints that a hundred crafts from thatching to cooking could have produced a material folk-culture as rich as that of the Danes or the Dutch. But the curse of history, from the piracies of the Vikings to the famine economics of the Victorians, "maimed us from the start".

I have thus far given a brief, and necessarily selective, summary of the "deprivation" view of Irish history as leaving us a (merely) verbal culture. To coin a phrase: we were robbed! There is however a more positive and interesting view of the matter which while not supplanting the first, modifies and complements it. It is this: the Irish are so good at verbalising, and so addicted to it, because they have two languages to play with.

This too of course is an over-simplification. Bilingual we may be, but, for practical purposes, only for about the last 150 years. Until the nineteenth century the common vernacular was Irish (*Gaeilge* ór Gaelic — a Celtic language, cousin to Welsh and to the ancient tongue of the Gauls). It had been so since before the dawn of history. Neither Vikings nor Anglo-Normans nor — until the time of the first Queen Elizabeth — the English had maintained their linguistic independence. Systematic plantation (i.e. land-robbery by the English) in Ulster and the Midlands created English-speaking "islands" from the seventeenth century onwards, but even some of these as well as the cities and towns (all old strongholds of English power) were often partly gaelicised through intermarriage with the Irish and the need for "native labour". Not until the end of the eighteenth century when legal relief from religious disabilities (the "Penal Laws") and some prospect of material advancement existed for Catholics, did the native Irish set about having their children taught English.

Long before English became Ireland's new spoken language, it had reigned high in the domain of the written word. Yet it never penetrated the Gaelic literary world, unlike Norman-French which brought to the English literary tradition a precious cargo from Provençal and from French itself. (The glittering impedimenta of Courtly Love which the bilingual Hiberno-Norman lords refashioned into Gaelic verses and which were later re-forged into the popular love songs are still sung in the Irish-speaking countryside.) English, I say, remained outside the Gaelic bardic circle. Even when that circle was broken with the collapse of the Gaelic aristocracy and its patronage at the beginning of the seventeenth century, only an occasional antiquarian acknowledgement (or the rare devotion of a Charlotte Brooke who collected and published "Reliques" in the manner of Percy) showed that even the most cultivated of the colonists had been at all aware of the cultural hinterland beyond the English Pale. Swift is sometimes said to have been an exception but, I believe, on very doubtful evidence. Not until bilingual Irish scholars emerged and could meet their peers on something like terms of equality was the work of publication and serious translation begun. Hardiman's *Irish Minstrelsy* (1831) is a landmark.

But if the Irish remained almost untouched by English and Hiberno-English literature until Tom Moore's time (1779-1852), they had long been all too aware of the written word of the colonists in another sphere. With the breakdown of Gaelic institutions in the early seventeenth century, spoken Irish lost all public function. English became the language of law and order, of commerce and communication, of "improvement" rural and urban, of schooling both established and informal and even of the Catholic Church (outside of the Latin liturgy). All over the country, grave-stones from the seventeenth and eighteenth centuries record in English the passing of men and women whose only tongue was Irish.

Left– The drama and tension of the storyteller's art is captured in this photograph of a travelling woman.

Below– Inside McDaid's, one of Dublin's literary pubs, where conversation was once as important as the drink.

And so was born a tension, a linguistic relationship which changed radically as the vernacular balance tipped from Irish to English. It was both guilt-ridden and liberated and charged with enormous creative capacity. The guilt, conscious or subconscious, came from the apparent rejection of the past and the attendant breakdown in communication between the generations — often, literally, between parent and child — which resulted from the widespread adoption of English as the spoken word. Balanced against this was the liberation which a second language always brings: the liberation from the automatic identification of word and thing, of idea and expression. Irish bilingualism does not mean that all or even most of us are equally at home in both languages. Indeed, as the vernacular shift from Irish to English took place, entire communities were left with only the vaguest memory of the speech of their grandparents, and today strenuous efforts to restore and revive Irish have only partially succeeded. Nevertheless it is important to recognise that the nation as a whole is bilingual, historically and actually (however imperfectly so) — in contrast to the situation of Belgium, say, or Canada, or Switzerland.

From the beginning of the present century, the potential of this cultural and linguistic condition has been recognised. And while its evaluation and interpretation have been a matter of deep and often furious debate, it has, in fact, been the seedbed for as diverse a literary flowering as *Ulysses,* the classic Abbey plays, the comic novels of Flann O'Brien and, most remarkable of all, a small but brilliant corpus of new writing in Irish of a quality and "modernity" which could hardly have been hoped for. It is a historical commonplace that the "Irish Renaissance" of the early twentieth century had its roots in that rediscovery of the Gaelic past which also gave Irish nationalism its distinctive tone and impetus. This rediscovery was both prompted and limited by the bilingual situation existing at the turn of the century which also had implications for the place of the word, in life as well as in letters, in the Ireland of today.

Before considering this last point however, it is convenient to ask a question already hinted at: is our "verbal emphasis" only partly a matter of historical condition, is it to some extent *de natura*? Without getting involved in the philosophical problem of what is inherent and what is learned in the nature of man, anyone who knows the Gaelic tradition must lean towards the view that the Irish are verbalisers because God made us so. All literature is made of words, but literature in Irish seems to use them not just as raw material but in a way I can only describe as ontological: the medium, if not the whole message, seems to be of its essence. There is a preoccupation — often a palpable delight, sometimes an obsession — with the selection, setting and shaping of words. In verse: from the "rhetorics" of the sagas and the first poetry of nature; in the highly wrought eulogies of the medieval professionals and the superb love lyrics of their amateur contemporaries; in the passionate political poems of the seventeenth and early eighteenth centuries; down through the declining days of the bardic tradition, one sees the work of men and women who were above all else masters of language. Many show a high talent and imaginative power; a few are fired by the vision of genius. All are craftsmen of words.

In prose too, from the early and medieval epics of "Gods and fighting men" to the smaller picaresque tales and satires, we find words used not just to tell the story but to embellish it, even at the cost of holding up the action. Perhaps there is nothing especially Irish in this, but what is of interest is the way in which much of the early art form has been inherited by the story-tellers of the Irish countryside, and has formed the core of their vast repertoire. Just how vast can be guessed at from the 2 million manuscript pages in the Irish Folklore archive in Dublin — and this is only the "remnant" still alive and recorded during the last fifty years. What the archive cannot possibly reproduce is the relish and critical discernment with which the storyteller's word-craft and word-play were received by his fireside audiences. The stories ranged from a classic tale to the re-telling of a tragic or comic event of a generation or two back. Or there might be an Irish version of some fragment of Indo-European, or even wider, heritage. In all cases the words are those of the artist-narrator and his masters and predecessors.

I have mentioned word-*play,* and this is an important part of it all. For it must be remembered about the telling of tales and hearing them, the making of verses and "swapping" them, the hand-copying of manuscripts (prose or verse) and circulating them, that none of these labours of love was confined to a small specialist circle. They have been the occupation and entertainment of what the outsider might call "simple folk" since at least the seventeenth century. I can recall a farmer in Co. Galway talking with enthusiasm of the poet Antoine Raifteirí who had died 120 years before, but whose verses he could quote with joy. He spoke of other versemakers, contemporaries and rivals of his hero, whom he dismissed as "mere peasants". (Poor Raifteirí was to the naked eye only a blind beggar-man!) Teasing my friend, I insisted that he tell me what makes one poet better than another. He thought a moment and then said, with great deliberation: "Better words, better placed. Like the way you'd be building a wall and you'd know where to put the bricks."

It was a good answer and a revealing one. I think it sums-up very well what I've been trying to identify as a central preoccupation of the Irish verbal tradition. Word-play in the most common sense is of course a prevailing feature of Irish conversation, the famous witty chat which we referred to earlier. In yet another sense, however, one may see it as having a more profound and sophisticated function. I was reminded of this recently when I read a perceptive article on Seán Ó Ríordáin, a Gaelic poet who died a year or two ago.[1] The journal in which this was published contained another essay which is also relevant to our argument. I will quote the opening paragraph:

It may seem ironic that the literature of a country notorious for its obsession with morals, and particularly with sexual morality, should be characterised by a relative indifference to moral issues and an almost total indifference to sexual morality, but such is the case with many of the major works of Irish literature in contrast to those of the literature of England, a country reputed to be more careless, at least of its sexual morality.[2]

The author deals almost exclusively with modern Irish writing in English and while she does not suggest that the Irish have substituted a verbal for a moral pre-occupation, verbalisation must of necessity be involved in what she calls the "self-delighting intellectualism... pedanticism and willfulness" of their work. This is not to be regarded as "just so much avid frivolity... not merely whimsical. Its detachment does not indicate a lack of intellectual conviction... The Irish tradition endorses Nietzsche's dictum: To mature; that is to regain the seriousness one had as a child at play."[3]

In the comedies of Oscar Wilde the word-play is as glittering and as mannered as the foil-play of fencers; with Shaw the game is more dangerous, the rapier strikes to wound. In Synge the syllables dance to an old tune, grave and gay by turn; in O'Casey's rememberings the tread is still measured though heavier. But for Yeats and Joyce the game is primal, cosmic, as on naming-day in Eden.

Names and what they mean, or can be made to mean, have had a long fascination for the Irish: place-names especially. Indeed, one of the classic categories of our early literature was the *Dindseanchas,* the lore of place-names. This was a corpus of verse and prose whose interest went far beyond the borders of the topographical, extending from the world of myth and ancestral memory, through the pieties of received tradition, to the irrepressible flowering of the gnomic and the anecdotal.

A sense of place is one of the most rooted of Irish characteristics, and its celebration has always been an occasion for the verbal salute, often in verse. The formal complexities of the *Dindseanchas* have their echoes in modern folk song and rhyme. The pangs of exile have inspired many, but the nostalgia is nearly always for a specific plot of earth, a beloved hillside, river-valley or townland, rarely for the country as a whole. But it is the sum of all these parts, the patchwork pattern of small places that make up the *grande patrie* and the larger patriotism. It is the great tapestry of Gaelic words which name the hills and valleys, the rivers and harbours and towns, the parishes and provinces of the island of Ireland, that bear witness to the common culture of the nation.

And there is more than all this, much more, to our concern with names and naming. As with our other verbal concerns, our preoccupation with names in, say, the political field has been called obsessive — perhaps not altogether unfairly. One notorious example of this is the way in which the words *republic* and *republican*, given a capital letter and an appropriate context, have become quite literally a matter of life and death.

I do not of course suggest that the placing of these words at the centre of a political debate which became a civil war was a frivolous matter, an example of the word-play of *homo ludens* gone into tragedy. One does

BRÍ GRAIGE

Brí Graige, whence the name? Not hard to say.
When Loegaire mac Neill, king of Ireland, went
to Ferta Fer Fecce to meet Patrick, when he
came to plant the Faith in Erin, there came,
through the miraculous power of Patrick,
great thunderings and lightnings, so that all the
studs of Erin were thrown into a panic. And
thus they were found there by the mountain.
So hence it is called Brí Graige, that is, the Hill
or Height of the Horses; for *brí* signifies 'height'
or 'hill'.

Right– An example of *Dindseanchas,* the lore
of place-names, translated from the Irish.

Below– Two men take time for a chat and a
rest on a roadside in Mayo.

not so easily dismiss the conflicting commitments of another generation, one deeply concerned with the structures of national liberation. Nor does one make little of the sincerity, however mistaken, of those to whom the implications of those commitments still point to violent action. But it has to be admitted that many times over the past sixty years the argument and the passion, the breaking of friendships, the sacrifices and the sufferings — yes, and the cruelties and barbarities — have seemed to be about words and names, however sacred, rather than about political realities. One can only turn gratefully from the darker tragic side of the story to the high comedy of a day some years ago in the national parliament when this central national debate was, quite seriously and formally, resolved by the Prime Minister by producing a dictionary! Still, one mustn't exaggerate, even in self-criticism, and it can be said in all fairness that quite a lot of the time realism keeps breaking in to save us from ourselves.

It is possible to argue that what may be regarded as undue concern with verbal niceties and definitions, even to a point of intolerance, is not specifically an Irish trait but is rather part of the common heritage of Roman Catholic culture. This is plausible but only partially valid for two reasons. First, one would be hard put to discover a similar concern, at least one as strong, among, say, the Italians or the Spaniards. They both have their dogmatisms but they differ from ours. And secondly, I would suggest that the dimension of intolerance in Ireland, the *shibboleth* of "reading the symbol too sharp" is comparatively new to our word-culture, a fairly recent accretion, another by-product of our later linguistic history, and a dangerous one.

As a result of the institutional breakdown of Gaelic culture in the seventeenth century, even those people who spoke Irish privately began to adopt a "public" English vocabulary, extensive or limited according to their needs and station. It might have been only a few words, and those only half-understood. It was essentially an artificial vocabulary lacking any direct relationship or "objective co-relative" to their inner lives or experience. The implication of some of the new words was gained gradually, often painfully: others remained mysterious though crucial, like formulas of an arcane ritual.

The adoption of English by native Irish-speakers continued and developed during the eighteenth and nineteenth centuries until the "public" words became integrated into private speech — but only partially. The words of law and order, of politics and administration still stood apart from the everyday words of everyday people. And, as the everyday people began to have attainable aspirations in the public sphere, they began to create special public words of their own: "emancipation", "coercion", "Repeal", "separation" . . . "Republic". Only at a very late stage in the process, did they reach into the old private vernacular for public words — *Sinn Féin* (ourselves) was probably the first of these. I don't think it fanciful to suggest that if native institutions had developed after 1600, a new public vocabulary in Gaelic would have developed quite naturally, and we would have been spared the hiatus and polarisation which occurred.

What is certain is that in the eighteenth century and well into the nineteenth, the world of the "public" vocabulary co-existed with the submerged life of what has come to be known as the *Hidden Ireland.* The name was coined by the Cork novelist and critic, Daniel Corkery (1878-1964), and formed the title of his important study of "Gaelic Munster" — a work which has been seriously criticised in detail but which remains an indispensable guide to understanding a most important chapter of the Irish past.

It is the story of the fragmentation of a national culture and its struggle to survive. Its heroes are neither resistance leaders nor freedom-fighters (at least not primarily, though some were) but poets: men who inherited the art and craft of Gaelic verse and whose achievement at a time of general social and cultural impoverishment was remarkable. Bereft of patronage, of libraries, of access to publishing houses — even to the printing press, they maintained their heritage and added to it. They circulated their work and that of their predecessors in manuscripts, hand-written with a skill and devotion that recalls the monks of a thousand years before. These men of the eighteenth century were no monks, and their exile was in their own land, but they too fought the darkness with the light of the Word. Some of them met together in "Courts of Poetry", and often started their proceedings with a proclamation in Irish verse or prose, but beginning with the English public word "Whereas". The court-house might be a tavern or *síbín,* and the presiding officer's coat in tatters: but the language was cloth of silver.

In any consideration of the Gaelic poetic tradition "singing" is a key-word. Literally from the earliest times down to the present-day, poetry in Irish has been made to be sung. The manner of the singing has of course changed. What we know of the earliest verse, and of the somewhat later classical "bardic" period, points to a formalised chanting of a kind not unknown in other early and medieval cultures. Certainly the verse-forms themselves bear witness to a continuing taste for verbal music and an extraordinary craftsmanship in its creation. Both the taste and the craft survived the disappearance of a professional poetic class. In the Hidden Ireland it met and mingled with a more popular tradition which shared many of the characteristics of the "higher" verse but in less sophisticated forms. Old moulds were broken, and the classic tradition was poured into the simpler but shapely vessel of the *amhrán.* This word in fact means "song" and though it can be used in a technical sense even where the verse is spoken, the fullness of the art comes to flower only when joined to that of the singer.

The singer's art too is a very special one. It is commonly known as *sean-nós* (old style), and it shares the "modal" quality of other folk-traditions. It has peculiarities of phrasing and intonation which make it an unique medium for a heightened articulation of the rhythms of Gaelic speech. It is a living art-form and although it survives a little elsewhere, it

Above– The *Fleadh Cheoil,* this one at Mullingar, Co. Westmeath, is Ireland's great festival of traditional music and song. While competitions are held in various halls, impromptu music takes place in the streets and pubs.

Left– "Both Barde and Harper is preparde, which by their cunning art, Doe strike and cheare up all the gestes with comfort at the hart." From John Derricke's *The Image of Irelande* (1581).

Traditional ballad singing in McLynn's Pub, Sligo. The singer is playing a *bodhrán*.

flourishes only where Gaelic is a living language. Its preservation and continuing development is an urgent national cultural priority.

The *sean-nós* does not confine itself to the human voice. In a secondary form, it gives Irish instrumental music its distinctive beauty and character, even in the playing of dance-tunes (some of which are not necessarily of Irish provenance) but, above all, in the performance of the great "airs" (*amhráin* "without words") which represent at least three centuries of composition for harp and pipe, violin and flute.

An ancient tradition of harping was unfortunately broken in the last century, and the same fate might have in time befallen the other instruments of the art. Fortunately, however, traditional piping, fiddling and flute-playing survived to provide a strong basis for the great folk-movement which began in the second half of this century. The Irish music revival has been immensely successful — certainly in popular appeal. The folk organisation *Comhaltas Ceoltóirí Éireann* spearheads a movement as young and vigorous as that of the contemporary pop-culture with which it sometimes overlaps. The *Fleadh Cheoil* is a festival of youth as much as it is of music.[4]

As to quality, as to the strengthening and enrichment of the tradition, one must speak with greater caution. On the face of it there are great grounds for optimism. The movement begat one man of genius, Seán Ó Riada, whose untimely death in 1971 at the age of forty, cut short an already brilliant achievement as a composer, performer, teacher and "animateur". He took the tradition in its integrity and made his own of it: he set it on a course of development, which, while rooted in the *sean-nós*, could appeal to the contemporary ear. Since his death other talented musicians have moved along the paths which he pioneered, and future developments could be radical and exciting.

But there remains one central problem, centred where words and music meet. The *sean-nós* can only survive and develop if the Irish language survives and develops, especially in those *Gaeltacht* areas where it is still a community vernacular — in a handful of parishes in Donegal, Mayo, Galway, Kerry, Cork, Waterford and Meath. What is at stake is the life or death of a whole culture.

FESTIVALS

Maeve Binchy

I USED TO LOVE them in fairy stories... festivals. Something would happen like the dragon being slain or the lost princess being found and the good wise King would be so happy he would order a festival for days and days and all the loyal subjects would cheer. And they used to have them in pantomimes too, all those half-insane people in peasants' skirts and leather jerkins were always "oohing" and "aahing" about festivals. A festival means banners and a band; it means somebody making an announcement from a stage and the main burden of the message is about enjoying yourself. A festival is an official license and encouragement to go a bit mad, to dance around some stage like the villagers in the opening chorus of the pantomime. There's a hint of headiness in it. And Ireland is full of festivals. If you could make a map of Ireland like those lovely maps of the Metro in Paris where stations light up when you press buttons, you would find a festival lighting up somewhere all the time. Even more exciting you could work out a festival circuit and follow it. A travelling festival-goer could have a magical journey... all the fairy stories and pantomimes brought to life.

In no way could you ever think of Ireland as a kind of dancing, yodelling Ruritania with bells of celebration pealing from coast to coast, but the country has a fair genius for festivity when it puts its mind to it. It's something which should not be remarked on perhaps or praised too much in case the Irish become too aware of it and really do become like the villagers dancing for an audience of tourists. Irish festivals come from within, they would fold up and collapse like cardboard scenery on a stage if they became two-dimensional and were put on only for the tourists. Festivals in Ireland are real and they are all-embracing: a horse fair is a festival; the crucifying communal exercise of scaling the second highest mountain in Ireland on an early Sunday morning in summer is as much a festival as it is a pilgrimage; a 325-yard sprint for greyhounds could be a festival as much as a sporting fixture.

Some are more real than others; some spring from Ireland's earliest history — the days before St. Patrick arrived with the news that was to change everything so much. Some are utterly contrived and oddly, often none the worse for it. A "walking festival" for example has no great roots in any tradition but it brings together people from all over the world in an entirely non-competitive way to walk for four days around some of the most beautiful countryside in the West. The people come and they walk and they meet other people and they like it and they leave... it's over. It was a festival surely? As real a festival as one which can find its pedigree enshrined in archaeology.

To be new is not to be non-authentic. I was actually there when a festival was conceived in front of my very eyes. I saw it begin. It began from chat. The chat was about *Cuirt an Mhean Oiche* (The Midnight Court) — the wonderful racey, rumbustious poem written in the eighteenth century by Brian Merriman. Its translations into the English language were being analysed. "Wouldn't it be great if we all went down to Feakle (in Clare) where it was written and had a reading of it at midnight?" asked one man. "And we could bring wine and food and have a feast," said another. "And we must invite..." The enthusiasm soared and a festival was on the way. Now a regular and respected occurrence, the Merriman Summer School invites scholars to address it and its participants to roam and play around the hills and castles of Co. Clare each summer. In winter time it has a weekend Winter School conducted through the medium of Irish. Always, summer and winter, taking a theme of Irish life. And it grew from one man's wish to read the poem where it was written and the conviction that it could be carried through.

I've been to festivals in other lands and they're not quite the same. You don't feel that you can join in just because you're there. Maybe that's because of their nature, who after all would want to join in the bull-running in Pamplona or some of the mysterious religious pilgrimages where local statues are carried through the streets? I've never quite known how much I was looking-in, slightly indecently, or how much the show was being put on for me and fellow standers. It's like watching the Battle of the Flowers or any huge parade of floral-decorated floats. There would be no point in making all those wild and magnificent arrangements if they were not to be shown to an audience, so the audience is essential. But since the audience can in no way be involved in choosing the flowers or sewing them together or designing the floats, then that audience must remain outsiders and in a way peripheral. I was at an Arts Festival in New England once where everyone in the small town was having a lovely time, but an outsider felt very odd indeed. I admired this lady's painting and read that one's poem, but it was a community effort. They didn't care if I or any passer-by ever read or saw their work, they were the community and their festival was for the community.

Now in Ireland I know I am right in saying that the festival, the gathering, the fair, the pilgrimage is for everyone. It expands to include all who arrive like some magic boat. And it's not a phoney inclusion, it's not like a nightmare MC who leans out of a complicated square dance and says to the most unlikely person, "Come on, join in. It's easy." There's nothing that smacks of bonhomie in an Irish festival. The interesting thing is that people feel no need to include outsiders in any deliberate way because there are no outsiders. If you have come along you are in some way part of the festival. Irish people don't think that there's anything strange about that until they go to other people's festivals. "I went to a folklore festival once," a man told me, "It was the biggest let-down of my life. They couldn't have been nicer. You know the Austrians, a very civilised and courteous people. You wouldn't meet nicer in a lifetime of looking. But the festival wasn't a festival at all. It was only a series of exhibitions. You just saw people dancing and heard them singing. Wasn't it very strange to call it a festival in the first place?"

I am naive enough to believe that the great majority of Irish festivals and gatherings happen because people actually enjoy them rather than from some mercenary motive about making money from the participants for the town. Of course a festival brings money, it stimulates the towns-people to paint their doors and windows, it means that the visitors will spend money in the shops, pubs and hotels, it means that spending power will be diverted from somewhere else to here. But that couldn't be the main reason. It can't be the real force behind the energy and enthusiasm that gets things going in a hundred places, a hundred different kinds of things too. One of the great joys of Irish festival spotting is seeing the enormous variety of interests that are represented. You'd be a poor person if you couldn't find something to please you in a selection that included railway preservation at one end of the country with gentle reflective people mourning the passage of the steam engine to the spectacle of 100,000 people all screaming *The Rose of Tralee* at the other end of the land in the climax to a talent-cum-beauty competition which has nearly driven everyone insane with excitement.

Some festivals have a glorious and spectacular vulgarity about them, as warm and welcoming as a hot bath at the end of a cold tiring day. Some are gentle and almost wistful, the kind of gracious, lightly-drawn happening that makes you wonder whether it was meant to be like this and fear that it could never be recreated next year. Within a few days of each other you might find yourself sitting in a beautiful drawing room with open windows letting in a night June breeze and letting out some exquisite chamber music — that would be the Festival in Great Irish Houses — followed by a blast of what they used to call the Gay Bachelor Festival in Ballybunion until the word gay changed its meaning even though the festival hadn't. Now it's the Ballybunion International Bachelor Festival, and men are judged on their eligibility as husbands by a tongue-in-cheek panel to the side-splitting amusement of everyone around. Both of these are Irish festivals, but the Irish are a many-sided people.

You need know nothing about oysters to have a good time at the Galway Oyster Festival. I actually met a couple once who nearly missed it because they thought you would have to be some kind of oyster expert

Above– A Mercedes provides a handy table from which to devour vast quantities of oysters and Guinness at the Galway Oyster Festival.

Left– Tralee, Co. Kerry. From Irish communities all over the world "Roses" are selected to compete for the title 'The Rose of Tralee".

and nearly didn't pay their fee. "Why do people pay fees and enroll and join and everything, if they aren't becoming members of something?" the puzzled Canadian asked me as his wife nodded. Eager to meet people, eager to join in, they were terrified also of looking foolish. "I think you only join in the sense that you pay for tickets to parties and receptions where they'll be eating oysters," I said helpfully. "Are you sure I won't have a number on my back and that I won't have to make some statement about them?" persisted the anxious man from Montreal. I took them by the hand and checked this fact out at the registration desk. "In fact," said the seller of tickets," We'd hate you to make a statement about the oysters." A holiday saved, a festival joined.

Since I genuinely believe that for many of us a holiday is the sum of the conversations, meetings and reactions rather than an album of the views or a guidebook listing the dates of castles, I believe that festivals and gatherings have a huge role in Irish life. They are more than little silli-nesses to enliven a town square with some coloured bunting. They are real forums for people to meet each other and to talk to each other. They are safety valves in lives which could become too caught up in odd priorities like working hard for a living whether on a lonely headland or in a lonely city and being too busy to stop and talk. Festivals are talking times; they are relaxing places. Few would argue that to feel a part of something moving and living is often more restful than the isolation of self-imposed solitude. Often a tired brain can be soothed more by the tap of dancing feet and the hum of good conversation than it can by silence and that velvety emptiness which is called "getting-away-from-it-all".

I've experienced the most unlikely soothings at festivals. Once when lonely and sad and not really knowing quite what to do, which is very alarming if you always know exactly what you are going to do, I headed on impulse to a deep-sea fishing festival. The man who was afraid he knew too little about oysters to go to the Galway Oyster Festival should have been a confident man compared to me and what I knew about deep-sea fishing. What I knew was nothing. I think I imagined you fished from a harbour but in the deep bit unlike those who did shallow-sea fishing and caught things in low water. Maybe I just liked the reassuring sound of the words Deep Sea. Anyway if I had planned for a month what to do, nothing could have been better. Elbow to elbow with overexcited Frenchmen and calm, unruffled Yorkshiremen I battled over the sides of trawlers for skate and shark. I became so involved with something at the end of a line that I nearly joined it in the Atlantic Ocean until I was dragged back on to the boat. Each evening I watched, sick with jealousy, while the other people's catches were weighed, but there would be matey advice and help in the pub with everyone still in their oilskins. My face became weatherbeaten and my soul calmer and I made a dozen new friends.

People are always making friends at the two huge Dublin shows – the Spring Show and the Horse Show. They are held in the gloriously old-fashioned RDS (Royal Dublin Society). There is something ageless about the way those bands play Strauss and Sullivan and something permanent in the way the elderly ladies sit down to listen to them, and the rest of us sit down pretending to listen but really to ease feet in shoes that are too tight.

The Spring Show, nominally an agricultural affair is on the first Tuesday of May. It is traditionally a fine day. It used to be said that if you wanted a sunny day for your wedding you should choose the first day of the Spring Show. Full of beautiful, bellowing bulls and small nervous chickens who had just come out of an egg and into a festival, the Spring Show is a marvellous part of Irish life. It mixes the social with the business, real life with relaxation in the most natural way. An overseas visitor would feel quite at home as he walked through the rows of prize-winning lambs or the fields of agricultural machinery. After all he is just as knowledgeable about it all as any city slicker from Dublin. I spent years of my young life nodding wisely at combine harvesters and at the fetlocks of a hunter as if I knew anything about either. You join in the excitement of the competition, share the pride of the red rosettes and the tears of disappointment for the calf or the vegetables or the young squat person on a young squat pony who don't make it.

I always find the Spring Show absolutely delightful but I cannot say the same for the Horse Show in August. This it must be said is a purely personal opinion and not at all shared by the rest of the world. The Horse Show attracts horses which is good and people who like horses which is also good. But it brings with it its own brand of "Hooray Henries" and terrible shouting, affected people which is bad. Or I think it brings them. One year I really did hear a group of appalling derby people who looked as if they had stepped out of a comedy film, screaming at each other on the steps of the Shelbourne Hotel. "Oh *do* hurry up Bunty," screamed one of them. "Old Pongo is getting the car around. What fun to be at Horse Show."

It sort of burned into my brain, and so did the stories about debs coming from other lands and attending the Horse Show Balls and behaving badly and throwing bread rolls at each other and at the waiters and squirting syphons of soda water. It all seemed a really idiotic and offensive way to carry on, and I never saw a strand of humour in it all. But as I say I am in the minority with this brooding prejudice about the Horse Show. Thousands of people who like horses and who like people have a marvellous time on green turf among white fences and bright flowers and lovely hats every August. My own sourness about the place is not echoed at all.

In fact I was once interviewed about the Horse Show on British television, and it's a bad memory. "Do many people come to the Horse Show?" the smiling David Dimbleby asked me. "No, its only a few upper class people," I said confidently and indeed wildly inaccurately as it turned out. The camera cut to thousands of people streaming in the gates. "Are the Irish people very interested in the results of the jumping?" he asked. "No, no only a few. The great mass of the people couldn't care

Lady riders, Dublin Horse Show.

less," I said with all the sureness possible. The camera cut to a shot of 10,000 Irish people screeching their support for the Irish horse and rider in the National Cup. My views on the Horse Show are obviously unsound.

There are festivals with charm and grace that comes from their being entirely unsuitable in the first place. I'm thinking of Wexford and its famous Opera Festival. It's known all over the world: an engagement at Wexford is as prestigious as you can find for a singer. No opera critic will miss the season there: the festival director's choice of operas is eagerly awaited by a music world every year. But Wexford is tiny, its minute little opera house holds about one fiftieth of the people who would like to get in when the festival is on. Its tiny streets defy parking and sometimes even the normal flow of traffic. But here is the reason for its success. Because it *is* small and inaccessible, and charming, and everyone in the town is so welcoming and becomes so involved... that's why the festival is there, why people will keep coming back to it. In Brasillia they probably have several stadiums which would hold all the disappointed opera-goers in Wexford, but that's not the point.

The point should never be too closely questioned anyway because nothing about festivals would stand up to heavy, logical analysis. Why do hundreds of people head to a town on the other side of the country when they hear a festival is taking place? Suppose all these people come from Dublin. Suppose they only met other people from Dublin while at the Wild Rose Festival in Manorhamilton, Co. Leitrim. Why, you might ask, could they not have met those people back in Dublin and saved everyone the journey? The answer is they didn't and they wouldn't. I've known people for years on one level and gone on to very different planes with them at festival time. I even managed to cure a long-standing feud and misunderstanding with a man I had always regarded as an enemy. Somehow we found the words to tell each other what had really happened as we danced an old-time waltz at Listowel Writers Week. I even heard of a woman who fell in love with her boss when she saw his profile during a film at the Cork Film Festival. She had always seen him full face before but she thought his profile revealed much better things about the man, and they were married not long afterwards.

You can even go to a festival with the intention of getting married if that's what you'd like. It often works very well too. This is at Lisdoonvarna in Co. Clare, a magic little place and the only town I have ever known to nestle in a valley. Other towns sit in valleys but Lisdoonvarna actually nestles; you get the feeling it might shift about to make itself more comfortable when you weren't looking. At the end of the harvest when the farmers had the important business of the year seen to, they used to think of getting themselves wives and would arrive in Lisdoonvarna, a spa town, "officially" to take the waters but unofficially and much more determinedly to find a bride. Unmarried women who were well aware of this practice happened to take the waters themselves at precisely this time. Wise local hoteliers and entrepreneurs decided that the town should not be short of romantic background music for this great blossoming, so dances were arranged, even afternoon dancing was encouraged, and the matches that were made from even the earliest days were legion. And it's not over yet. At the end of the summer the two sexes flock into the town, with a hefty sprinkling of those already attached and not wanting to make any further arrangements. The Lisdoonvarna festival is a non-stop party, good humoured bubbling, the ideal background to romance no matter how prosaic the elderly farmers are reputed to be in their demands and however much they are reported to prefer a potential bride to own her own tractor or combine harvester than to have golden hair and blue eyes.

The festivals can totally supersede the actual reason for them. This happens quite a lot at race meetings. In most other countries you would have to be interested in horseflesh, gambling or in looking stylish and hoping to be admired before you would go to the races. In Ireland none of these needs or interests have to be met, and you can still have a great day out at the races. There is a sense of fun and excitement about races generated of course by the pounding hooves of the horses themselves, but spreading into the bars, the tents, the sideshows, the thousand and one places where you meet people you haven't seen for years or strike up new and totally acceptable conversations with strangers simply because the Races is a defined day out. The old rules about being reserved don't apply on a day out, it's as if we were all at the same picnic and it's only natural to be relaxed with your fellow picknickers isn't it?

So race meetings have characters all of their own which have little to do with the calibre of the horses or the amount of the prize money. People have personal preferences about them. I find Galway and Killarney a bit too smart for me in the sense that people seem to dress up a lot and parade up and down. I'd prefer Listowel and Tramore. But that's a one-woman opinion. No one can agree on which is the most stylish, and therefore Ireland really has no Ascot in terms of fashion parades. Which I think is no harm anyway.

The participation which makes Irish festivals so splendid is something to be treasured, a lot of it is nurtured and helped along by the notion of a festival club. Now let us not be coy or over-romantic at this point. The point of a club has a lot to do with the licensing laws of the country which say that public houses close at 11.00 p.m. in winter and at 11.30 in summer. A club can stay open till all hours or say 1.00 a.m., 2.00 a.m., 3.00 a.m. depending on the club and the licence applied for. This for drinking folk is very good news. A place that is going to be open till all hours so you can drink with your friends has to be seen as manna of the best possible kind. But it is not the only reason for a club, and I will not go along with a cynical viewpoint which thinks that festivals develop only after the club licence has been applied for and secured. I don't think we invent festivals as an excuse to drink later into the night. We can do that in each others' homes anyway. No the festival club revolved around the notion that the actors and audience are one at an Irish festival and therefore they should drink together, and they do. An English visitor told me once that he had absolutely worshipped a famous actress for years. He had written letters to her and got no reply, he had hung like a traditional stage-door Johnny around the entrance to the theatre in London's West End but never a glance. Then she was performing in Dublin, so he saw and enjoyed the play. He was drinking in the Festival Club afterwards never thinking that she would be there or that he would get within a mile of her if she was. But lo. He bought her a half pint at the bar; she thanked him; they talked for an hour; she danced with him twice. His friends still don't believe him. At times he says he has difficulty in believing it himself.

It happens at the Cork Film Festival too, and an American show-business journalist admitted that he sometimes came to Cork to do interviews because he found film stars relaxed and just sitting about and he didn't have to go through a long procedure of applying for interviews through press agents and publicity people at the studios. You just went up and sat down beside them.

Visiting bands and visiting performers like this too; its exhilarating to meet your audience later on that night and be told personally that they liked the performance. People who have come to Ireland to buy or sell horses at a fair want to talk to their opposite numbers late into the night, so a club doubles the pleasure for them too. A club is a place where the visiting teams can relax and get to know each other if it has been a day of competitions. I once heard two show jumpers talking and laughing in a festival club, obviously having become lifemates. "Why am I giving you all this advice?" one asked suddenly, "I'm jumping against you tomorrow." In sport particularly this kind of thing should happen more often. Quite enough of the fun has been taken out of games by people who have defined the word professional too literally.

Goodwill gets extended or shared or whatever happens to goodwill, it happens greatly at Irish festivals. I remember once at Tralee when the organisers had decided to fill every minute of the waking day with activity, they made a mistake in what they defined as the waking day. For most of the revellers it was not time to wake up when a German band began to play goodwill music in the town square directly below the bedroom windows of the sleepers. Almost in unison the window sashes were raised and a loud cacophony drowned the little band below. The words may have been indistinguishable, but the message was clear. It was a dismissive message asking the band to go away and stop playing.

Later I thought sadly about the incident, even though I had been one who had roared from a window. I felt ashamed that the band should have come the whole way from southern Germany to play at an Irish festival and then get such an appalling welcome. I decided to take upon myself the collective guilt of everyone who had been so rude and make a personal thank you and apology to them that night at the festival club. But when I got to them, they were surrounded by a crowd of equally guilty people and seemed in high spirits. "It was very funny was it not?" said one of the bandsmen holding a big glass of beer and looking like a stage German. "It was most amusing ja? All the peoples were asleep and when they heard

Above– The Spring Show, Ireland's great agricultural exhibition, held each year at the Royal Dublin Society showgrounds at Ballsbridge.

Top– After the harvest country people traditionally met at Lisdoonvarna, a spa town, "officially" to take the waters but unofficially to find a mate.

our music, they thought they were in Hell." He beamed with delight at all his new friends. And we all felt much better, and that marvellous shmaltzy thing goodwill was flying all around the place. As I think it does always at Irish festivals.

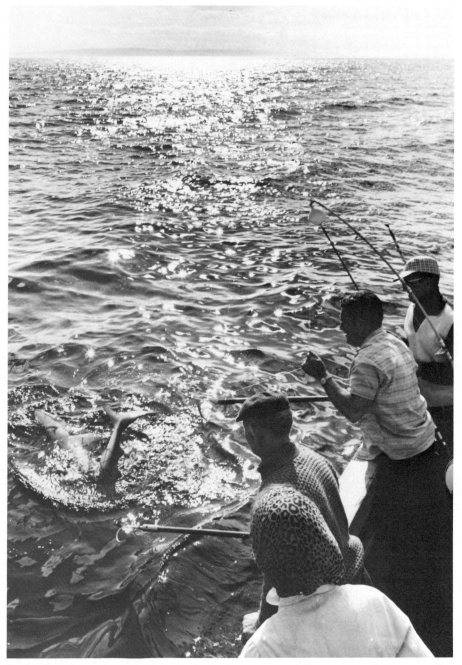

Fishing festivals are popular on lakes and rivers in the open sea. Here a group of deep sea anglers struggle with a shark off Dungarvan, Co. Waterford.

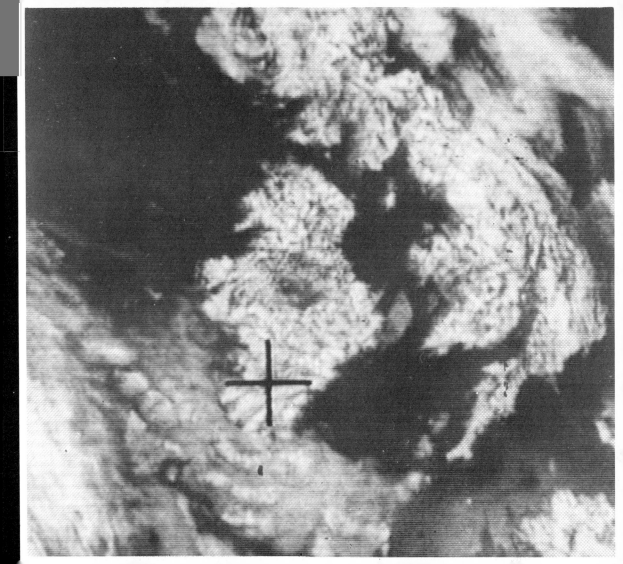

Lights along the Liffey, Dublin.

IRELAND
IN THE
MODERN WORLD

Sean MacBride

IT CAN BE said that the "Irish Republican Tradition" dates from 1798 when John Moore of Moore Hall, Carra Lake in Co. Mayo was appointed the first President of the Irish Republic. The Republican Tradition had been spelled out in no uncertain terms by Theobald Wolfe Tone who made his appeal to the "numerous and respectable class of the community − the men of no property". The respective roles of the fathers of Irish nationalism were set forth by Pádraic Pearse in *The Sovereign People:*

> Tone is the intellectual ancestor of the whole modern movement of Irish nationalism, of Davis, and Lalor, and Mitchel and all their followers; Davis is the immediate ancestor of the spiritual and imaginative part of that movement, embodied in our day in the Gaelic League; Lalor is the immediate ancestor of the specifically democratic part of that movement, embodied today in the more virile labour organisations; Mitchel is the immediate ancestor of Fenianism, the noblest and most terrible manifestation of this unconquered nation.[1]

If from a short-term policy point of view, the execution of the 1916 leaders was an indefensible and counter-productive British blunder, the long term results for Ireland were disastrous. The thinkers and leaders, on whose ideals and philosophy the revival of Irish nationalism and republicanism had been built, were eliminated in one fell swoop. They were no longer there to lead the Irish people in the crisis that followed 1916. While retribution, and a desire to destroy the concept of Irish separatism and republicanism were the reasons which prompted the British Government to execute the leaders of the Rising in 1916, their executions undoubtedly were counter-productive. The executions led to the destruction of the Irish moderate constitutional political party − the Irish Party. As a consequence, Sinn Féin, the Irish Republican Army (I.R.A.) and the Irish Republican Brotherhood (I.R.B.) were swept into power as a challenge to British rule in Ireland.

The rejuvenation and revival of Irish nationalism had been brought about by the combined idealism and determination of men such as Pádraic Pearse, James Connolly, Tom Clarke, Thomas MacDonagh, the O'Rahilly, Seán MacDiarmada, Joe Plunkett and Éamonn Ceannt. Those that survived the 1916 Rising were good men, but they lacked the long standing motivation and tradition of the leaders they replaced. The Irish people unhesitatingly, in a period of resentment and euphoria, gave their full support to the new leadership that had survived the 1916 Rising.

It is no criticism of that leadership to say that they occupied their position of leadership solely because they had survived the Rising. They had not formed part of the leadership that had planned the Rising and organised the spearhead of the revolutionary tradition inspired by Tone. In a difficult situation, they sought to provide a leadership that would maintain the unity of the Irish people. But, unfortunately, they were unable to do so. The truce, the Treaty negotiations and the Civil War created a deep cleavage from which Ireland is only now recovering. During the Civil War period we lost many more of our leaders: Michael Collins, Arthur Griffith, Liam Mellows and Rory O'Connor.

It should be borne in mind that Michael Collins accepted the Treaty because he believed it could be used as a "stepping stone" towards the achievement of an independent Republic. The death of Michael Collins and the bitterness of the Civil War, however, made many forget the basis upon which he had advocated its acceptance.

By a strange reversal of roles it was Eamon de Valera who proceeded to implement the "stepping stone" policies adumbrated by Michael Collins; he gradually chipped at, and removed some of the most objectionable limitations of Irish sovereignty contained in the Treaty of 1922. Conversely, *Cumann na nGaedhael* (Fine Gael) drifted into an attitude of defending the Treaty as an acceptable solution. By another strange evolution it was Mr. de Valera's party, Fianna Fáil, which having successfully eliminated the British Crown from our Constitution reintroduced it in 1939 by way of the External Relations Act. This limitation on our Sovereignty was finally eliminated by the Repeal of the External Relations Act and the enactment of the Republic of Ireland Act in 1950.

One of the unaccountable features of the controversies concerning the Anglo-Irish Treaty of 1922 was that its effect on the partition of the country escaped attention. In point of fact, while the British Government had provided for the partition of the country in the Ireland Act of 1920, partition had never been accepted by the Irish people. The Treaty, however, made provisions which were bound to lead to partition of the country; acceptance of the Treaty involved an acceptance of partition. It is quite surprising that in the course of the Treaty debates in *Dáil Éireann*, this aspect received little attention.

Full credit must be given to Mr. de Valera for his policy of neutrality and for his leadership during the last World War. It was the only possible policy, and he handled it superbly. While the basis for our policy of war-

Top— History repeats itself. British soldiers at Butcher Gate, Derry, 1969.

Above— British troops prepare to leave Ireland; Irish troops prepare to take over, in January 1922.

time neutrality and of non-involvement in NATO was originally due to partition, the reasons behind our adoption of non-alignment and neutrality as a permanent basis for our foreign policy deserves attention.

The bitterness engendered by the Civil War and the resulting conflict of personalities eroded the political life of the country for well over thirty years. *Clann na Poblachta* in 1948 represented the first serious attempt to eradicate the divisions that were based on the Civil War. The major parties were not overly anxious to eradicate the memories of the Civil War. Both parties had acquired a certain automatic electoral support derived from the Civil War split. This automatic electoral support nearly amounted to a vested interest in the continuance of Civil War divisions.

During all this period we lacked the kind of leadership that was necessary to heal the differences of the Civil War and to lay the necessary basis for our economic independence. We needed during this period the type of leadership which Pádraic Pearse proposed in 1913, in the following terms:

> I propose that we take *service* as our touchstone, and reject all other touchstones; and that, without bothering our heads about sorting out, segregating, and labelling Irishmen and Irishwomen according to their opinions, we agree to accept as fellow Nationalists all who specifically or virtually recognise this Irish Nation as an entity and, being part of it, owe it and give it their service.[2]

Leaving aside the barren political controversies which dominated political discussion, the main criticism which can be justly levelled against our governments since 1922 has been in the failure to plan for the economic development and independence of the country. For the first twenty-five years following the Treaty, Ireland did not really pursue an independent economic policy of its own. It continued to pursue a policy which made our development subservient to British financial policies.

This subservience to the British economy in our country was, in the main, due to the uninformed and conservative views that dominated the Irish Department of Finance and the Irish Central Bank. Willynilly our financial establishments anchored Irish economic policies to the requirements of the British treasury. Accordingly, while we had acquired a large measure of national independence for this part of Ireland and while we busied ourselves painting our letterboxes green, we continued to pursue the same old economic and financial policies as those that had been instituted while we were a British dependency. The Civil Service machinery, which we took over, remained unchanged. No progressive thinking was permitted within the walls of the Department of Finance, and Ireland was to be kept solidly anchored to sterling and the requirements of British financial policies. Even the Shannon electrification scheme and the setting up of the ESB (Electricity Supply Board) were opposed and delayed by the pundits of the Department of Finance. Had it not been for the determination of Patrick McGilligan and Dr. McLoughlin, the Shannon scheme would not have been built.

Eamon de Valera at Árus an Uachtaráin at the end of a long political career.

At one stage when Mr. de Valera set up the Currency Commission in 1938, it was hoped that an independent Irish financial policy would be developed. These hopes were finally shattered, when Mr. de Valera accepted the conservative policies of the Department of Finance rather than those set forth in the O'Loughlen Minority Report of the Currency Commission. The restrictive policies of the Department of Finance were again challenged by *Clann na Poblachta* in the Inter-Party Government, 1948-1951; they were breached to the extent that the government insisted on a much higher rate of investment in afforestation and land reclamation than before. This was done in spite of the overt and covert opposition of the Department of Finance and the Central Bank.

Our membership in the European Economic Community has at long last broken the total dependency of our economy on the British market and on the requirements of British financial policies. Britain is a large, wealthy, highly industrialised country; Ireland is a small, underdeveloped agricultural country. It is nearly axiomatic that the policies that are suitable for the British economy are unsuitable for the Irish economy.

I am somewhat uneasy as to our industrialisation policies. I fear that we place too much emphasis on selling Ireland as a country where labour is cheap; inevitably, wages here will never fall far below wages in Britain. We should also be careful not to induce the establishment of industries here that cannot be viable. Foreign entrepreneurs should be selected with care to ensure that enterprises that are set up here are viable. Otherwise, there is a danger that foreign entrepreneurs may come here to obtain the government grants made available to them, and to off-load some obsolescent plant. Having thus profited at our expense, they can then close up, or go bankrupt, and blame industrial strife.

We should promote a much higher rate of public investment in afforestation and land reclamation. Afforestation is of very special importance for four reasons. First, the labour content in afforestation is higher than in any other public work. In a country with such a high rate of unemployment, this is a very important consideration. Secondly, forestry is highly profitable. Thirdly, timber is an increasingly important raw material for many industrial uses — including the production of energy. And finally, we have the best possible climate for rapid growth of timber. Let us now double our plantation rate of trees; this is an investment upon which we cannot lose.

There should also be a much greater emphasis placed on quality food production and exports. Our industrial policies should be, wherever possible, based on raw material which we can produce. In particular, we should seek to process the mineral resources which we undoubtedly have.

In common with the rest of the world, we face serious oil shortages. We must plan for alternative sources for energy. Instead of rushing into vast expenditure for nuclear energy which will make us dependent on imported uranium, let us concentrate on the sources of energy that are available to us here: timber, biomass, wind, tide and waves. We have in Ireland at least five universities, each of which has available to it

Top– The ESB peat-fuelled generating station at Ferbane, Co. Offaly. The station has the capacity of 90 mw, and the fuel is supplied by Bord na Móna from the adjoining bogs.

Above– The Turlough Hill Pumper Storage Scheme was the biggest civil engineering project ever carried out in Ireland. It generates 292 mw of electricity by the transfer of millions of gallons of water from the top of the hill to the bottom. Designed by ESB engineers, it took six years to build and has proven to be one of the most efficient of its kind in the world.

efficient and devoted scientists. Many of our physicists and other scientists have earned international recognition for their work. Why do we not seek their aid and advice in the search for solutions to our energy problems? They are highly qualified and would readily respond to any research projects which the Government might invite them to undertake. I would therefore propose that the Government should make available to University College Dublin, Trinity College, University College Galway and University College Cork, together with Queen's University in Belfast, a research grant of 1 million pounds to each of these five universities, to enable them to undertake research projects into the field of alternative sources of energy. I am certain that 5 million pounds invested in this way in the brains of our scientific academics would give a much better return than the nearly 11 million pounds which has been spent on a new Central Bank building in Dublin!

Our Civil Service is badly in need of reorganisation. The inadequacies of our telephone services are, I am afraid, a reflection of the incompetency of our Civil Service. Generally, I fear that we are living through a period of mediocrity. We need more imaginative thinking and a greater degree of idealism in our public life.

Overshadowing all the other problems that confront Ireland is the problem of partition. It intrudes into every aspect of life — North and South. People try to ignore it or to pretend that it is not a serious problem, but it keeps intruding itself into all aspects of our religious, political, social, moral and economic life. Indeed, perhaps some of the violence that disrupts life in the North arises from attempts that have been made to underplay or minimise the gravity of partition.

The test as to what area constitutes a national entity which is entitled to exercise the right of national self-determination is that its boundaries should be clearly defined and that its population should be reasonably homogeneous. The national boundaries of the island of Ireland are beyond dispute. The population of Ireland is probably more homogeneous than the population of most other independent states; it is a white population which shares Christian beliefs. True, there are Catholics and Protestants, but both denominations share the same Christian beliefs. Many countries with far less well defined boundaries and a multiplicity of ethnic origins, languages and religions are recognised as national entities having the right to exercise self determination as national units. Accordingly, none of the usual criteria applicable to the definition of nationhood can be used to justify the partition of Ireland.

The concept of partition was evolved to suit the requirements of British policy in Ireland. In fomenting divisions in Ireland, based on religion and "culture", the British Government found many willing agents in Ireland. This process was intensified in the eighteenth, nineteenth and in the first part of the twentieth century. Until the Catholic emancipation, all Catholics were denied elementary fundamental rights. The non-Catholic population were given special privileges which gave them a vested interest in the maintenance of the division thus created. From the point of view of the British rulers the policy of divisiveness based on religion, was merely the application of the age-old colonial concept of "Divide and Rule".

When after World War I it became obvious that Ireland would have to be granted a measure of self government, the British Government formalised the divisions which had been carefully fostered for a couple of centuries, and provided for the political partition of Ireland by the Ireland Act of 1920. Unfortunately, the partition provided for by the 1920 Act was reinforced by the Anglo-Irish Treaty of 1922 and by the subsequent Boundary Commission.

By creating a "Northern Ireland – Six County State", Britain assured the strengthening of the vested interest which the Protestant majority in the new State had, and ensured that that segment of the Irish population would become more and more dependent on Britain for its powers and privileges. When the actual boundaries of the six county area were under consideration, the British representatives were guided by two main considerations: that the maximum area should be included in the six county State, and that there should be a permanent Protestant pro-British majority in the new State. As a result, the six county State included vast areas which were predominantly nationalist or Catholic. However, by reason of the fact that the Catholic population grew more rapidly than the Protestant population, the British Government began to fear that in a relatively short period of time the Catholic/nationalist population would outnumber the Protestant/pro-British population. This development posed a real threat to the continued domination of this area by a Protestant-British hegemony.

This was ever present in the minds of the Northern Ireland Government and the British Government in the 1920s and the 1930s. Ways and means had to be found to prevent such a development – which would have inexorably led to the reunification of Ireland. It is for these reasons that a systematic process of discrimination against Catholics was instituted in regard to housing, employment and representation on public bodies. In this manner it was hoped that the Catholic population would regress and certainly would not be permitted to increase. A process of fierce and rigid discrimination was instituted and continued right up to the 1960s.

While the older generation tended to accept the discrimination as endemic in the system to which they had become accustomed, a new young generation arose that had different views. They rejected the old leadership and refused to allow themselves to be treated as third-rate citizens. This led to the birth and development of the Civil Rights Association. It was a new brand of democratic republicanism. All the forces of repression and sectarianism were then directed against the Civil Rights movement. The police and the more extreme sectarian element joined forces to eradicate this new movement. The Burntollet attack on Civil Rights marchers in 1969 and the Derry massacres, coupled with extensive use of internment, drove many of the Civil Rights workers into the Republican physical force movements. This led to the growth of the I.R.A. and the setting up of physical violence. Cycles of repression and violence succeeded each other. The policy of sectarian murders was, if not encouraged by the authorities, for a time tolerated by them. Gradually, over a period of some three years, a tacit understanding was reached between the Protestant paramilitary element and the Republican paramilitary element that sectarian killings must be ended. A further development of interest was a tacit agreement between some of the Protestant paramilitary groups and the I.R.A. that the British forces should be withdrawn from Northern Ireland. There was, however, little or no agreement as to what would happen after their withdrawal. A strong movement developed within the Protestant paramilitary groups in favour of the setting up of an independent State that would have no links with either Britain or the Republic. This was not acceptable to the I.R.A.

Nevertheless, one is conscious that an evolution has been taking place whereby the viewpoint of the paramilitary groups on both sides has been getting closer together. They are at least prepared to recognise each other's standpoint and to discuss possible solutions. There also seems to be a consensus developing in favour of a complete British withdrawal. To that extent despite the horror and the bloodshed that has taken place, there is room for some measure of optimism. The ultimate solution may well lie in a confederation that would provide for a wide measure of regional autonomy: in the meanwhile, why not accept the provisions of the European Convention for the Protection of Human Rights and Fundamental Freedoms as forming a basis for the constitutional guarantees for the rights of the minorities in both North and South. This Convention and the mechanisms created by it have been accepted by Dublin, Belfast and London. By agreement, the mechanisms of the Commission and of the Court of Human Rights could be extended to provide for a special jurisdiction to apply to all human rights issues arising in Ireland.

Notes

FIVE CITIES

1.   *Town and Country Planning*, London: Thornton-Butterworth Ltd., 1933, pp.25-26.

THE 1890s & 1900s IN CLARE

1.   When drafting this sentence I used the comprehensive colloquial word "yoke" (contraption) spontaneously. I have left it unaltered because it exemplifies an element of our country life, viz. Hiberno-English speech. There are at least 300 such words and phrases, mainly taken from the Irish language, only a few of which, such as brogue and galore, have found their way into standard English dictionaries. I wrote a series of articles on this subject in *An Sguab* in 1923, and it has recently been pursued at length by the Royal Irish Academy.
2.   See E. A. MacLysaght, *Short Study of a Transplanted Family in the Seventeenth Century.* Dublin: Browne and Nolan, 1935.
3.   The West Clare Railway was closed down as obsolete in 1961. We should not forget however that during World War II, owing to the scarcity and bad quality of the coal available, mainline trains repeatedly broke down, sometimes requiring two or three locomotives to complete their journey. The despised West Clare managed to keep going quite steadily by using local turf as fuel.
4.   E. A. MacLysaght, *Interesting Times.* London: Colin Smythe, 1978.
5.   Biddy Early, baptized Bridget Ellen Connors, was born in 1798 in Co. Clare, the daughter of a poor peasant family. During her lifetime she acquired a widespread reputation as an herbalist, curer and diviner. The dark-coloured, "magical" bottle she used as an aid in divination became the object of intense curiosity and superstition. It disappeared mysteriously after her death in 1874.
6.   See E. T. Craig, *An Irish Commune: The History of Ralahine.* Dublin: Martin Lester, 1920.

THE 1920s IN DONEGAL

1.   A caul is part of the membrane enclosing the foetus which is occasionally found on a baby's head. It is believed to be a good omen and a charm against drowning.
2.   S. Pender (ed.), *The Census of Ireland, 1659.* Dublin: Irish Manuscripts Commission.
3.   See *Donegal Annual*, vol. 10, 1971, p.9.

THE 1930s ON ARAN

1.   Surnames are rarely used in speech in Aran when Gaelic is spoken. Translated into English my mother would be "Delia, daughter of Michael son of Michael son of Patrick etc.". In Gaelic it is simply "Michael's Delia" and in turn her father is "Michael's Michael". In English one used the Gaelic names or else used the English name and surname, which led to problems in an island where so many families shared the same surname and so many children were christened Mary or Patrick. In these cases the child would be called Mary Flaherty (Pat) or Patrick Flaherty (Michael Tom). Only in Gaelic could the whole genealogy be rattled out, using only christian names.
2.   Liam O'Flaherty is one of Ireland's leading novelists and short-story writers. He is the author of *The Informer* (1925), *The House of Gold* (1929), *Famine* (1937), *The Pedlar's Revenge* · (1976) and other works. See *The Novels of Liam O'Flaherty.* Dublin: Wolfhound Press, 1977.
3.   Pat Mullen was a native of Inishmore. He worked with Robert Flaherty on the filming of *Man of Aran* and published an account of Flaherty's sojourn on the island — *Man of Aran* (1934). He also wrote *Hero Breed* (1936); *Irish Tales* (1938) and *Come Another Day* (1940).
4.   The Congested Districts were defined under the Land Purchase Act of 1891 as part of an attempt to relieve the poverty of the West of Ireland. As originally conceived, they consisted of all those electoral divisions with a valuation of less than thirty shillings per head of population, but in 1909 they were re-defined more simply as the counties of Donegal, Leitrim, Sligo, Roscommon, Mayo, Galway and Kerry, together with West Cork and part of Clare. Abolished in 1923, the Congested Districts reappeared in the Underdeveloped Areas Act (1952) as the region eligible for special government grants.

FAIRS AND PILGRIMAGES

1   John Millington Synge, *In Wicklow, West*

Kerry and Connemara. Dublin: Maunsel & Co., 1911, pp.43-46.
2. Dialogue adapted from field notes and Patrick Kavanagh, "November Fair". *Ireland of the Welcomes,* vol. 17, Nov.-Dec. 1968, pp.6-9.
3. Synge, *In Wicklow, West Kerry and Connemara.* p.120.
4. From a survey of religious practices and beliefs in the Republic conducted in 1973 and 1974 by Máire Nic Ghiolla Phádraig of the Department of Sociology, University College Dublin.
5. Jonathan Sumption, *Pilgrimage: An Image of Medieval Religion.* London: Faber & Faber, 1975, p.114.
6. Gerald Simons, *Barbarian Europe.* New York: Time-Life Books, 1968, p.90.
7. Quoted in T. F. O'Sullivan, "Pattern Day at Saint Moling's", *Irish Times,* 8 July 1976, p.10.
8. Sir William Wilde, "Memoir of Gabriel Beranger, and his Labours in the Cause of Irish Art, Literature, and Antiquities from 1760 to 1780." *Journal of the Royal Society of Antiquaries of Ireland,* vol.2, 1873, pp.449-50.

THE SPORTING TRADITION

1. Eugene O'Curry, *On the Manners and Customs of the Ancient Irish.* London: Williams & Norgate, vol.2, 1873, p.237.
2. Rev. Patrick S. Dinneen, *Irish-English Dictionary.* Dublin: Irish Texts Society, 1927, p.602.

WORDS: WRITTEN, SPOKEN & SUNG

1. Tadhg Ó Dúshláine, "Sean O Riordáin Homo Ludens." *Maynooth Review,* vol.4, May 1978, pp.53-62.
2. Mary Fitzgerald, "Out of Eure Sands Creek." *Maynooth Review,* vol.4, May 1978, pp.63-72.
3. Ibid.
4. *Fleadh Cheoil,* literally "music-feast": a network of these festivals – local, regional and national – attracts large attendances most week-ends from spring and autumn.

FESTIVALS

Festivals and Events mentioned in the text

Ballybunion International Bachelors Festival (Ballybunion, Co. Clare) 22 June-1 July.
Cork Film Festival (Cork City, Co. Cork) 23-30 June.
Festival in Great Irish Houses (various large houses) 3-15 June.
Galway Oyster Festival (Clarenbridge, Co. Galway) 19-21 October.
Galway Races (Galway City, Co. Galway) 30 July-3 August.
Horse Show (Dublin, Co. Dublin) 7-11 August.
Killarney Races (Killarney, Co. Kerry) 16-19 July.
Lisdoonvarna (Lisdoonvarna, Co. Clare) early Autumn.
Listowel Races (Listowel, Co. Kerry) 24-28 September.
Listowel Writers Week (Listowel, Co. Kerry) 26 June-1 July.
Merriman Summer School (Ballyvaughan, Co. Clare) 24-30 August.
Merriman Winter School (Ballyvaughan, Co. Clare) 9-11 February.
Rose of Tralee Festival (Tralee, Co. Kerry) 1-6 September.
Spring Show (Dublin, Co. Dublin) 1-5 May.
Tramore Races (Tramore, Co. Waterford) 14-17 August.
Wexford Opera Festival (Wexford Town, Co. Wexford) 24 October-4 November.
Wild Rose Festival (Manorhamilton, Co. Leitrim) 19-26 August.

For further details on these and other events contact Bord Fáilte Éireann, Dublin, or any local tourist information centre.

IRELAND IN THE MODERN WORLD

1. Pádraic Pearse, *The Sovereign People.* Dublin: Whelan & Son, 1916, p.20.
2. Pádraic Pearse, *From a Hermitage.* Dublin: Irish Freedom Office, 1915 (originally published June 1913), p.3.

Acknowledgements

This book was made possible through the help and co-operation of many people. I would like to begin by thanking the following individuals and organisations for their help with photographic research: Commandant Kevin Hogan of Baldonnel for his assistance with Department of Defence aerial photographs; the staff of Bord Fáilte's photographic division, especially Margaret McGahon; John Scarry and Con Brogan of the Board of Works; Mr. W. G. Callaghan from the Irish Meterological Service; Mike Ryan and Tony Lennon of *The Irish Times* library; Anne O'Dowd of the National Museum for her tireless assistance with the Mason, Stephens and Welsh collections; Tom Kennedy of Source Photographic Archive; the staffs of the Ulster folk Museum, the National Library, Northern Ireland Public Records Office, Northern Ireland Tourist Board, RTE Guide Library and the Railway Record Society. I would also like to thank Pat Langan, Tom McElroy and Richard Mills for the use of numerous of their outstanding photographs, and Tom Donnelly who produced photographs at such short notice.

To my husband and colleague, George Gmelch, I owe many thanks not only for the use of several of his photographs but for his frank opinions and valuable advice during the course of putting this book together. To Michael O'Brien, my publisher, I owe a debt of gratitude for many things, but especially for his patience and humour in dealing with a sometimes distraught editor. I also wish to thank Brian Cullen for his editorial assistance and Nuala Gunn for her excellent typesetting. And finally I wish to thank the contributors to this book without whose time and considerable talents it would not have been possible. To those who were prompt; to those who were helpful in other ways; and to those who retained a sense of humour to the end, a special word of thanks.

Sharon Gmelch, May 1979

List of Illustrations

The Authors

Sean MacBride is a founder member of the Irish section of Amnesty International and vice-president of the World Federation of United Nations Associates. He was born in 1904. He received his higher education from the National University of Ireland. He had a prominent role in Ireland's fight for freedom. In 1937 he was called to the Bar and in 1943 to the Inner Bar. He founded the political party *Clann na Poblachta* (Republican Party) in 1946. He has been a member of *Dáil Eireann,* serving as the Irish Minister of External Affairs from 1948-51; vice-president of the Organization for European Economic Cooperation; president of the Foreign ministers of the Council of Europe; United Nations Commissioner for Namibia; and secretary-general of the International Commission of Jurists, Geneva. Mr. MacBride is a recipient of the Nobel Peace Prize (1974), the Lenin Peace Prize (1977) and the American Medal of Justice (1978).

▼

▲

Edward MacLysaght was born in 1887 on a ship off the Cape of Good Hope, later to be baptised in Co. Clare. As a youth he attended public school in England. He received his M.A. and D.Litt. in history from the National University of Ireland at Cork. He has led an active and varied life, working as a farmer, businessman, writer, political activist, member of the first Senate, journalist, archivist and historian. He is the author of fifteen books and several times as many articles in both English and Irish. He is perhaps best known for his work on Irish surnames. Most recently he was chairman of the Irish Manuscripts Commission, a position he held until 1973 when he retired at the age of 85. Dr. MacLysaght is married and has five children and fourteen grandchildren. He divides his time between Dublin and his family home in Co. Clare.

Sharon Gmelch received a Ph.D. in anthropology from the University of California, Santa Barbara, and is now an associate professor at Union College in Schenectady, New York. She has done extensive research with Irish Travellers and is the author of *Tinkers and Travellers* (Dublin: The O'Brien Press) and *Nan: The Life of an Irish Travelling Woman* (New York: W. W. Norton). Her professional interests include ethnicity, applied anthropology and life history. Other interests are photography and squash. She is married and the mother of one child.

▼

Joseph Raftery was born in Dublin in 1913. He received his B.A. in Celtic Studies from University College Dublin in 1933 and an M.A. in archaeology the following year. He was awarded a Ph.D. in archaeology from Philipps-Universitat, Marburg/Lahn, Germany, in 1939. He then joined the staff of the Irish Antiquities Division of the National Museum of Ireland. In 1949 he was appointed Keeper of Irish Antiquities. He is a former president of the Royal Irish Academy and of the Royal Society of Antiquaries of Ireland, former chairman of the National Monuments Advisory Council and former director of the National Museum of Ireland. He is now retired. Dr. Raftery is the author of *Prehistoric Ireland* (1941), editor of Volume Two of *Christian Art in Ancient Ireland* (1951) and author of over 120 papers in scientific journals in English and German.

▼

Maeve Binchy was born in Dublin in 1940. As a youth she attended the Holy Child Convent in Killiney and later University College Dublin where she received a B.A. and H.Dip. in education. She taught history and Latin in a girls' school until 1969 when she left to begin work with *The Irish Times.* Since then she has become one of Ireland's most popular and entertaining journalists. Ms. Binchy is the author of *My First Book* (1977), *Central Line* (1978), *End of Term* - a one-act play , *Light a Penny Candle* (1982) and *Echoes* (1985). She is currently London columnist for *The Irish Times.* ▶

▲

Antony Orme is Professor of Geography and Dean of Social Sciences in the University of California, Los Angeles. Born in Somerset, he received a First Class Honours B.A. in 1957 and a Ph.D. in 1961. From 1960 to 1968, he was Lecturer in Geography at University College Dublin. He was also President of the Association of Geography Teachers of Ireland and editor of their journal *Geographical Viewpoint.* His professional interests straddle the earth sciences and the social sciences, and among his sixty publications are several dealing with the Irish landscape, including a book *Ireland* published by Longman in 1970. Formerly a keen player of cricket, rugby, and soccer, he is now an avid tennis player.

Patrick Shaffrey is an architect and town planner. He was born in Bailieboro, Co. Cavan, in 1931. He received his secondary education at St. Patrick's College, Cavan. He studied architecture in University College Dublin and town planning in Heriot-Watt University, Edinburgh. He is a former honorary secretary of *An Taisce* — The National Trust for Ireland — and a founder member and first president of the Irish Planning Institute. He is the final adjudicator in the countrywide Tidy Towns Competition. Mr. Shaffrey is the author of *The Irish Town: An Approach to Survival* (1975), and, with his wife, Maura, of *Buildings of Irish Towns* (1983) and *Irish Countryside Buildings* (1985). ▼

Seán MacRéamoinn was born in Birmingham, England, in 1921. His family returned to Ireland when he was still an infant. He attended school in Clonmel, Co. Tipperary, and following that at Coláiste Iognáid (S.J.). He received a B.A. in Irish, French and English from University College Galway and an M.A. in Old and Middle Irish. From 1944 to 1947 he worked in the Department of Foreign Affairs. Thereafter he began his long association with the Irish broadcasting service, first as a producer and writer for *Radio Eireann,* later as controller of radio programmes and currently as head of External Affairs in *Radio Telefis Eireann.* He has been active in the promotion of the Irish language and is a member of both *Bord na Gaeilge* and the board of *Gael Linn.* His special interests are religion, politics, the arts and "in talking about them all".

▼

▲

Oscar Merne was born in Dublin in 1943. He has long been interested in wildlife, especially birds, first joining a wildlife society at the age of twelve. Since then he has been active in many wildlife organisations, both national and international, and was a founder member of The Irish Wildbird Conservancy. His main interests are seabird breeding, waterfowl and wetland conservation and the ecology of coastal habitats. In 1968 he was appointed the first Wildlife Warden of The Wexford Wildfowl Reserve. He is now working with the Research Branch of the Forest and Wildlife Service. Mr. Merne has published numerous scientific papers and several books on wildfowl, most recently *Wading Birds* (1979).

Garry Redmond, Dubliner, formerly sports editor for *The Irish Press,* then managing editor of the *RTE Guide,* currently works on the staff of *Radio Telefis Eireann.* For thirteen years he was the sports correspondent in Ireland for *The Observer,* covering all Irish games and pastimes. He played rugby for over twenty years in Lansdowne Football Club (he wrote its centenary history in 1972). He has also done some hurling, Gaelic, soccer, cricket, tennis and although he's never ridden at Punchestown, he's at least "walked the course". He golfed ceaselessly until recently when a "football-back" curtailed his swing.

▼

George Otto Simms was born in Dublin in 1910 but soon after moved to Lifford, Co. Donegal. As a youth he attended public school in England but returned to Ireland for his higher education. He received a Ph.D. in 1950 from Trinity College Dublin for work on the Latin text of the Book of Kells, and a Doctor of Divinity in 1952. He has had a long and distinguished career in the Church of Ireland, first becoming a deacon in 1935. He was elected Bishop of Cork in 1952, Archbishop of Dublin in 1956, and Archbishop of Armagh and Primate of All Ireland in 1969. He is now retired. His publications include *The Book of Kells: A Short Description* (1961), *Christ Within Me* (1975) and collaboration on *The Book of Durrow* (1961). Archbishop Simms is married and has five children. ▼

▲

Breandán Ó hEithir was born on Inishmore, Aran Islands, and educated by his parents at Kilronan National School. His mother was a sister of novelist Liam O'Flaherty. He attended the Coláiste Einde, Galway, and spent three years studying in University College Galway. He worked as a fisherman in England, an itinerant book salesman, a publisher's editor and freelance broadcaster before becoming Gaelic Editor of *The Irish Press*. From 1963 to 1965 he lived in Germany, since then he has worked as a journalist, writer and broadcaster in Dublin. His first novel was *Lig Sinn i gCathú*, later translated into English as *Lead Us Into Temptation*. He has also written *Willie the Plain Pint agus An Pápa* (1978), *Over the Bar: A Personal Relationship with the GAA* (1984), and sixteen film scripts. He has worked with *The Irish Times* and with Radio Telefís Éireann.

▲

Nell McCafferty was born in Derry City in 1944. After taking a "useless" arts degree from Queen's University, Belfast, she travelled on the Continent and in the Middle East, finishing with a year on Kibbutz Maa 'yan Baruch in Upper Galilee, where she weeded the orchard. She returned to Derry in 1968 and joined the dole and Derry Labour Party in quick succession. She moved to Dublin and *The Irish Times* in June 1970, doing the usual bit of television, radio and public speaking extras, with specific reference to feminism and malpractice in court. A collection of her articles, *The Best of Nell*, was published in 1984, and *A Woman to Blame* in 1985. She is now working as a freelance journalist in Dublin.

Index